ZION: CANYONEERING

ZION: CANYONEERING

Trail Hiking & Technical Canyon Adventures in & Around Zion National Park

TOM JONES

Tom's Utah Canyoneering Guide

Published by Canyoneering USA
PO Box 5532
Mount Carmel, Utah 84755
www.CanyoneeringUSA.com

First edition 2006

Cover, book design and layout: Marge Mueller, Gray Mouse Graphics
Maps and illustrations: Tom Jones
All photos by author, unless otherwise noted.
Photos p. 27 and 29, Public Domain photographs courtesy U.S. Geological Survey.

Cover photo: *Tom Wetherall rappelling in Kolob Creek*
Frontispiece: *First rappel in Engelstead Canyon*

ISBN 0-9789614-0-4

This book is dedicated to my father, Nolan Jones, who infected me, at an early age, with a love of outdoor adventure–from which I have never recovered.

WARNING

Canyoneering is a sport where you may be seriously injured or die! Read this warning before using this book.

You are responsible for your own safety.

This book describes a wide variety of adventures, some of which involve considerable risk. Understand the risks involved and take steps to minimize them, including:

- CONSULT with other information sources about current conditions and to verify the information in this book;
- APPLY COMMON SENSE in regard to current, past and likely future weather conditions, and condition of the environment, and your own capabilities to deal with emergencies;
- CARRY PROPER EQUIPMENT such as a map and compass, plenty of drinking water, cold-water protective clothing and technical equipment that may be needed.

Tackle adventures in Zion that are appropriate to your physical conditioning, experience and skill set. If in doubt, enjoy the easier ones first, and work your way up.

- ON-TRAIL HIKES will be fun for most hikers;
- OFF-TRAIL HIKES require greater fitness and more advanced skills, such as reading topographic maps, assessing natural hazards and taking care of yourself. These hikes carry considerably more risk than on-trail hikes.
- TECHNICAL CANYONEERING requires downclimbing, ropework and canyoneering-specific skills. Before venturing into technical canyons, you must be proficient at rappelling, setting anchors and, in many cases, canyoneering-specific skills. Obtain these skills by training or experience before venturing into technical canyons.

While a few hints about technique may be included, this book is NOT an instruction manual. Obtain proper instruction BEFORE entering the canyons.

The information in this guide was compiled over many descents, and was most likely accurate at the time of publication. However, **canyons change rapidly and the wise canyoneer expects the unexpected, and is prepared to find or create anchors as needed. Where reality and this book disagree, make decisions based on reality.**

THERE ARE NO WARRANTIES, EXPRESSED OR IMPLIED, THAT THIS GUIDEBOOK IS ACCURATE OR THAT THE INFORMATION CONTAINED IS RELIABLE. BY USING THIS BOOK YOU ASSUME THE RISK OF DESCRIPTIVE ERRORS AND SOLE RESPONSIBILITY FOR YOUR SAFETY.

Table of Contents

LIST OF MAPS AND ILLUSTRATIONS

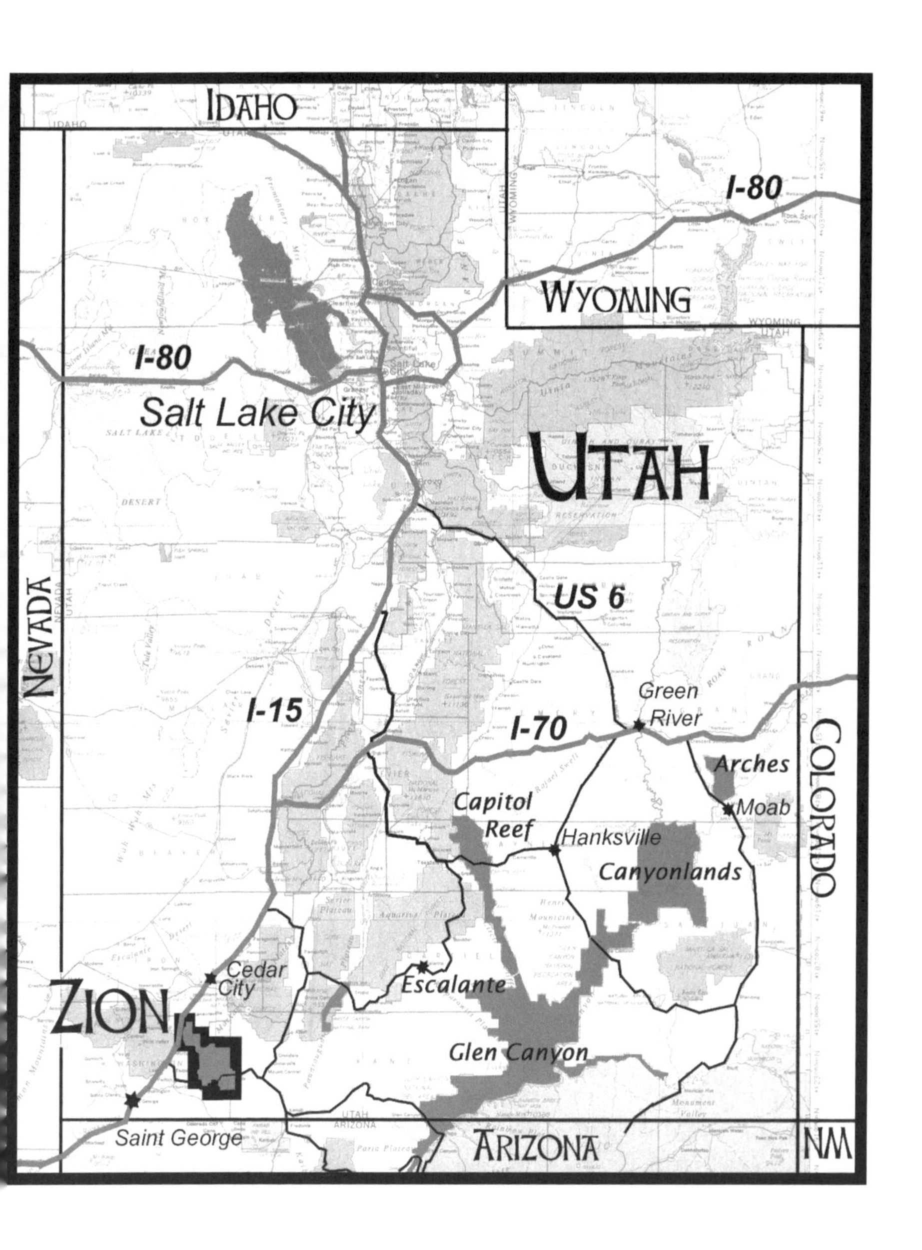

IDAHO
WYOMING
I-80
I-80
Salt Lake City
UTAH
US 6
NEVADA
I-15
I-70
Green River
Arches
Moab
COLORADO
Capitol Reef
Hanksville
Canyonlands
Cedar City
Escalante
ZION
Glen Canyon
Saint George
ARIZONA
NM

CHART OF CANYONS

Star Rating System: *** - a classic; ** - good, worth doing; * - OK, do others first; (no stars) - not recommended.

Canyon or Hike	Page	Area	Rating	Star Rating	Hours	Longest Rappel	Protective Clothing	Notes
ON-TRAIL DAYHIKES 59								
1. Emerald Pools Trail	59	Main Canyon	1A II	***	1-2	none	none	
2. Angels Landing	61	Main Canyon	1A II	***	3-5	none	none	
3. Hidden Canyon	63	Main Canyon	1A II	***	2-4	none	none	
4. Observation Point Trail	64	Main Canyon	1A III	**	4-6	none	none	
5. Observation Point via East Mesa Trail	67	East Side	1A II	**	3-4	none	none	
6. Middle Fork Taylor Creek	68	Kolob Canyons	1A II	***	2-4	none	none	
7. West Rim Trail in a Day	71	KT/Main Canyon	1A III	***	6-12	none	none	
ON-TRAIL OVERNIGHT HIKES								
8. West Rim Trail Overnight	75	KT/Main Canyon	1A IV	***	6-12	none	none	
9. LaVerkin Creek and Kolob Arch	77	Kolob Canyons	1A IV	***	6-10	none	none	
OFF-TRAIL HIKES 79								
10. The Narrows from the Top	89	East/Main Canyon	1B III or IV	***	8-14	none	none	
11. The Narrows and Orderville Canyon from the Bottom	96	Main Canyon	1B III	***	4-10	none	none	

Canyon or Hike	Page	Area	Rating	Star Rating	Hours	Longest Rappel	Protective Clothing	Notes
12. Orderville Canyon	101	East/Main Canyon	2B III	***	6-10	15 ft (3 m)	Wetsuit except in summer	
13. The Subway from the Bottom	105	Kolob Terrace	1B III	**	6-10	none	None	
14. The Right Fork from the Bottom	111	Kolob Terrace	1A III	**	8-12	none	None	
15. Lower Pine Creek	112	Main Canyon	1A II	**	1-2	none	None	
16. Middle Echo from the Bottom	114	Main Canyon	1B III	***	3-5	none	None	
17. South Fork Taylor Creek	116	Kolob Canyons	1A II	**	1-3	none	None	
CLASSIC MODERATE TECHNICAL CANYONS 135								
18. The Subway from the Top	135	Kolob Terrace	3B III	***	6-12	30 ft (10 m)	Wetsuit except in summer	
19. Pine Creek	142	East/Main Canyon	3B II	***	2-6	100 ft (30 m)	Highly variable	
20. Keyhole Canyon	146	East Side	3B I	**	1-2	60 ft (20 m)	Wetsuit	
21. Middle Echo Canyon	148	Main Canyon	3B II	***	3-6	30 ft (10 m)	Wetsuit	
22. Mystery Canyon	150	East/Main Canyon	3B III	***	5-8	120 ft (38 m)	None	
23. Behunin Canyon	158	Main Canyon	3B III	***	5-9	165 ft (50 m)	None	
TECHNICAL CANYONS 163								
24. Fat Man's Misery	163	East Side	3B III	***	6-10	40 ft (15 m)	None	
25. Englestead Hollow	167	East Side	4B III or IV	***	6-10	300 ft (91 m)	Wetsuit except in summer	
26. Birch Hollow	169	East Side	3A III	**	5-10	100 ft (30 m)	None	
27. Spry Canyon	171	East/Main Canyon	3B III	***	5-7	165 ft (50 m)	none	

Canyon or Hike	Page	Area	Rating	Star Rating	Hours	Longest Rappel	Protective Clothing	Notes
28. Lodge Canyon	174	East/Main Canyon	4A III R	*	5-7	200 ft (60 m)	None	
29. Grotto Canyon	176	East/Main Canyon	3A III	(0 stars)	4-6	260 ft (80 m)	None	
30. Hidden Canyon from the Top	177	East/Main Canyon	3A III	**	5-7	100 ft (30 m)	None	
31. Corral Hollow	179	KT/Main Canyon	3A IV	**	8-12	200 ft(60 m)	None	
32. Upper Telephone Canyon	180	Main Canyon	3A III	***	6-8	200 ft (60 m)	None	
33. Refrigerator Canyon	181	Main Canyon	3A III	(0 stars)	3-5	200 ft (60 m)	None	
34. Spearhead Canyon	182	Main Canyon	4B V	**	12-16	200 ft (60 m)	None	
35. The Right Fork	183	Kolob Terrace	3B V	***	16-24	60 ft (20 m)	Wetsuit except in summer	
36. Russell Gulch	189	Kolob Terrace	3B III	**	7-10	100 ft (30 m)	Wetsuit except in summer	
37. Das Boot	191	Kolob Terrace	3B III	***	7-10	60 ft (20 m)	Wetsuit at all times	
38. Full Left Fork of North Creek	194	Kolob Terrace	3B IV	**	10-14	60 ft (20 m)	Wetsuit at all times	
39. Goose Creek Direct (closed)	194	KT/Main Canyon	4A V	***	16-24	240 ft (75 m)	None	
40. Boundary Canyon	195	Kolob Terrace	3A or C III	***	8-10	200 ft (60 m)	Wetsuit when running	
41. Kolob Creek	197	Kolob Terrace	3C IV or V	***	9-12	165 ft (50 m)	Full wetsuit or drysuit	
42. The MIA Trail	201	Kolob Terrace	MIA 5	(aargh)	2-4	none	none	
43. South Fork Oak Creek	203	Kolob Terrace	3C III or IV	***	8-12	150 ft (45 m)	Full wetsuit or drysuit	

Canyon or Hike	Page	Area	Rating	Star Rating	Hours	Longest Rappel	Protective Clothing	Notes
44. Icebox Canyon - North Pass	206	Kolob Canyons	3B IV	**	8-12	165 ft (50 m)	Wetsuit except in summer	
44. Icebox Canyon - Slickrock Pass	00	Kolob Canyons	4B IV	**	8-12	165 ft (50 m)	Wetsuit except in summer	
45. Imlay Canyon from Potato Hollow	214	KT/Main Canyon	4B V R	***	12-16	165 ft (50 m)	Full wetsuit or drysuit	
46. Imlay Canyon Sneak Route	217	Main Canyon	4B IV R	***	9-14	130 ft (40 m)	Full wetsuit or drysuit	
47. Heaps Canyon via Phantom Valley	218	KT/Main Canyon	4B V R	***	12-16	280 ft (90 m)	Full wetsuit or drysuit	
48. Heaps Canyon via The Gunsight	222	Main Canyon	4B IV R	**	10-14	280 ft (90 m)	Full wetsuit or drysuit	
49. Isaac Canyon via The Gunsight	222	Main Canyon	4B V	**	12-16	280 ft (90 m)	Wetsuit at all times	

Zion National Park — Overview

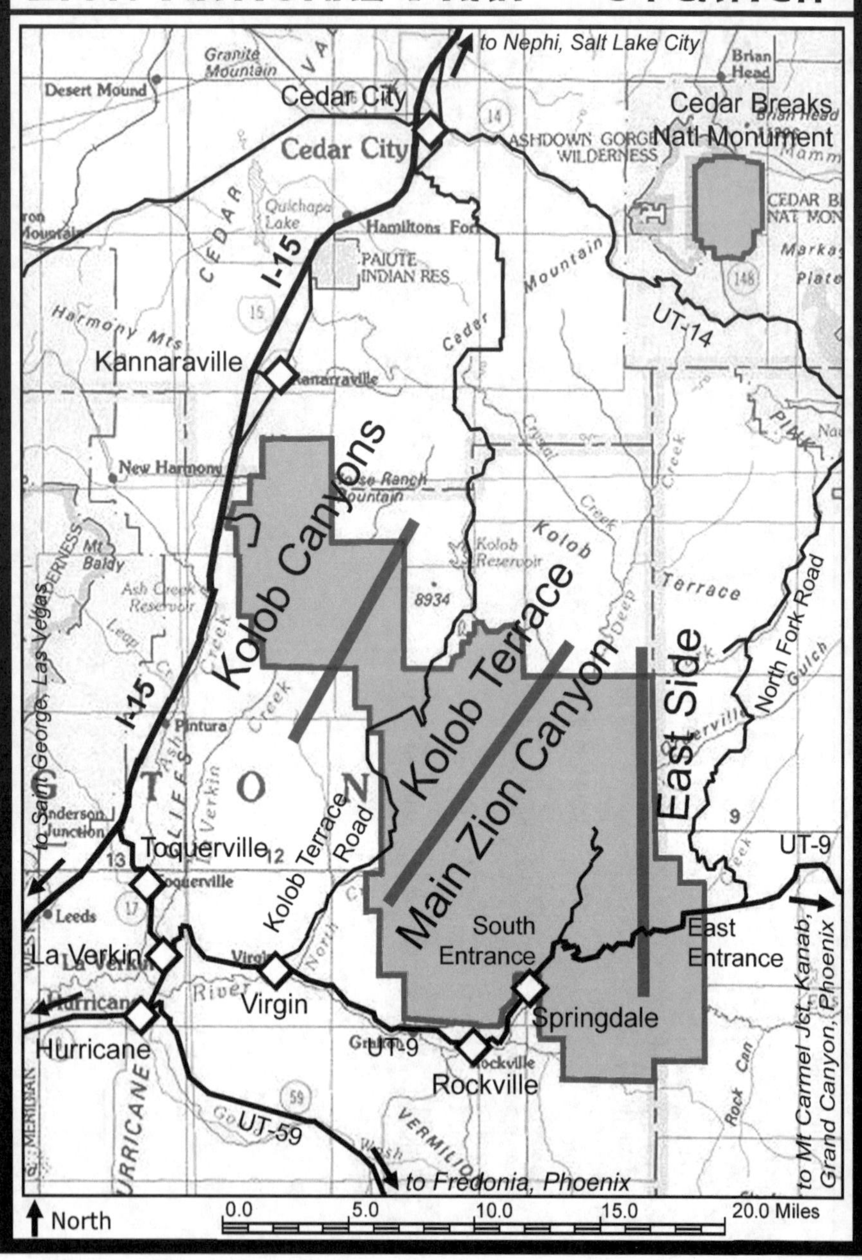

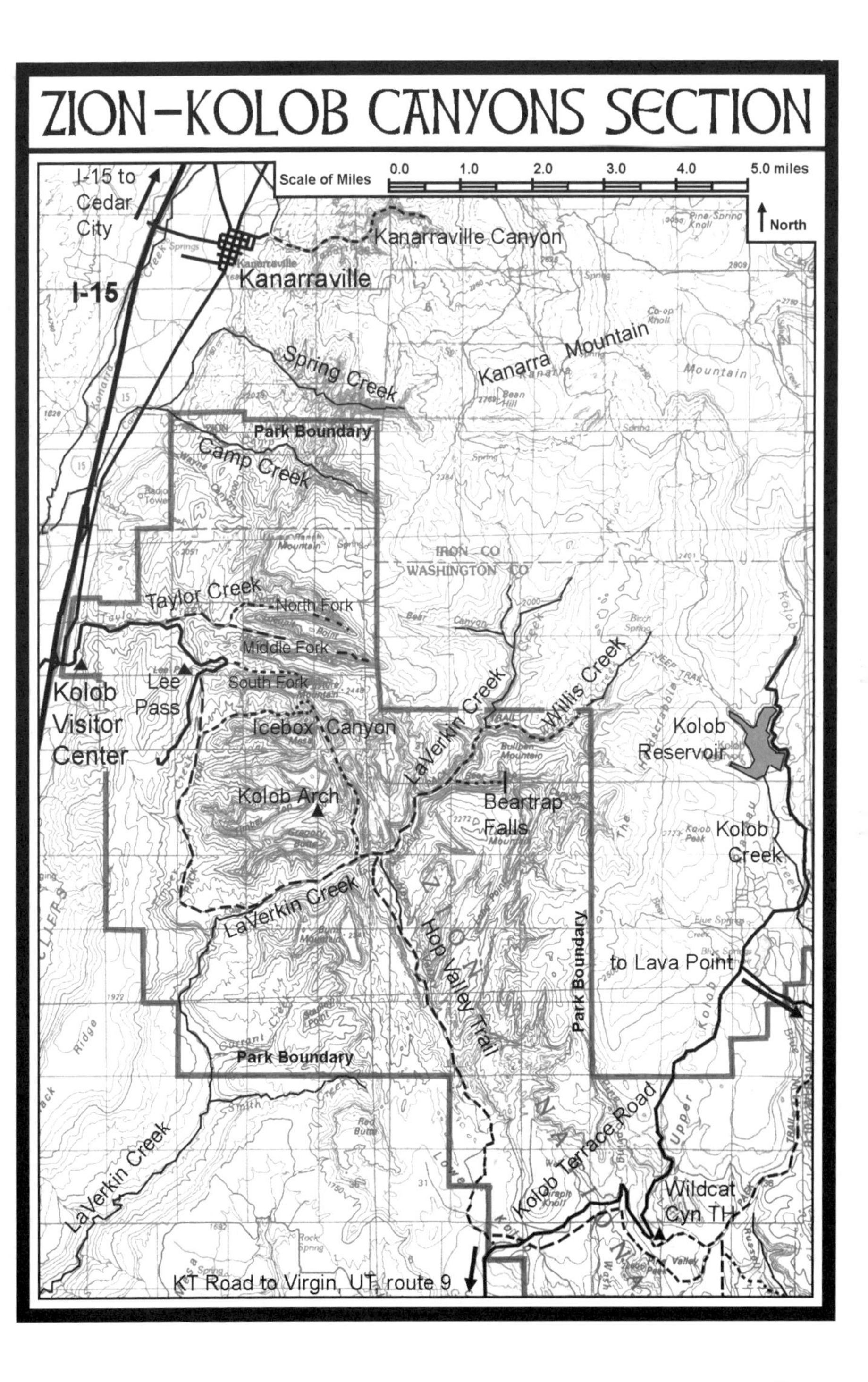
ZION-KOLOB CANYONS SECTION
I-15 to Cedar City
Scale of Miles
0.0
1.0
2.0
3.0
4.0
5.0 miles
North
Kanarraville Canyon
Kanarraville
I-15
Spring Creek
Kanarra Mountain
Park Boundary
Camp Creek
IRON CO
WASHINGTON CO
Taylor Creek
North Fork
Middle Fork
South Fork
Kolob Visitor Center
Lee Pass
Icebox Canyon
LaVerkin Creek
Willis Creek
Kolob Reservoir
Kolob Arch
Beartrap Falls
Kolob Creek
LaVerkin Creek
Hop Valley Trail
Park Boundary
to Lava Point
Park Boundary
Kolob Terrace Road
LaVerkin Creek
Wildcat Cyn TH
KT Road to Virgin, UT, route 9

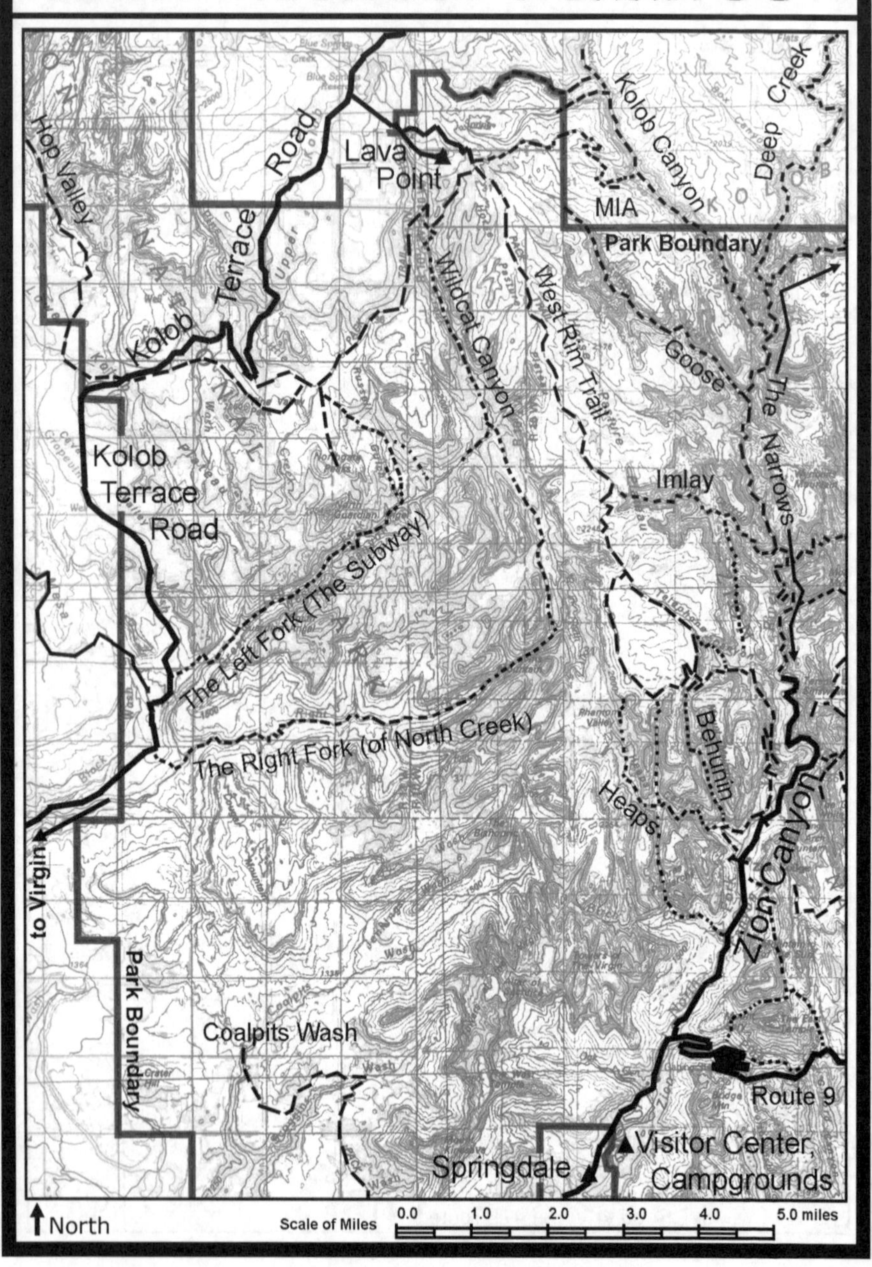
ZION–KOLOB TERRACE
Kolob Terrace Road
Lava Point
Hop Valley
Kolob Canyon
Deep Creek
MIA
Park Boundary
Wildcat Canyon
West Rim Trail
Goose
The Narrows
Kolob Terrace Road
Imlay
The Left Fork (The Subway)
The Right Fork (of North Creek)
Behunin
Heaps
Zion Canyon
to Virgin
Park Boundary
Coalpits Wash
Route 9
Visitor Center, Campgrounds
Springdale
North
Scale of Miles
0.0
1.0
2.0
3.0
4.0
5.0 miles

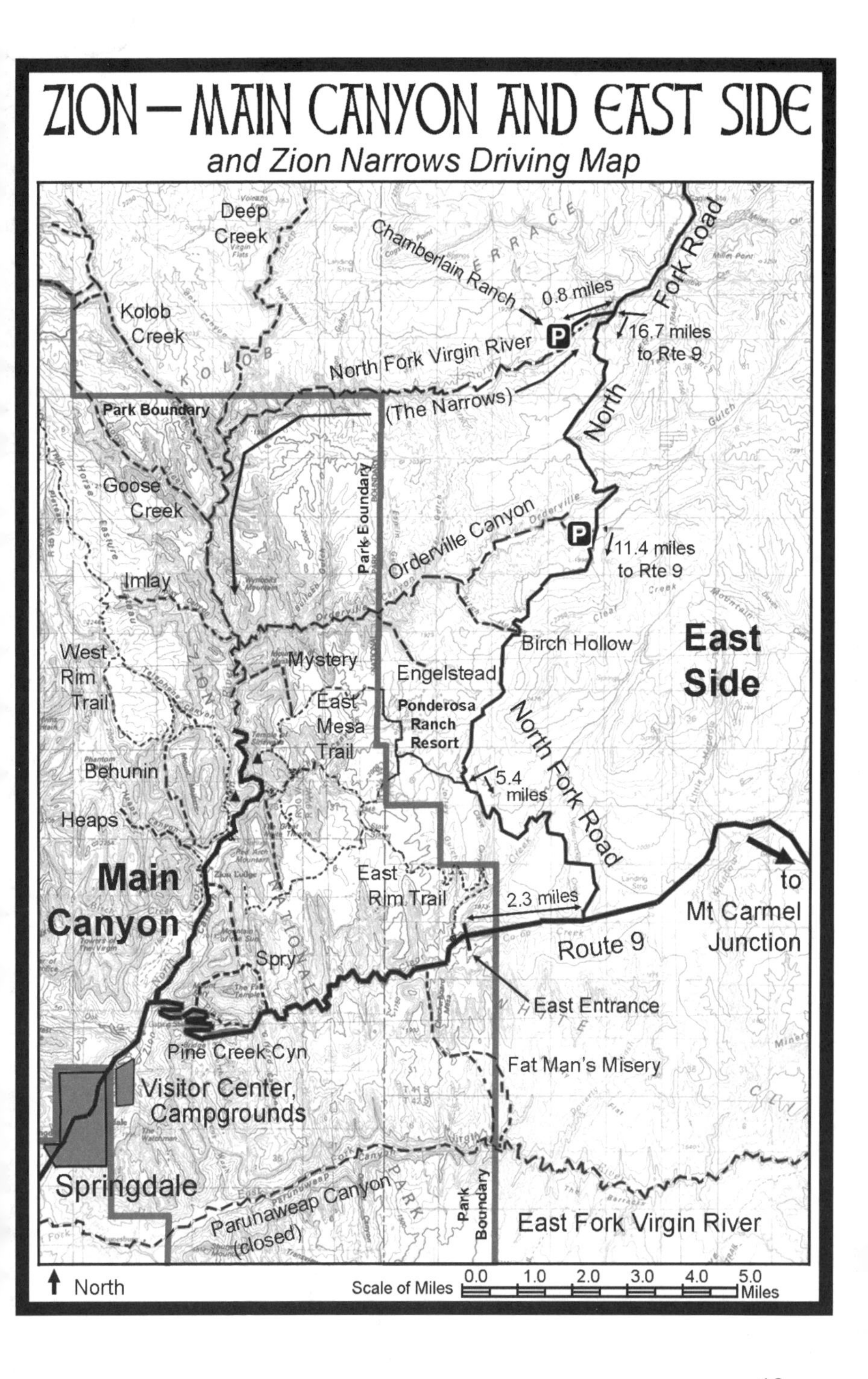
ZION – MAIN CANYON AND EAST SIDE
and Zion Narrows Driving Map
Deep Creek
Chamberlain Ranch
0.8 miles
North Fork Road
16.7 miles to Rte 9
Kolob Creek
North Fork Virgin River
(The Narrows)
Park Boundary
Goose Creek
Orderville Canyon
11.4 miles to Rte 9
Imlay
Birch Hollow
East Side
West Rim Trail
Mystery
Engelstead
East Mesa Trail
Ponderosa Ranch Resort
North Fork Road
Behunin
5.4 miles
Heaps
Main Canyon
East Rim Trail
2.3 miles
to Mt Carmel Junction
Route 9
Spry
East Entrance
Pine Creek Cyn
Fat Man's Misery
Visitor Center, Campgrounds
Springdale
Parunaweap Canyon (closed)
Park Boundary
East Fork Virgin River
North
Scale of Miles
0.0
1.0
2.0
3.0
4.0
5.0
Miles

Foreword

A few of us had been visiting some challenging canyons in the Escalante region. We had come to town, soon to head to Zion, and stopped briefly at the Escalante Ranger Station. The station was populated by the usual assortment of folks. All were dressed neatly, washed and scrubbed... except for a pair of fellows over in the corner. Both were destined to become close friends and frequent adventure partners. I strolled toward them—noting torn and soiled shorts, a shirt discolored with sweat and grime, legs with long scrapes and blood streaked scabs alongside ground-in dirt. I realized . . . my partners and I looked just like them! Seeing a potential soulmate in canyoneering, I strode over with a big smile and said "looks like you've been doing what we've been doing!" This fellow looked at me strangely and subtly turned away. I guess I was less appealing than he was. Thus started my association with Tom Jones

Soon, he would answer me and we would schedule many an adventure together, forming a complimentary partnership, exploring many canyons new to us both. Tom showed himself to be an exceptional problem solver, using gadgets of his own invention, to help extract us from tight spots that our curiosity and drive had led us into.

Tom found his way to the outdoors hiking and climbing in the White Mountains, back in New Hampshire. He soon headed west and dove in to the sports of rock climbing and mountaineering, accumulating a long list of ascents, including Longs Peak, Mt. Whitney and El Capitan. Similar to many like-minded souls, he dabbled in other outdoor disciplines, including paragliding. Paragliding went well, except the last time, when gravity won the day in a rout. After a bit of convalescing, not quite ready for the mountains yet, Tom tried canyoneering, and it was love at first experience. Never to do anything half way, Tom has explored 100's of canyons since that fateful day.

Tom has a strong drive to know how things work. It led him to an engineering degree from MIT. He combined this need to tinker and experiment with his love of the outdoors. Soon he was inventing gear, and improving other manufacturer's gear. It was a natural progression for him to create an outdoor gear company, and for it to become successful and a known organization. JRAT was his baby. Eventually, he sold the company and started a long association with Black Diamond. But innovation is best fostered in an environment of complete control and as such,

Opposite: *Rylin LaPlante rappelling in Birch Hollow*

Tom started Imlay Canyon Gear, where he designs, produces, markets and sells innovative canyon-specific gear.

All this tinkering hasn't gotten in the way of Tom devoting large chunks of time to exploring the canyons. I have enjoyed accompanying him on many of these days. Among the ways Tom gives to the community is: a fantastic website CanyoneeringUSA.com, sharing information, ethics and education with a whole new generation of canyoneers; organizing canyon fests, where interested novices meet with more experienced locals for several days of doing canyons, sharing knowledge, skills and an environmental ethic. Tom has organized several service projects, working with land managers to do trail work and minimize impacts in sensitive areas. He is the chairman of the Zion Canyoneering Coalition, which is working hard to keep open access to "our" National Parks.

As busy as he has been, he has found time to reach deep into his notes and put together this comprehensive and user friendly guidebook, to the canyons of Zion National Park and adjacent areas. Zion is a canyon Mecca and here, in one book, is a guide to keep an adventurer busy for a long time. Thanks Tom, for everything you do and let's schedule that next trip soon.

Steve Ramras
Fort Collins, Colorado
July 2006

Preface

Zion is an exceptional place, best explored by visiting the backcountry on its own terms, in a word, by canyoneering. Some have questioned the wisdom of having a guidebook and bringing more people to these canyons, but they are coming already. My intention is to provide accurate information, and to get in front of newcomers to Zion with a strong environmental, leave-no-trace message so that they, too, can become good stewards of these remarkable canyons.

Please enjoy these canyons, and remember that many have been there before you, and many will come after. Do a good job of leaving the canyons the way you found them (or cleaner!) and we can all share them in a natural state for years to come.

The use of bolts is a controversial subject in canyoneering, and Zion is no exception. While bolts have a long history in Zion, and have a place in popular canyons to keep visitors in the watercourse, protect live trees and minimize impacts, in the rest of Zion their use tends to dumb-down the canyons and diminish the wilderness experience. There are plenty of bolts in Zion, please do not place more. Learn the skills necessary to traverse Zion's canyons using natural anchors, and bolts will not seem like quite so wonderful a solution.

Tom Jones
Mt. Carmel, Utah
September, 2006

Welcome to Zion

There is an eloquence to their forms which stirs the imagination with a singular power and kindles in the mind . . . a glowing response.
— Clarence E Dutton reflecting on Zion Canyon, 1880

Zion enjoys a geologic configuration that leads to especially magnificent canyons. Cut into the southern edge of the Markagunt Plateau, the dramatic rise in elevation results in steep canyons with big drops. The 7000 foot (2000 m) altitude of the plateau top attracts considerable precipitation, and the porous nature of the Navajo sandstone allows that moisture to work its way through the rock, then along less-porous rock layers to emerge from the walls in the form of springs and seeps. The canyons are lush, steep and deeply cut.

Human History

Ancestral Pueblo Indians (Anasazi) lived in Parunaweap Canyon from 500 AD to about 1300 AD. These settlements were the furthest west Anasazi villages, and were somewhat isolated from the main culture, developing unique styles.

When the first white settlers arrived in the 1860's, Southern Paiute Indians sparsely inhabited the area. The Paiutes shunned Zion Canyon as a place of mysterious happenings—not a good place to be after dark! Many Zion place names come from Paiute theology including Mount Wynopits (after Wynopits, the God of Evil) and Mount Kinesava (after Kinesava, the Trickster).

Guided by a friendly Paiute, Nephi Johnson was the first pioneer to visit Zion Canyon in November 1858, riding in as far as the Great White Throne and perhaps to The Narrows. He returned to the Virgin River valley a month later with a settlement group and founded the town of Virgin. The next wave of settlers led by Orson Pratt arrived in December 1861, settling Rockville and Shunesberg, three miles east of Rockville on

Opposite: *The Great White Throne*

the East Fork of the Virgin River. Springdale was established in the fall of 1862, the town laid out and irrigation ditches dug. By 1864, an LDS church census counted 765 persons living in the Upper Virgin valley, from Virgin to Springdale.

The first of the new settlers to visit upper Zion Canyon was Joseph Black, who made the arduous exploration in 1861 or 1862, and talked up the glories of the canyon to the unbelieving pioneers. He did, however, catch the interest of Isaac Behunin, who visited upcanyon in the summer of 1863, built a summer cabin near the present day site of Zion Lodge, and planted a few crops. By 1864, the Behunins had dug an irrigation ditch and placed several acres under cultivation, for corn, fruit trees and tobacco.

Within a few years, William Heap (or Heaps) and John Rolf had settled their families in the same area, though they wintered in Springdale, as did the Behunins. John Rolf built two houses, one down by the Behunins and one up by The Grotto.

Isaac Behunnin (later Behunin) was born in Oswego County, New York in 1803, and baptized into the LDS Church on New Year's Day, 1833. He soon moved to Kirtland, Ohio, and later (1837) to Randolph County, Missouri. He was with the Saints through numerous persecutions in Missouri, escaping to Nauvoo, Illinois in 1839. Thence to Winter Quarters, then to Salt Lake City in 1848. He was the first settler in Ephraim, Utah, helping found the town in 1852. He was called upon by the church elders to help settle Springdale in 1862. By the time he got to Zion Canyon at the age of 60, he was ready for a little rest and respite. Isaac is oft-quoted as naming Zion, reflecting on the LDS Temple being built in Salt Lake City: "These are the Temples of God, built without the use of human hands. A man can worship God among these great cathedrals as well as in any man-made church—this is Zion."

The first wagon road into the upper canyon was constructed in the winter of 1864-65. The years of 1866 and 1867 were less idyllic, as fighting broke out in southern Utah between the settlers, the Paiutes and the Navajo. The pioneers concentrated into Springdale, then to Virgin, for better defense, and outlying fields were tended by armed parties. With the arrival of peace in 1868, the former prosperity was gradually restored. Isaac Behunin left Zion Canyon in 1874 to join the United Order in Mount Carmel, and helped found the town of Orderville, where he died in 1881.

John Wesley Powell visited the area in 1872, making the first modern descent of the East Fork of the Virgin River (Parunaweap Canyon). His party left the village of Mount Carmel on September 10th, spent an uncomfortable night in the canyon and arrived at the settlement of Shunesberg the next day.

The same year, 1872, geologist and explorer Grove Karl Gilbert, working with the Wheeler survey, led the first European-American party down the North Fork of the Virgin from Navajo Lake through The Narrows to Zion Canyon. Major Clarence Dutton, working for the 1875 Powell Survey, visited Zion and waxed poetic about the view: "In an instance, there flashed before us a scene never to be forgotten. In coming time it will, I believe, take rank with a very small number of spectacles, each of which will, in its own way, be regarded as the most exquisite of its

The Dome on the Virgin River. Photo by J. K. Hillers (1872)

kind which the world discloses. The scene before us was The Towers of the Virgin."

The Cable

In the meantime, Mormon settlers were prospering in Springdale and the surrounding communities. Timber was needed for building houses, but not available locally. David Flanigan remembered great stands of timber up on the East Rim; and in 1900, unable to convince others of the practicality of lowering timber on a cable, packed 50,000 feet of wire to the top of Cable Mountain. His job was made easier by John Winder's 1896 work on the old Indian trail up Echo Canyon (now the East Rim Trail) making it barely passable to horses. Over the course of three years, Flanigan perfected a rig for lowering timber and, in 1904, hauled an old sawmill to the top and began operations. By Christmas 1906, 200,000 feet of milled lumber had been lowered on his cable.

The sawmill was located at what is now Stave Spring. At the height of operations, between 30 and 45 men were employed, and lived in the summer, with their families, up by the mill. "Riding the Wire" both up and down became commonplace after 1910, when Quimby Stewart, part of a group sent in to survey the area for the National Monument, made the descent for a reward of watermelon. The ride took two or three minutes.

The cable was used for lowering lumber for the building of Zion Lodge in 1924, but this was the last big contract. The cable was dismantled in 1930, after the death of Orderville schoolteacher Mr. Albin Brooksby, clocked on the head by a sliding piece of iron while chasing one of his charges off the bottom towers. The parking lot at Weeping Rock is located where the bottom towers used to be.

National Recognition

One hardly knows just how to think of it. Never before has such a naked mountain of rock entered our minds. Without a shred of disguise its transcendent form rises pre-eminent. There is almost nothing to compare to it. Niagara has the beauty of energy; the Grand Canyon of immensity; the Yellowstone of singularity; the Yosemite of altitude; the ocean of power; this Great Temple of eternity–"The Titan fronted blowy steeps, that cradled Time."

—Frederick S Dellenbaugh, "A New Valley of Wonders," Scribner's Magazine, January 1904 (in reference to the West Temple).

While the writings of John Wesley Powell and other explorers sparked interest in the West, the beauties of Zion were lost in a vast river of

Entrenched meanders of the Virgin River at the upper end of Zion Canyon, Temple of Sinawava. The walls of Navajo Sandstone rise 1,800 to 2,200 feet above the river. Photo by Army Air Corps, 1950

churning prose. National interest in Zion Canyon was enflamed by the efforts of Frederick S. Dellenbaugh, a member of John Wesley Powell's second Grand Canyon float trip. Dellenbaugh visited Zion Canyon in 1903, took photographs and painted a few paintings. His article and photos in the January 1904 Scribners Magazine created a sensation, as did the exhibit of his paintings at the St. Louis 1904 World's Fair.

A National Park

The nation was growing up rapidly, and with the invention of the automobile and increasing prosperity, interest grew in the new leisure activity of tourism—and touring the scenic wonders of the American west. The National Park System was created in this era—Zion being added as Mukuntuweap National Monument July 31, 1909; then expanded and renamed Zion National Monument in 1918. By act of Congress, it became Zion National Park on November 19, 1919.

Frederick Vining Fisher, Methodist minister of Ogden, Utah, visited Zion in September 1916. Shown Zion canyon by the son of the Rockville LDS Bishop, the two played a game of naming the scenic points as they traveled up-canyon. Returning in the late afternoon, Fisher was awestruck by a great monolith gleaming in the late afternoon sun—which he named The Great White Throne.

Southern Utah was promoted as a scenic destination. The WW Wylie Company ran auto tours from the railhead at Cedar City, through Zion to the North Rim of the Grand Canyon and back to Cedar, operating a tent camp at the site of the Zion Lodge. President Warren G Harding visited Zion on June 27, 1923 on his one-way trip to Alaska.

All this interest led to better roads as automobiles started to transform the nation. A connection between Mount Carmel and Zion canyon was desired—but the terrain was difficult. John Winder, builder of the East Rim Trail and current operator of the Cable Mountain lumber operation, thought he had the perfect place for it. He proposed a road up Pine Creek, then punching a tunnel right through the Great Arch. The engineers were unimpressed, but realized a road up the south side of Pine Creek and through the cliffs above might just be feasible. The mile-long Zion-Mount Carmel tunnel was started in 1927 and completed in 1930. It was an engineering marvel.

In Zion canyon, the road was extended from the base of the cable to the Temple of Sinawava in 1925. The Gateway to The Narrows trail was built that same year, as was the West Rim Trail, the Lady Mountain Trail, and a trail along the west bench under the cliffs. The following year, the trail to the tip of Angels Landing was completed, plus two suspension bridges over the river. The West Rim Trail was worked on some more, and the East Rim Trail was upgraded to its current condition. The steep trail up Lady Mountain became problematic for the park Service, due to the large number of people that became stranded, and was closed in the 1960s.

Zion Lodge was built with the cooperation of the Union Pacific Railroad, opening in 1925. The original main building burned to the ground in 1966, and a replacement was built in 108 days. The replacement was described as "hideous," but was partially restored to the original lodge plans in 1992.

Rock climbing came to Zion in 1927 with the first recorded ascent of the Great White Throne by "daredevil" William H. W. Evans on June 27th via the south face. He built a fire on the summit to prove his accomplishment, but did not return to the valley the next day. A rescue team was organized and found him several days later lying at the base of the upper cliffs, bruised and delirious. The rescue effort led to the discovery of Hidden Canyon, and a trail was constructed to it the next year.

The Great White Throne was climbed again by Dan Orcutt in June 1931. Walter Becker, Fritz Becker and Rudolph Weidner climbed Cathedral Mountain on August 31, 1931. Other early peaks climbed include the West Temple (1933), the East Temple (1937) and the Sentinel (1938). Modern climbing came to Zion with the 1967 ascent of the Northwest Face of the Great White Throne by Fred Beckey, Galen Rowell and Pat Callis, after extensive wrangling for permission from the park.

Canyoneering history is more obscure, as writings from the original canyoneers are lost in the murky depths of time. Mystery Canyon and Goose Creek were descended in the sixties, as was the Right Fork of North Creek. Royce D. Trapier forged many descents of local canyons including Pine Creek, Keyhole, Echo and Behunin. Dennis Turville explored much of the Zion backcountry in the seventies; and Norman Harding and Royce D. Trapier descended the last of the main canyons, Heaps, through The Narrows in October 1982.

Geologic History

A quick glance around Zion reveals that the geologic story is about sandstone. The most obvious formation, the Navajo, is an orange to white sandstone that forms huge cliffs. Standing 2200 feet tall in Zion, the Navajo was formed by sand dunes about 180 million years ago. The Navajo's tendency to form huge cliffs is largely responsible for Zion's stunning, high-wall scenery.

Zion sits on the southern end of the Colorado Plateau, an area stretching from central Utah and western Colorado down to northern New Mexico and Arizona. It is a vast landscape of desert sandstone with rock layers generally laying flat.

Let's start from the beginning, and look at the rocks as they were deposited.

The sedimentary rocks of Zion were laid down as loose sediment—

sand, clay and silt—between 210 and 160 m.y.a., during the Jurassic period, when dinosaurs were the dominant species. After being deposited, the sediments were covered with more sediment and pushed down into the earth, where with pressure and elevated temperature, the loose sediments were pressed and baked into rock. During the last 80 million years, forces deep within the earth uplifted the Colorado Plateau, the overlying rocks and sediments were eroded off and canyons were formed.

While the geology is evident throughout the area, a good place to view the layers talked about here is from the bridge across Pine Creek, looking up at the East Temple.

Geologists talk in terms of rock *formations*—a group of rock layers laid down in a specific order over a short period of time—and *layers* or *members*—a specific rock layer. Formations consist of several layers or members much like a paragraph consists of several sentences.

Moenave and Kayenta Formations *(Mo-en-A-vee, Ka-YEN-ta)*

210 to 190 million years ago

In geology, the beginning is at the bottom, where the oldest rocks are. In Zion, the crumbly rocks leading up to the base of the Navajo are the Moenave and Kayenta layers. Both are deep red, look like piles of boulders or talus, and form steep slopes that are not quite cliffs. There are short cliff bands in each.

The Moenave Formation (400 to 570 feet thick) is at the bottom, and has two members. It starts with a crumbly siltstone—the Dinosaur Member—that was deposited in a rainy, equatorial environment by slow streams and ponds, like a Louisiana bayou. Above the Dinosaur is the Springdale Member—a solid, blocky sandstone that forms a 30 m (100 foot) sheer cliff. These sands were left behind by a faster flowing river that left the sand, but swept the lighter clays and silts out to sea. The Springdale Member forms the charming gorge and waterfalls above the bridge in lower Pine Creek, in addition to the cliffband just above the town of Springdale.

The Kayenta Formation (500 to 700 feet thick) starts immediately above the Springdale Sandstone with more of the crumbly red siltstone that forms steep, loose slopes. Near the top, just below the Navajo, the Kayenta is a solid, red sandstone that forms long ledges and benches. The floor of The Subway and the red waterfalls below The Subway are Kayenta.

The Kayenta formed from silt and sand left behind by streams at the southern edge of a great desert. Rainy summers and dry winters left behind a mix of sediments.

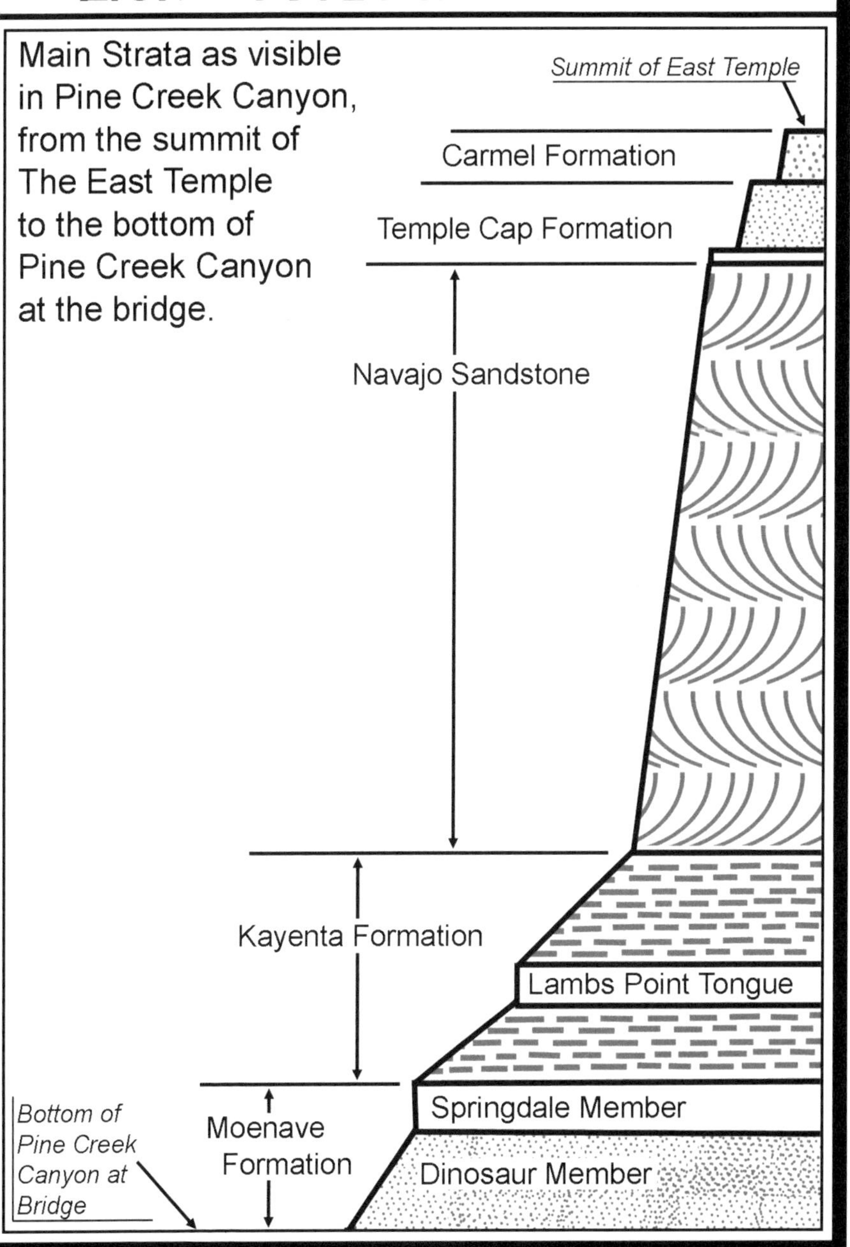
ZION GEOLOGICAL PROFILE
Main Strata as visible in Pine Creek Canyon, from the summit of The East Temple to the bottom of Pine Creek Canyon at the bridge.
Summit of East Temple
Carmel Formation
Temple Cap Formation
Navajo Sandstone
Kayenta Formation
Lambs Point Tongue
Springdale Member
Moenave Formation
Dinosaur Member
Bottom of Pine Creek Canyon at Bridge

The East Temple. Keyenta (brushy slope) to Temple Cap (summit)

Navajo Sandstone *(NA-va-ho)* 190 to 180 million years ago

The Navajo Formation consists of one rock layer, Navajo Sandstone. While the Navajo is a dominant rock layer across the Colorado Plateau, it is thickest in Zion National Park—2200 feet (700 m) thick. Navajo is a cliff-forming sandstone, but soft and easily cut by flowing water. These somewhat contradictory characteristics result in the formation of dramatic canyons.

A vast area of sand dunes that stretched, at one time, from central Wyoming to the southeastern point of California left behind the sand that became Navajo Sandstone. The climate was much the same as the current Sahara desert, and the sand accumulated in a slowly sinking basin. The sand blew back and forth, rounding the crystals and allowing impurities such as clay and silt to blow away. The rock shows traces of the dunes that formed it as *cross-bedding*—short horizontal layers of diagonally banded rock. The diagonal bands are layers left behind by the lee faces of the dunes. The cross-bedding is seen best on the upper layers of the Navajo beside the road near the East Entrance.

Sandstone is held together by impurities such as clay and lime that are deposited with the sand. Navajo lacks these impurities and thus is poorly held together. The rock is weak and often crumbly, but still forms huge cliffs. The rock near the top is especially pure, white and weak, partly because it was deposited as pure sand, and partly because rainwater, over tens of thousands of years, has dissolved what little binding material was available and carried it down through the rock to the lower layers.

Temple Cap and Carmel Formations 180 to 160 million years ago

At the top of the stack, above the Main Canyon and visible as flat caps on the higher peaks, the Temple Cap Formation was deposited atop the sand of the Navajo desert by streams carrying red mud, leaving a couple of feet of bright red clay and silt. Just above this, desert conditions resumed, though a little wetter, and 100 feet of orange sand was deposited, now forming towers and short mesas atop some of the peaks. Soon after, a shallow sea like the Mediterranean flooded the area, and a thin layer of very hard limestone was deposited. This is the lowest layer of the Carmel Formation.

More Rocks 160 to 20 Million Years Ago

More rocks were deposited on top of this, but in the Zion area they have mostly been eroded off. Some of these rocks can be found on the east side of the park, and are responsible for the terrible sticky clays that make the North Fork Road impassable after rain.

Interleaving

In some places, the laying down of the rocks was not quite so orderly as the description above might imply. The contact between the Navajo and Kayenta was, in places, much like the shuffling of cards. This is seen clearly in The Subway by the many spring layers apparent between the first obstacle and the Red Ledges. A 90-foot thick layer of Navajo Sandstone (called the Lambs Point Tongue) is visible halfway down the Kayenta in Pine Creek Canyon. This forms a vertical cliff that is rappelled when exiting Spry Canyon.

What Would Water Do?

Knowing about rocks allows us to understand how the rock eroded to the dramatic scenery we find in Zion today. Let us imagine ourselves as a raindrop falling on the very top of the West Temple, to see how the various layers interact with the erosive power of water.

Falling on the flat limestone layer atop the West Temple, raindrops don't do much. The limestone is very resistant to weathering, and is responsible for the very flat tops of the Temples. Softer rock above broke up and was carried away—but the thin layer of limestone remains.

For the sake of our story, let us imagine the rain collecting and finding its way to the edge of the limestone and dripping onto the Temple Cap sandstone beneath. The Temple Cap sandstone is strong but porous, allowing the water to penetrate the surface. The Temple Cap is like the Navajo, in that it likes to form vertical and near-vertical cliffs, by shedding massive blocks rather than by wearing down grain by grain and forming lower-angled slopes.

Our imagined raindrop flows down the cliff and soaks through the rock until it finds the bottom of the sandstone, where it encounters a thin layer, the bottom of the Temple Cap, a non-porous layer of siltstone that stops downward progress. Again, the moisture runs slowly across the surface until if finds the edge. Undulations in the siltstone concentrate the flow of water like small streams in the porous rock above. These are seen all over the park where they reach the edge, producing springs and seeps at the top of the Navajo. The West Rim Spring just off the West Rim Trail is such a seep, but there are many other examples easily seen when climbing the West Rim Trail toward Behunin Pass.

Our raindrop has now arrived at the top of the Navajo sandstone, dripping onto the soft, white rock and quickly soaking in. Many hundreds of years are required for our little raindrop to find its way through 2000 feet (600 m) of porous rock to somewhere near the bottom of the Navajo. Where the rock becomes less porous, our raindrop moves sideways to find a path to continue its downward journey, often finding a zone of weakness. Eventually, it reaches the non-porous Kayenta layer and moves directly sideways looking for a way out. Joined with other raindrops, the moisture follows weaknesses in the rock caused by previous faulting and natural variation, and finds a place to seep out of the canyon walls. These are the springs and seeps found throughout the park at the bottom of the Navajo, from Pine Creek to Weeping Rock to The Subway.

Below this, our raindrops become a swift-flowing stream of naturally-filtered, fresh, clean water.

Creating Canyons

Zion's canyons form along faults in the Navajo Sandstone that run north to south and east to west. Beginning 80 million years ago, the Colorado Plateau was uplifted and compressed when the Pacific Ocean plate ran into the North American continent. Over 50 million years, east/west compression formed the Rocky Mountains and Sierra Nevada, and the Colorado Plateau was lifted 7000 to 10,000 feet. The Navajo Sandstone stayed mostly intact, but fractured or faulted in places in response to the compressive forces. These fractures run mostly north/south.

More recently, in the last 20 million years, the forces reversed and a great expansion has been taking place, as California is stretched away from Utah. The result is the Great Basin, which starts just west of Zion with the Hurricane Fault, running along I-15. This expansive stress added more fractures to the Navajo Sandstone, many running east-west.

When water falls onto the Navajo, it soaks into the rock and seeks the easiest path. The water seeps to the fracture zones, where the rock is slightly broken up. As more water flows through a fracture zone, the binding minerals are carried away and the rock becomes weaker. This first forms a shallow canyon that attracts more water at the surface, causing more erosion and a deeper canyon. In this way, canyons form along the lines of the N-S and E-W fault lines.

Much of Zion is characterized by *headward erosion*. Pine Creek is a good example. The big canyon at the bottom is working its way upcanyon by eroding the rock away at the base of the Navajo. The canyon above concentrates the water, which seeps through the Navajo to the top of the Kayenta, where it runs horizontally to burst out of the canyon wall as a spring. The flow of water carries away the binding minerals, making the rock weak, and the rock erodes away at the base of the Navajo, forming spectacular alcoves. Eventually, the undercut rock breaks away in blocks, and the large canyon progresses, headward.

When Did the Canyons Form?

The present canyon system started to take form about 15 million years ago, at first shallow then developing into the canyons we know and love today in the last 3 to 5 million years. Much of the carving was probably done during the wet period at the end of the last ice age, 100,000 to 2 million years ago.

Rock Slides and Hot Lava!

Due to the expansion starting 20 m.y.a., the crust became thin in places and hot lava was able to push its way to the surface. Rather than forming volcanoes, this type of lava flowed out of rifts and small cones. These can be seen along the Kolob Terrace Road leading to Lava Point. On at least 20 occasions, lava flowed from rifts and created flows a couple miles long and a couple hundred feet thick. These flows date from 1.5 million years ago to about 200,000 years ago. Lava flowed into the already-formed canyons of the Left and Right Forks, damming them, forming lakes. In the Left Fork, the flow came over the edge near the current trailhead, forming a dam that backed water up as far as The Subway. The lake filled with sediment and the stream overflowed the dam, cutting a new channel in the soft sediments. Sediments from the lake can still be seen at the top of the lava when hiking out of The Subway.

Massive landslides formed other lakes in Zion. The most famous is Sentinel Lake, formed by a giant slide 4000 years ago. This slide came off The Sentinel, just north of the Streaked Wall, and dammed the canyon above Canyon Junction, backing water up past Angels Landing. The floor of Zion Canyon is wide and flat from Zion Lodge to the Temple of Sinawava—this is the lakebed of Sentinel Lake. The lake was at least 350 feet deep, and filled with sediment over about 400 years. Eventually the lake filled and the river was reborn, piercing the dam and cutting sharply through the sediments to form the V-shaped canyon between the Court of the Patriarchs and Canyon Junction. Continued slumping of lakebed sediments continues to this day. A slide in 1995 dammed the river, which overflowed the road. The river is insistent and soon swept the sediments away.

In Zion today, many of the flat-bottomed valleys (Hop Valley, South Fork Taylor Creek, Left Fork, Right Fork and the Main Canyon) are due to lakes formed by landslides and lava flows. Two slide-lakes currently exist in Zion—the Mystery Canyon seasonal lake, and Chasm Lake hidden in the backcountry between Kolob Terrace and LaVerkin Creek.

What Makes Zion Special?

Why is Zion different than other areas on the Colorado Plateau? Zion in located on the southern edge of the Markagunt Plateau—a section of the Colorado Plateau that extends from Springdale 60 miles north and east past Cedar Breaks. This particular chunk of rock has been uplifted and tilted in the last 10 million years. Rivers and streams were already established heading southward down the Plateau, and they had to cut deeply to keep up with the uplift. The highlands created by the uplift attract more rain and snow than the surrounding desert, a lot of which ends up draining through Zion. So, combine a rapid uplift, an established drainage system and plenty of water to provide cutting power—and we end up with a dramatic concentration of incredible, deep canyons–Zion National Park.

Opposite: *Canyon wall and tree in the South Fork of Taylor Creek*

PART I

Hiking and Canyoneering in Zion

CHAPTER ONE

Your Visit to Zion

A wide variety of canyon adventures are concentrated in Zion National Park. Most of the technical canyons are cut deeply into the Navajo sandstone, forming narrows sections 10 to 40 feet (3 to 12 meters) wide and 50 to 300 feet (15 to 100 m) deep. Flowing water is rare in Zion's technical canyons. At the bottom of the Navajo sandstone, springs emerge from the rock, and a flow of beautiful clear water often marks the end of the technical portion of the canyon.

Canyons in Zion usually involve a series of short rappels, though raps up to 300 feet (100 m) are not unknown. More frequently, rappels are in the 40 to 100 foot (10 to 30 m) range, with lovely hiking and downclimbing sections between. Rappel counts range from one or two short ones, to 30 or 40 rappels in some of the more involved canyons.

When difficult, Zion canyons are difficult due to potholes, and because of exposure to cold water. The deep canyons hold water from snowmelt within their bowels, and are refreshed by summer thunderstorms. That water is cold, and some canyons involve being in and out of potholes and cold water for several hours at a time. For this reason, a few canyons require dry suits or heavy wetsuits even in the hottest weather. Other canyons require use of a lightweight wetsuit to be descended enjoyably.

Escaping potholes is a technical challenge found in some canyons. When full, potholes present few challenges, but as the summer progresses without rainfall and the water level lowers, potholes become difficult and strenuous to exit. In canyons with keeper potholes, gear for exiting potholes should be taken at all times. Check for the current conditions.

Anchors in the easier canyons are well-established and rely upon bolts. Venturing away from the trade routes, natural anchors are used, and canyoneers will need to be familiar with more advanced techniques.

Most canyons in Zion are done in one day, though the experience of spending a planned night in one of Zion's canyons should not be missed. Longer routes such as The Narrows, Kolob, Imlay and Heaps are commonly done in two days, though bivy equipment should be kept to a minimum.

Rappel in Little Blue Canyon, Right Fork

The experience of canyoneering in Zion focuses on the sublime scenery and magnificent variety of natural forms, rather than on technical difficulty. With a few exceptions, the technical difficulties to experienced, well-equipped canyoneers are few. The play of light upon the walls, the fluted and sculpted sandstone, the call of the canyon wren, the mystery of what is around the next corner—these are the wonders that the canyoneer delights in, that make Zion a magnificent playground.

For the windshield tourist, Zion makes for a nice day. For the on-trail dayhiker, there are worthy hikes for a few days. For the backpacker, a small selection of overnight trips is available.

For the more adventurous spirit, there is a cornucopia of off-trail exploration in Zion. Sixty percent of the park is considered "inaccessible"—the focus of this book. The best in Zion is found by getting off the trails, heading into the backcountry, and using ropes and canyoneering techniques to descend the maze of canyons that dissect Zion's improbable geography.

Who This Book is For:

This book is for advanced hikers and technical canyoneers. First, the text describes a selection of on-trail hikes. Next, it describes more adventurous off-trail hikes. Thirdly, the most popular of Zion's technical canyons are described in detail. They range from fairly easy to fairly difficult, and provide a starting point for people with technical skills wanting to visit Zion's beautiful canyons. Lastly, this book describes more adventurous and less-traveled canyons in brief.

Zion Logistics

Getting To Zion National Park

Zion is in the southwest corner of the state of Utah. The closest city with an airport, rental cars and amenities is Saint George, Utah. Out-of-state and international visitors might find it easiest to fly to Las Vegas, Nevada, and rent a car. Bus service is available from Las Vegas to Saint George, and then a taxi can be taken to Springdale.

Zion is about 5 hours south of Salt Lake City, Utah; 3 hours northeast of Las Vegas, Nevada; and 6 hours northwest of Phoenix, Arizona.

Springdale, Utah

Life in Zion centers on the town of Springdale, the park Visitor Center and the campgrounds that are just north of town. Springdale was settled as a farming community in 1862, and is now a small town that has maintained much of its charm.

Zion Canyon (The Main Canyon) lies north of Springdale. From the entrance to Zion National Park on the north edge of town, the canyon extends 10 miles north to where the North Fork of the Virgin River emerges between soaring canyon walls. This dramatic place has been known as "The Narrows" for 140 years.

From April to October, the Main Canyon north of Canyon Junction is served by a free shuttle-bus system, and private vehicles are prohibited in the upper six miles. The shuttle is convenient—unless you start or finish a canyon when the service is not running.

Utah State Highway Route 9 runs north from Springdale a few miles to "Canyon Junction," then east up Pine Creek Canyon and through the Mount Carmel Tunnel to the East Side of the park. Just outside the park boundary on the east side, the North Fork Road runs north from the highway and provides access to adventures including The Narrows (from the top, starting at Chamberlain Ranch), Orderville Gulch, and Mystery Canyon. Route 9 runs to Mount Carmel Junction, providing access to Bryce Canyon (north), the city of Kanab (south) and the Grand Canyon (further south).

North and west of the Main Canyon is a plateau area known as The Kolob Terraces, accessed by driving west from Springdale to the town of Virgin, then north on the Kolob Terrace Road (also known as the Kolob Reservoir Road). The Subway and The Right Fork are accessed off the Kolob Terrace Road. The highest point of Kolob Terrace is Lava Point, and the trailhead nearby is the West Rim Trailhead. The West Rim Trail runs south from Lava Point to the floor of the Main Canyon, and is the start for many canyons that drain into the Main Canyon, such as Kolob Creek, Goose Creek, Imlay Canyon and Heaps Canyon.

Further north and west is the Kolob Canyons Section of the park. This is home to the famous Kolob Arch, and is connected to Kolob Terrace by the Hop Valley Trail. There are interesting canyoneering adventures here, including Icebox Canyon. Driving west from Springdale to Interstate 15 (I-15), then north 13 miles to a well-marked exit accesses the Kolob Canyons Section. Cedar City is 18 miles further north. The Kolob Canyons Section has its own Visitor Center.

Where to Stay

The best camping is inside the park, just inside the South Entrance. The **Watchman Campground** (435-772-3837) is a reservation-only campground, and the adjacent **South Campground** is first-come, first-served.

The Watchman is a much nicer campground, and well worth the effort to secure a reservation. Visit the park website for more information: *www.nps.gov/zion*

Park campgrounds do not offer showers. These can found for a small fee at the **Zion Canyon Motel and Campground** (479 Zion Park Boulevard, 435-772-3237); at **Tsunami Café** (180 Zion Park Boulevard) just outside the South Entrance (Tsunami has only one shower); and at **Zion Rock and Mountain Shop** (1458 Zion Park Boulevard, 435-772-3303). If you are up on the east side, showers can be purchased at the **Mukuntuweap Resort and Campground** a mile outside the East Entrance.

There are several commercial campgrounds in Springdale.

A nice place to stay is the **Zion Ponderosa Resort**, high on the East Side, adjacent to the park. They have both cabins and campsites, and very clean showers. *www.ZionPonderosa.com 1-800-293-5444*

Free Camping can be had at **Mosquito Cove**, a casual, non-fee (as of 2006) area along the highway between Rockville and Virgin near milepost 23.5. Being informal, it tends to be loud, dirty and messy. Needless to say, do NOT leave anything there in your absence.

There is a six-site, first-come, first serve campground at Lava Point. No water is available, and sites often fill up early.

Springdale has many **motels.** Reservations are recommended at ALL times. My favorite inexpensive motel is the **El Rio Lodge** (995 Zion Park Boulevard, (435) 772-3205 or toll free (888) 772-3205, Fax (435) 772-2455, E-mail: Elrio@infowest.com). Another inexpensive choice is the **Pioneer Lodge** (838 Zion Park Boulevard, 888-772-3233).

For those willing to spend a little more, The **Desert Pearl Inn** (707 Zion Park Boulevard, 435-772-8888) is a very nice place to stay.

Inside the park, in the Main Canyon, the **Zion Lodge** (435-772-3213) is a fabulous grand hotel from the days of the railroad. Reservations are required year-round, and the price is not outrageous, considering the location.

If heading east to Bryce or the Grand Canyon, the **Best Western Thunderbird Motel in Mount Carmel Junction** (Toll Free: 888-848-6358; Local Phone: 435-648-2203) is a great place to stay, and maybe play a quick round of golf.

More information on businesses in Springdale can be found at the chamber of commerce website: *www.zionpark.com*

Restaurants

The **Mean Bean Café** (932 Zion Park Boulevard) is the popular hang in the morning, the best place to get a decent dose of Joe. Hang around for lunch and try the Mushroom Cloud—it's awesome!

The Pioneer Lodge and Restaurant (838 Zion Park Boulevard) offers a classic American menu at reasonable prices, and is open for breakfast at 7 AM in summer.

For lunch, **Sol Foods** (95 Zion Park Boulevard), just outside the South Entrance offers an excellent deli selection convenient to the park; and the **Zion Park Deli** (866 Zion Park Boulevard) next to the Pizza Noodle offers a worthy rendition of the traditional American sandwich.

For dinner, my favorites are the **Bit and Spur** Mexican restaurant (1212 Zion Park Boulevard) on the south end of town, and the **Pizza Noodle** (868 Zion Park Boulevard) downtown. The Pizza Noodle only takes cash—there is an ATM across the street.

Groceries

Springdale has a couple of small grocery stores. **The Sol Foods Market** (95 Zion Park Boulevard) is conveniently located next to Sol Foods just outside the South Entrance to the park, and can be walked to from campsites in the park. The **Springdale Market** (865 Zion Park Boulevard) has a slightly larger selection, but is still rather limited.

More serious shopping trips require the 19-mile drive to LaVerkin and the **Farmer's Market** found at the intersection of Route 9 and Route 17. A larger, better-stocked grocery store (open on Sundays, unlike the Farmer's Market) is **Lin's Grocery** (1120 West State Street), 4 miles south of LaVerkin in Hurricane.

Internet

The Internet can be accessed at many restaurants in town including Oscar's (934 Zion Park Boulevard) and Sol Foods. You can also connect at the town library (898 Zion Park Boulevard, next to the elementary school) for a nominal fee.

Gear (Purchase or Rental), Outfitting, Guiding, and Training

Guiding is not permitted in Zion National Park, however, there are very good canyons and crags just outside the park that are guided by two local companies.

Zion Adventure Company (36 Lion Boulevard, about 470 Zion Park Boulevard) offers an assortment of canyoneering gear for rent including shoes, packs and dry suits. ZAC offers an informative introductory talk on the Zion Narrows; rental gear for Narrows hikers in all seasons; plus a comprehensive menu of canyoneering courses and adventures, as well as guided technical rock climbing. *www.ZionAdventures.com* 435-772-0990.

Zion Rock and Mountain Guides (1458 Zion Park Boulevard) offers a

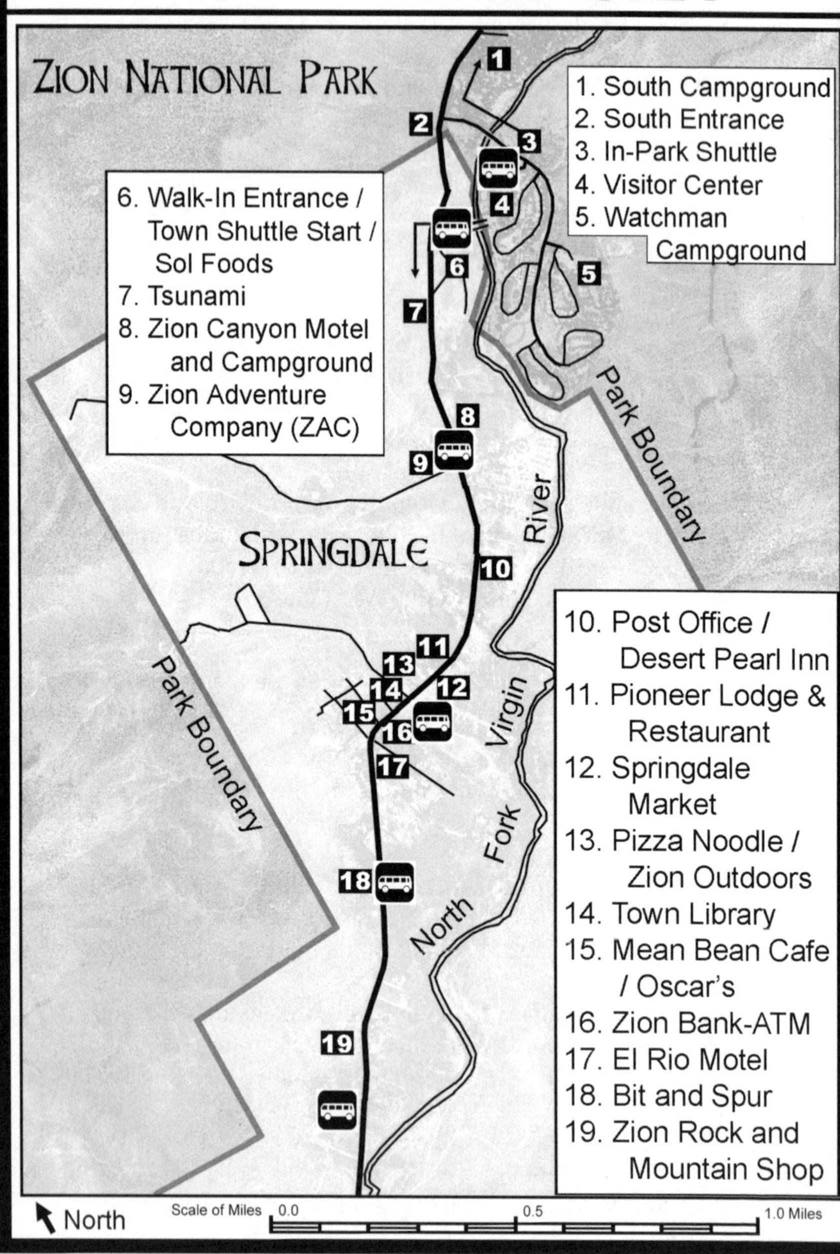
TOWN OF SPRINGDALE
ZION NATIONAL PARK
1. South Campground
2. South Entrance
3. In-Park Shuttle
4. Visitor Center
5. Watchman Campground
6. Walk-In Entrance / Town Shuttle Start / Sol Foods
7. Tsunami
8. Zion Canyon Motel and Campground
9. Zion Adventure Company (ZAC)
SPRINGDALE
Park Boundary
River
Virgin
Fork
North
Park Boundary
10. Post Office / Desert Pearl Inn
11. Pioneer Lodge & Restaurant
12. Springdale Market
13. Pizza Noodle / Zion Outdoors
14. Town Library
15. Mean Bean Cafe / Oscar's
16. Zion Bank-ATM
17. El Rio Motel
18. Bit and Spur
19. Zion Rock and Mountain Shop
North
Scale of Miles 0.0 0.5 1.0 Miles

good selection of rock climbing and canyoneering gear, as well as canyon shoes, wetsuits and dry suits for rental. They are experts on rock climbing in Zion, and offer guided rock climbing and canyoneering just outside the park, as well as curriculum-based canyoneering courses that can be adjusted to fit your current skill set. *www.ZionRockGuides.com* 435-772-3303

The Zion Outdoor Center (868 Zion Park Boulevard, behind the Pizza Noodle) offers a selection of gear, including specialized canyoneering gear, for purchase or rent; and outfitting for the Zion Narrows. 435-772-0990

For a wider selection of gear, **The Outdoor Outlet** in Saint George (1062 East Tabernacle, 435-628-3611) and the **Mountain Shop in Cedar City** (1067 South Main Street, 435-586-7177) stock a good selection of canyoneering and backpacking gear, and are both managed by experienced canyoneers.

Also of note, the **American Canyoneering Association**, located in Cedar City, Utah, offers courses in canyoneering technique for beginner and experienced canyoneers. Find them on the net at *www.Canyoneering.net*, or call 435.590.8889

Getting Around

Hiker Shuttle Service

Zion Rock and Mountain Guides offers shuttle services, with daily shuttles to Chamberlain Ranch and special services by arrangement. Call 435-772-3303.

Zion Adventure Company: Shuttle service to Chamberlain Ranch and other East Side trailheads departs from 36 Lion Boulevard every day at 6:30am and 9:30am. Reservations required. Custom shuttles available upon request. Call 435-772-0990.

Free Shuttles

In town, Springdale has the best public transit system of any town of 500 in the US! Free shuttles run up and down Zion Park Boulevard as far south as the Majestic Inn (the west end of town) on a regular basis. Shuttles start just outside the walk-in entrance to the park, next to Sol Foods and close to the Main Visitor Center. If staying at one of the park Campgrounds, hopping on the shuttle is easy.

In the park, the shuttle system serves the Main Canyon from the Visitor Center, and is convenient for canyon and hiking adventures. Shuttle schedules vary with the season, but in summer, the first shuttle is at 6:30 AM, and the last at 11:00 PM. If you miss the last shuttle, walk to Zion Lodge and someone there might find you a ride out.

If your backcountry plan does not fit with the shuttle schedule, it may be possible to obtain the coveted **Red Pass** that allows off-hours car-access to the main canyon in special circumstances. When getting your permit, make your plea for a Red Pass.

Shuttles run from approximately April 1st to November 1st.

Permits, Reservations, Quotas and Lottery

Zion National Park Visitor Center

The Visitor Center has a gift shop and book store (including maps and guidebooks), really nice bathrooms, and the all-important Backcountry Desk. **Permits are REQUIRED** (as of 2006) for many of the adventures in this book, and are obtained at the Backcountry Desk (435-772-0170). The backcountry staff is friendly and knowledgeable, and often has information about conditions in the canyons.

Since permits are required, there is often a line. Permits can be picked up the day before, or the day of, your adventure, and careful planning will keep you out of long lines. Visit the VC as early as practical to get your permits. The line forms at 6 AM.

Reservation System

Zion has an Internet-based reservation system that helps avoid some frustrations. In addition, you can sign up for the Zion Express Permit Program at the backcountry desk. The ZEP Program allows you to make reservations and print permits from the convenience of any Internet Portal. For more on the current system, visit the park's webpage: *www.nps.gov/zion/Backcountry/Backcountry.htm.*

Backcountry Permits are required for all overnight trips (including climbing bivouacs), all through-hikes of the Virgin River Narrows and tributaries, any trip into the Left Fork of North Creek (The Subway), and all canyons normally requiring the use of descending gear or ropes.

Permits must be obtained the day before, or the day of, the start of your adventure. This allows you to check the latest weather forecast before entering the canyons.

The person who obtains the permit must be 18 years of age or older, and must participate in the trip. The person named on the permit is held responsible for the actions of the group and for compliance with permit conditions and backcountry rules and regulations.

Permits are obtained in person at the Backcountry Desk, at the Kolob Visitors Center (435-586-9548), or using the Internet-based Express Permit System. Hours vary with the season. A Permit Window at the main visitors center opens at an indecently early hour in the summer—and can have a long line even then.

The Backcountry Desk staff is not responsible for the inconvenient rules and regulations that manage use of the backcountry canyons. Please accord them respect and civility. If you have frustrations to take out, write a letter to the park superintendent.

Limits and Lottery

In 2002, the park instituted Interim Use Limits for all technical canyons, in order to limit use while the backcountry planning process is under way. Limits (quotas) vary from canyon to canyon. It is fair to say that many of the canyons in this book are popular and can be difficult to obtain a permit to enter. Make reservations early, obtain your permit as early as possible, and have alternate plans at hand. Fridays and Saturdays are the most popular days.

Reservations can be made for the most popular canyons by signing up for a **Lottery** held three months in advance. After the lottery, reservations can be made via the internet.

Climate, Weather and Canyoneering Season

Zion is blessed with an unusually long and wonderful canyoneering season. Let's start with the "High Season" and proceed from there:

May 15ish–September 15 (High Season/Summer). Summer in Zion is hot. Sometimes scorching hot, sometimes just hot. Approaches in the full sun are best hiked early in the morning. Canyons with just a bit of cold water exposure can be done without protective clothing, but many require wetsuits, and some require full, thick wetsuits or dry suits even in the hottest weather.

September 15–November 1 (Autumn). A wonderful time in Zion. Cooler temperatures and fall colors make this my favorite season. Canyons with any water at all are normally done with wetsuits. Short days often require early starts and careful planning; and make carrying a headlamp essential.

November 1–March 15 (Winter). Winter is a harsh time to canyoneer in Zion. Short days, cold temperatures and accumulated snow in the high country make this a time for very limited technical canyoneering–and then only in the best conditions by experienced canyoneers. Danger!

The Kolob Terrace Road is often closed 1 mile before the Wildcat

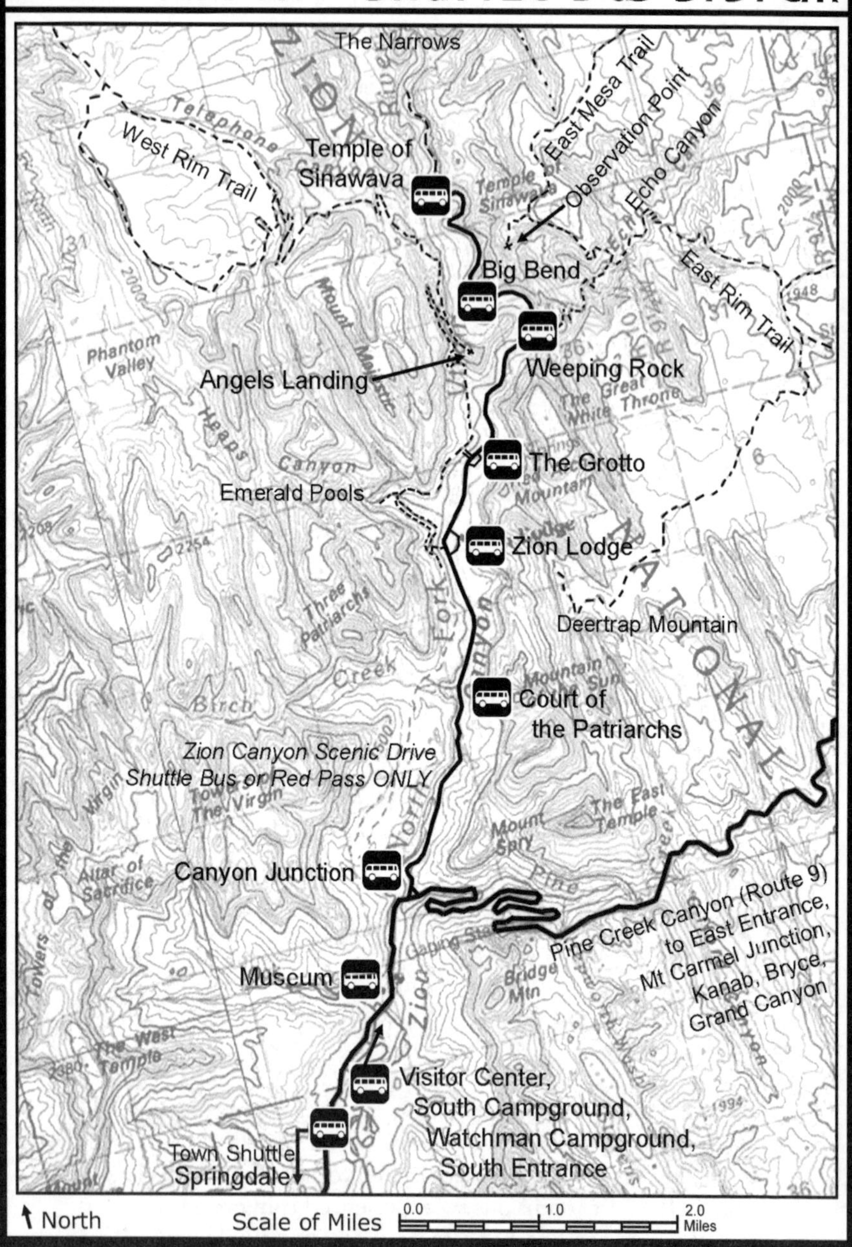
ZION CANYON — SHUTTLE BUS SYSTEM
The Narrows
West Rim Trail
Temple of Sinawava
East Mesa Trail
Observation Point
Echo Canyon
Big Bend
East Rim Trail
Weeping Rock
Angels Landing
The Grotto
Emerald Pools
Zion Lodge
Deertrap Mountain
Court of the Patriarchs
Zion Canyon Scenic Drive
Shuttle Bus or Red Pass ONLY
Canyon Junction
Pine Creek Canyon (Route 9)
to East Entrance,
Mt Carmel Junction,
Kanab, Bryce,
Grand Canyon
Muscum
Visitor Center,
South Campground,
Watchman Campground,
South Entrance
Town Shuttle
Springdale
North
Scale of Miles
0.0
1.0
2.0
Miles

Canyon trailhead. The road to Lava Point may be closed longer, and the road down to the West Rim Trailhead is the last to get open. How long these closures last depend on snow conditions.

March 15–May 15ish (Spring). The weather is most unstable in spring. Many canyons are difficult and dangerous due to snow, meltwater, and melting, overhanging ice. Melting snow raises the height of the North Fork of the Virgin River, often making it impassable, and causes flooding in many other canyons. Very cold water and extended exposure times makes this a very dangerous time to do difficult canyons.

The Narrows is impassable when the water level is high. During such times, permits are not issued for The Narrows and canyons that end in The Narrows (such as Orderville and Mystery). High country snowpack feeding The Narrows varies widely from year to year. Typically, The Narrows is closed for 30 days from mid-April to mid-May, but there are years with no closures, and years with quite long closures. In 1995, The Narrows was closed from March 11th to July 15th.

The Subway is also impassable for a few weeks in the typical spring. Since there is no gauge on the Left Fork, it is up to you to make your own judgment of how difficult it will be. The last few springs, rescues have been called out for people in The Subway who over-estimated their abilities, and spent an uncomfortable night in the canyon.

The Monsoon. Thunderstorms and flash floods can occur at any time of the year, but during the summer, a special pattern sets up that produces big thunderstorms day after day. The Monsoon weather pattern can set up for a few days or a few weeks, anytime in the summer or fall. Warm, moist air is drawn from the Gulf of California, and produces powerful thunderstorms each afternoon. Thunderstorms lead to flash floods—not good for canyoneers.

The Monsoon works like this: It rains in the afternoon or during the night. The morning dawns clear and hot, and all that moisture starts evaporating off into the sky. Unfortunately, the air aloft is already holding a lot of moisture. Thunderhead clouds start to build, often being prominent as early as 10 AM. The clouds build and build, eventually collapsing in huge thunderstorms.

How can you tell if the Monsoon has set up? Pay close attention to the weather report, and note large thunderheads beginning to build as early as 10 AM.

How can you canyoneer in the Monsoon? You can't. Go hiking, visit Vegas, or carefully choose short adventures and start very early in the day. Assess the risk carefully.

Desert Traveling—Being Kind to Yourself and the Landscape

Hiking in the desert is quite different than hiking in other environments, and requires special preparations. Following these guidelines will improve the quality of your experience, minimize your impact on the park, and improve the quality of other people's experience.

Taking Care of Yourself

- **Bring plenty of water.** Dry air, hot sun and high temperatures combine to suck water right out of you. There is very little drinkable water in the Zion backcountry even with filtering, so carry plenty from the start of the day. In summer, this means at least three quarts for a half-day hike.
- **Plan your hike.** In summer, get up early and get the bulk of the uphill done while the air is still cool. Figure out the sun exposure of the hike, and plan around it. Take a siesta in the hottest part of the day, or at least plan to be in the bottom of a nice cool canyon for the scorching hours.
- **It is hard work.** Hiking off-trail, even on such well-established routes as The Narrows and Orderville Gulch, is slow and strenuous. Allow plenty of time to complete your hike before dark.
- **Carry less stuff.** Zion is steep, and carrying a bunch of stuff up hill and over dale is tiring. Inform yourself on up-to-date backpacking techniques, and carry less weight–you will have a better time.

Taking Care of the Landscape

- **Watch your step.** Pay attention to where you walk. Stay on established trails, or walk on zero-impact surfaces such as slickrock and wash bottoms. When following social trails (trails made by the passage of people, rather than by deliberate trail building), stay on the main trail to minimize the proliferation of trails. Walk single file rather than side by side. When given the choice, follow the edge of the stream rather than taking a side-trail that climbs over a hill.
- **Leave nothing, not even footprints.** Carry out all you bring in. No one likes looking at your litter, so take care and leave no refuse behind. When possible, don't even leave footprints.
- **Your poop stinks.** Your poop and toilet paper are one of the worst

Opposite: *Walking between rappels in Spry Canyon*

things you can leave in a canyon. Don't. Make an effort to do your daily duty in the morning, before the start of the hike. If you must go in the canyon, pick a spot with lots of vegetation, as far from the normal line of travel, and as far from the watercourse, as possible. Dig a shallow cathole in the sand, do your business, cover with sand, then cover that with a large rock. Carry a Ziploc bag and pack out your used toilet paper. On overnight trips, get a "Rest-Stop" poop bag from the backcountry desk, or carry a sturdy Tupperware container with double Ziplocs to pack out your poop.

- **Your pee stinks, too.** In the desert environment, that pee smell can last for months, even for years. Urinate where others will not smell it. Don't pee right next to the obvious rest-stop–walk off a few minutes. In a narrow canyon, hold off until a place out of the normal flow of traffic can be found to leave your aromatic brew. In The Narrows, pee directly into the flowing river when possible.
- **When in Rome...** Utah is less vulgar than some parts of the US. Be a sport, respect the local way of doing things. Don't pee in front of other people–go find some cover. Casual nudity is offensive to many Utahans–wear shorts or a swimsuit when swimming, and find some cover when changing into or out of your wetsuit.
- **Social impacts count.** Don't rain on other people's wilderness experience. Respect other parties right to quiet–give them space to do the canyon without YOU breathing down their neck. In narrow canyons, invite faster parties to pass. Create separation between parties either by speeding up or slowing down, or by taking a break to let the other party get a ways ahead.
- **Travel in small groups.** Large groups tend to have significantly more physical impacts per person than small groups, and have a greater impact on other people's feeling of solitude. Limit yourself to parties of 6 or less. If need be, split into two groups and start an hour apart. In small groups, people tend to appreciate the canyon more. In large groups, they tend to appreciate each other. Nothing wrong with that, but there are more appropriate places for a party than on backcountry trails and in wilderness canyons.

Make showing respect for the natural world and other adventurers your first priority when you visit Zion.

Opposite: *View from Angels Landing*

PART II

TRAIL HIKING IN ZION

Chapter Two

Introduction to Trail Hiking

Zion is blessed with a small selection of very spectacular trails. The selection is small and the trails spectacular for the same reason—the terrain is so steep that there are a limited number of places trails can be built. Zion's trails were constructed in the 1920's, and major engineering was required. Most of the trails were built for horses—thus they are wide, paved and well graded.

This section provides information on my favorite trail hikes in Zion. For hiking in the park, you will need to carry a MAP. The Trails Illustrated map of Zion works well.

A few cautions: Some trails have steep dropoffs on one or both sides, carved steps or walkways in the rock, and chains for handholds. Zion is not a place for acrophobes. If you are seriously scared of heights, do not attempt the Angels Landing Trail, Hidden Canyon Trail or Observation Point Trail.

Summer heat calls for careful planning. Get an early start—the earlier the better. Zion trails are steep. Climbing steeply in the cool of the morning is one thing, but climbing steeply in the heat of the day is quite another. Plan your day to avoid sun exposure.

In winter, the plan is reversed. The canyon bottom is cold and shaded much of the day, but with careful planning, your day's hike can be mostly in the sun.

There is very little drinkable water on Zion's trails. Even if water looks clear, filter or treat all backcountry water before imbibing. After years of drought, many of the upland springs dry up. CARRY ALL YOUR WATER FOR THE DAY. In summer, this might mean starting the day with 5 liters of water! About half of the shuttle stops have drinking water and bathrooms.

Opposite: *Double Arch Alcove, Middle Fork Taylor Creek*

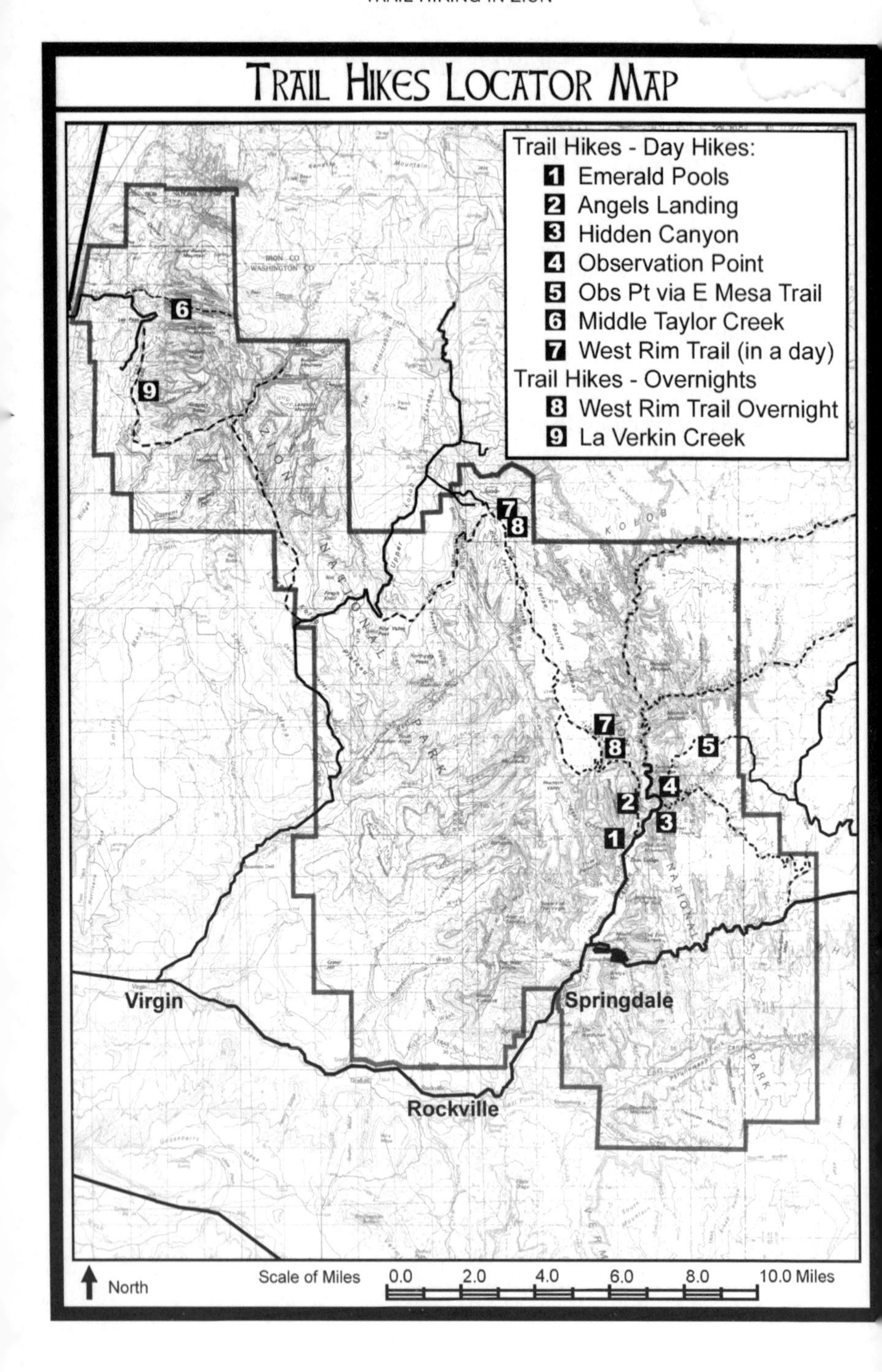

Trail Hikes Locator Map
Trail Hikes - Day Hikes:
1 Emerald Pools
2 Angels Landing
3 Hidden Canyon
4 Observation Point
5 Obs Pt via E Mesa Trail
6 Middle Taylor Creek
7 West Rim Trail (in a day)
Trail Hikes - Overnights
8 West Rim Trail Overnight
9 La Verkin Creek
Virgin
Springdale
Rockville
North
Scale of Miles
0.0
2.0
4.0
6.0
8.0
10.0 Miles

ON-TRAIL DAY HIKES

1 Emerald Pools Trail

Type: There and back, out and around
Length: 2.1 miles to 3.0 miles, total (3.4 to 4.8 km, total)
Time: 1 to 2 hours
Altitude gain: 400 feet (120 m)
Start: Zion Lodge Shuttle Stop (water, bathrooms)
Cautions: Somewhat exposed. Lower Trail suitable for all; other trails not suitable for small children.
Shade: Tends to be shaded in the afternoon.

A short little hike, the Emerald Pools "trail" visits a couple of wonderful waterfalls and the amazing cirque where Heaps Canyon and Behunin Canyon drop in. There are five parts to the trail, and before doing Heaps or Behunin, it is helpful to head up there and figure the network out. It is especially beautiful in the spring, or after a thunderstorm in the summer, when water is flowing out of Heaps and Behunin, and over the ledges into the lower pool.

GETTING THERE: The Emerald Pools Trail starts and finishes at Zion Lodge. A side trail connects to The Grotto.

THE TRAIL(S): The trail system consists of five parts. From Zion Lodge, cross the road and then the river on a suspension bridge.

The LOWER TRAIL leads from this point north along the river 0.2 miles (300 m), then west into a side canyon 0.4 miles (600 m) to the lowest Emerald Pool. This part of the trail is paved, and pretty much flat.

Surprisingly, the main attraction of the Emerald Pools Trail(s) are the spectacular waterfalls. The pools themselves are rather unexciting–the waterfalls and the trails are really nice. The lower trail runs along the base of the Lamb's Point Tongue Formation cliffband, the same 100 foot (30 m) sandstone cliff over which the waterfalls plunge.

Continue along the trail around the Lower Pool and behind the waterfalls. The trail then climbs a hundred feet to reach the MIDDLE TRAIL.

The GROTTO TRAIL proceeds east (right) from this point, then north 0.7 miles (1100 m), mostly along the top of the Lamb's Tongue cliffband, to The Grotto picnic area and shuttle stop.

The MIDDLE TRAIL cuts back west (left) 0.2 miles (300 m) back to the

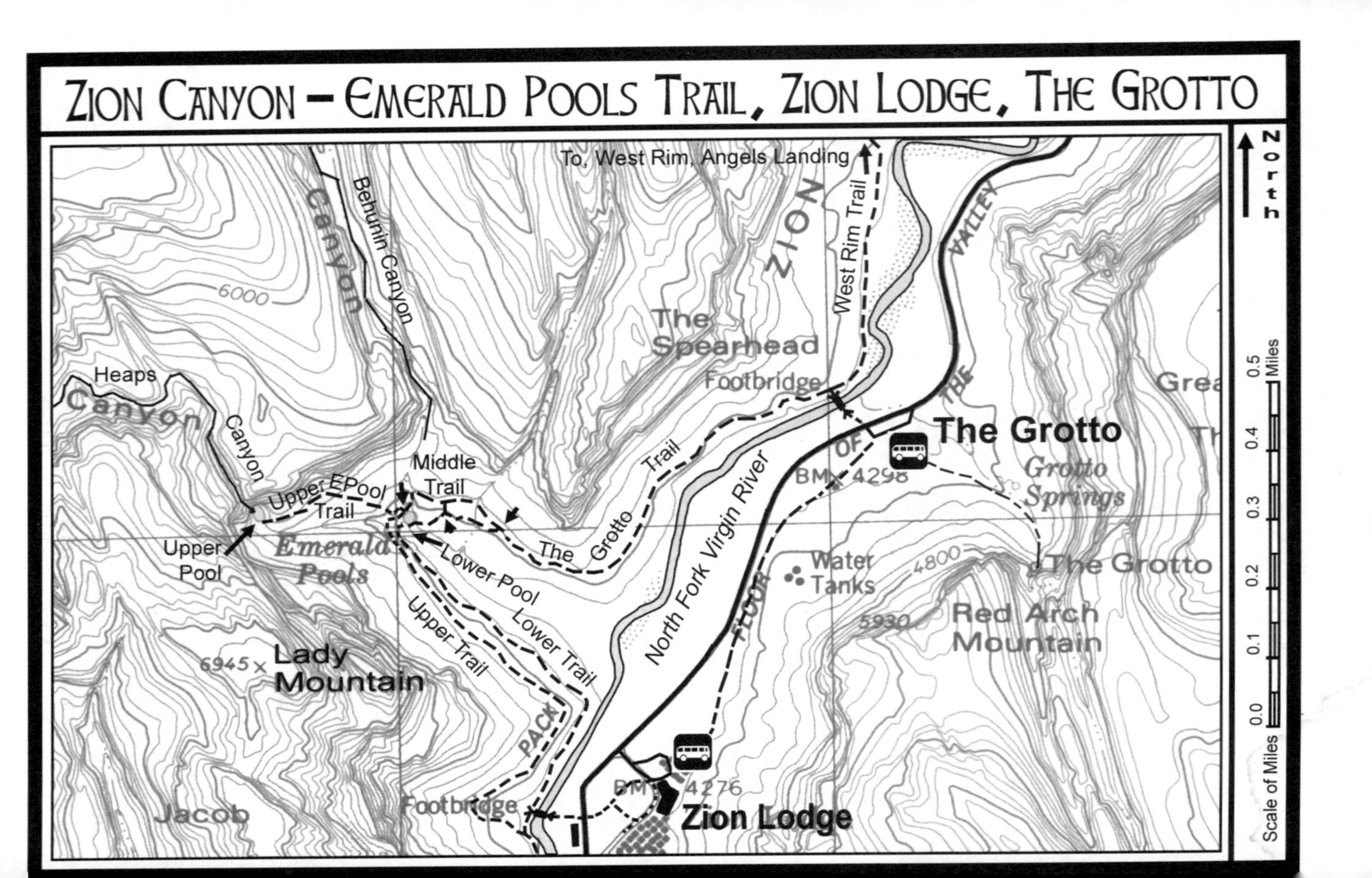

Zion Canyon – Emerald Pools Trail, Zion Lodge, The Grotto
North
To, West Rim, Angels Landing
West Rim Trail
Zion
The Valley
Of
The
Floor
Behunin Canyon
Canyon
6000
Heaps
Canyon
Canyon
The Spearhead
Footbridge
The Grotto
Grotto Springs
The Grotto Trail
Middle Trail
Upper EPool Trail
Upper Pool
Emerald Pools
Lower Pool
Lower Trail
Upper Trail
North Fork Virgin River
BM 4298
Water Tanks
4800
The Grotto
Red Arch Mountain
5930
Lady Mountain
6945
Pack
Footbridge
BM 4276
Zion Lodge
Jacob
0.0
0.1
0.2
0.3
0.4
0.5
Miles
Scale of Miles

top of the waterfall, and an area known as the Middle Pool, though in this case, the pool is more of a wide area in the stream than an actual pool.

From here, the UPPER EMERALD POOL TRAIL branches right and climbs steeply for 0.3 miles (450 m) to the upper pool, and the amazing walls of stone that surround it. The luminous 2000-foot (600 m) sheer wall of Lady Mountain soars to the south, while Heaps Canyon drops 450 feet (130 m) into the talus behind the pool. That nice, green ivy growing among the rocks is Poison Ivy, so watch what you touch. This is an awesome place to sit and watch the light change on the sandstone. (Return the way you came).

Back at the end of the Middle Trail, continuing straight (south) is the UPPER TRAIL. This soon crosses the top of the waterfall (caution!), and then follows the top of the cliffband back out to the main canyon, and eventually down a break in the cliff to the end of the suspension bridge.

When exiting from Heaps or Behunin, it is easier and faster to take the Middle Trail to the Lower Trail and hence to Zion Lodge, rather than the Upper Trail.

The top of the waterfall has been the site of a few tragedies in the past decades. Small children, straying from their parents' close supervision, slipped on the smooth rock at the stream edge and were swept over the falls. A reminder that even on the paved trails of Zion, the dangers of a natural environment are present.

2 Angels Landing

Type: There and back
Length: 2.4 miles (3.8 km) each way
Time: 3 to 5 hours
Altitude gain: 1500 feet (450 m)
Start: The Grotto Shuttle Stop (water, bathrooms)
Cautions: Very exposed, not for acrophobes. Not suitable for small children.
Shade: Lower part shaded in the afternoon. Refrigerator Canyon is shaded most of the day, and the final stretch is fully in the sun.

Zion's easiest rock climb? Or most thrilling hike?

The Angels Landing Trail was built in 1926 as an extension of the West Rim Trail. In many places, steps were hewn out of the rock and thick chain installed along the knife-edge ridge to provide security for the non-mountaineer. Many find the final ridge too much, and wait at the

ANGELS LANDING, HIDDEN CANYON AND OBSERVATION POINT

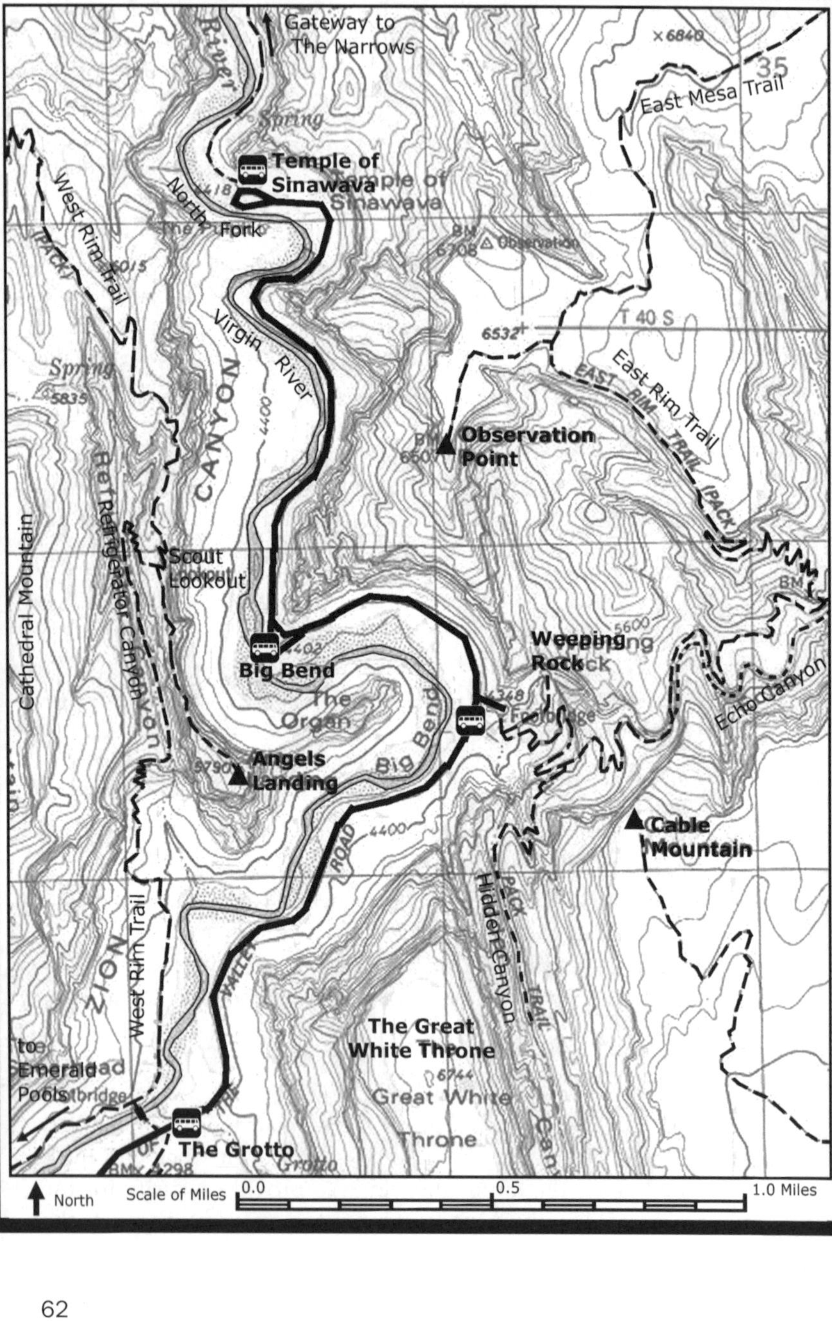
Gateway to
The Narrows
East Mesa Trail
Temple of
Sinawava
North Fork
West Rim Trail
Virgin River
CANYON
East Rim Trail
EAST RIM TRAIL (PACK)
T 40 S
Observation
Point
Spring
Cathedral Mountain
Refrigerator Canyon
Scout
Lookout
Big Bend
The Organ
Weeping
Rock
Echo Canyon
Angels
Landing
Big Bend
Cable
Mountain
ROAD
Hidden Canyon
PACK TRAIL
ZION
West Rim Trail
The Great
White Throne
to
Emerald
Pools
The Grotto
North
Scale of Miles
0.0
0.5
1.0 Miles

"Widow's Tree" for their companions to return from the summit. Those who continue to the top will enjoy amazing views of Zion Canyon, from a lofty perch.

The Grotto was, for many years, the center of activity in Zion. The first ranger cabin was built here, at the end of the road. This used to be THE campground, so if you are in South Campground, and wonder where North Campground was—it was at The Grotto. There is an alcove and spring 0.25 mile (400 m) southeast of the shuttle stop.

The lower section of the West Rim Trail was immortalized in Clint Eastwood's classic film "The Eiger Sanction."

GETTING THERE: Angels Landing is approached via the West Rim Trail. Start at The Grotto picnic area and shuttle bus stop.

THE TRAIL: Cross the road and take the suspension bridge across the river. Turn right. At first the trail is flat and follows along above the river, but soon it starts switchbacking up the steep, south-facing hillside. The trail gets steeper, until it actually cuts into the cliff face, climbs around a buttress and enters Refrigerator Canyon—and the cool shade. Halfway there.

Enjoy the frigid air of Refrigerator Canyon. All too soon, the trail starts climbing again, up the 21 constructed switchbacks of infamous Walt's Wiggles, named for Zion's first superintendent, Walter Ruesch. At the top of the Wiggles, the trail comes out to a sandy area at the top of the ridge known as Scout Lookout. The West Rim Trail turns left and heads north up the ridge. The Angels Landing Trail follows the knife-edge south. Bathrooms are available a short walk to the north (not always open).

Hike south along the ridge. Spectacular views of the North Face of Angels Landing are hard to miss. After climbing a warm-up bump on the ridge, the trail really gets western. A combination of carved steps and fixed chains provide extra security as the trail works up the knife-edge ridge to the top. Return the way you came.

3 Hidden Canyon

Type: There and back
Length: 1.1 miles (1.8 km) at least each way
Time: 2 to 4 hours
Altitude gain: 970 feet (300 m)
Start: Weeping Rock Shuttle Stop (bathrooms)
Cautions: Very exposed, not for acrophobes. Not suitable for small children.

Shade: Lower part shaded in the morning. The canyon itself is shaded all day.

While Angels Landing satisfies the macho, goal-oriented hiker, Hidden Canyon is more of a sublime, spiritual experience. A nice place to while away a few hours on a hot summer day, the beautiful, well-shaded grotto offers no specific objective—and is better for it.

The trail to the mouth of Hidden Canyon was constructed in 1928. Like its sibling across the way, the HC Trail is hewn into a steep rock buttress, with chains anchored to the rock for security. Don't bring small children or the faint of heart.

Hidden Canyon also makes a fine, moderate technical canyoneering adventure. See "Hidden Canyon from the Top" under "Technical Canyons."

GETTING THERE: The Hidden Canyon Trail starts at the Weeping Rock shuttle stop, in the Main Canyon. Bathrooms are available there, but no drinking water.

THE TRAIL: Ascend the East Rim Trail on the painfully obvious switchbacks for 0.66 mile (1 km), gaining 600 feet (180 m). The signed Hidden Canyon Trail branches right, climbing to the crest of a buttress, then slicing across the cliff face to the back of a notch. Follow the trail cut into the rock around another buttress to the mouth of Hidden Canyon. The official trail ends here.

But that's no reason to stop! Explore up the canyon as far as nerve, skill, time and sense allow. There is a delightful arch on the right about half a mile up. Further along, a few obstacles block the way, surmountable by the more vigorous and or foolish. Remember that the climb down is more difficult than the climb up. Several hikers have broken legs here over the last couple of years, and the carryout is slow, painful and difficult.

Return the way you came.

4 Observation Point Trail

Type: There and back
Length: 3.25 miles (5.2 km) each way
Time: 4 to 6 hours
Altitude gain: 2270 feet (700 m)
Start: Weeping Rock Shuttle Stop (bathrooms)

Cautions: Exposed, not for acrophobes. Not suitable for small children.

Shade: Lower part shaded in the morning. Upper half exposed to the full sun all day.

Observation Point offers a tremendous view from high on the east canyon rim. From here, Zion can be seen as a vast, dissected plateau. The view is not as intimate as Angels Landing, and the effort substantially more, so there tend to be many fewer people, making for a quieter experience.

The Observation Point Trail was constructed during the trail-building frenzy in the late 1920's, however, the trail up Echo Canyon follows an old Paiute Indian trail that was expanded to handle pack horses and cattle by pioneer John Winder in 1896.

GETTING THERE: The Observation Point Trail starts at the Weeping Rock shuttle stop, in the Main Canyon. Bathrooms are available.

THE TRAIL: Ascend the East Rim Trail on the painfully obvious switchbacks for 0.66 mile (1 km), gaining 600 feet (180 m). The signed Hidden Canyon Trail branches right. Continue up the East Rim Trail, passing under the impressive, smooth face of Cable Mountain and into Echo Canyon. The trail soon exits the canyon bottom and climbs moderately for a mile or so to another trail intersection. The East Rim/Observation Point Trail is the main trail, while the Echo Canyon Trail branches right and descends into Echo Canyon. Follow the trail up a series of steep, airy switchbacks to the rim of the canyon. Traverse left to intersect with the East Mesa Trail, then continue along the rim another 0.4 mile (0.6 km).

The view at Observation Point is tremendous, sweeping around almost 360 degrees. To the east is the deep cleft of O-Point Canyon, and expanses of slickrock leading over to Echo Canyon. Across Echo Canyon is the

Mileage Log—Observation Point Trail

Landmark	Distance Miles	Distance Km	Gained Feet	Gained Meters
Start of Trail	0.0 mile	0.0 km	0 ft	0 m
Hidden Canyon Trail	0.5 mile	0.9 km	600 ft	180 m
Echo Canyon Trail	1.7 mile	2.7 km	1240 ft	380 m
East Mesa Trail	2.9 mile	4.7 km	2140 ft	655 m
Observation Point	3.3 mile	5.2 km	2270 ft	690 m
Return to Weeping Rock	6.6 mile	10.4 km		

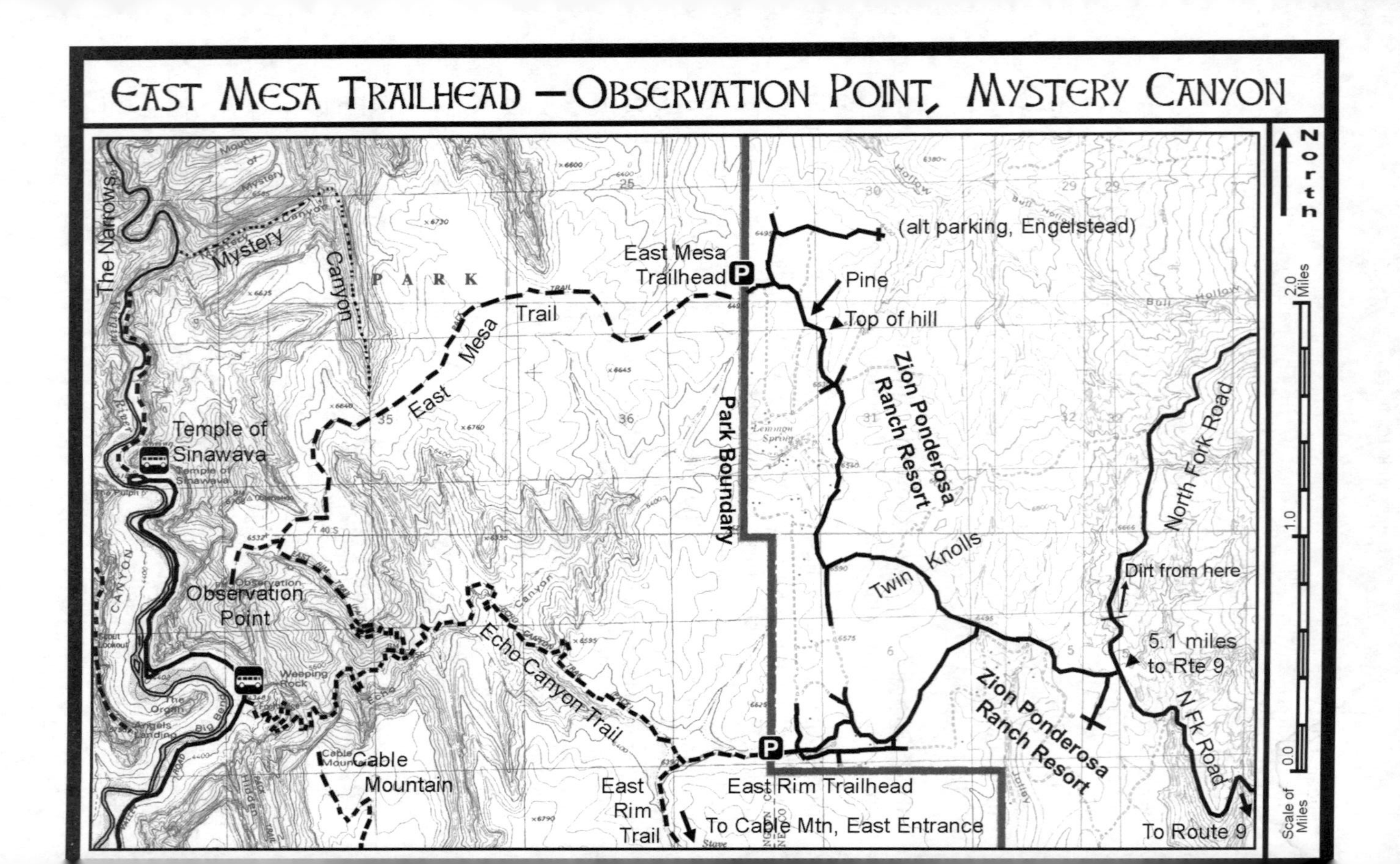
East Mesa Trailhead – Observation Point, Mystery Canyon
North
Scale of Miles
0.0
1.0
2.0
The Narrows
Mystery
Canyon
PARK
Temple of Sinawava
Observation Point
Weeping Rock
Cable Mountain
East Mesa Trail
East Mesa Trailhead
Park Boundary
(alt parking, Engelstead)
Pine
Top of hill
Zion Ponderosa Ranch Resort
Twin Knolls
North Fork Road
Dirt from here
5.1 miles to Rte 9
N Fk Road
To Route 9
Echo Canyon Trail
East Rim Trail
East Rim Trailhead
To Cable Mtn, East Entrance

sheer, 1200-foot (400 m) rock face of Cable Mountain, and to its right, first Hidden Canyon then The Great White Throne. Across the river and far below is Angels Landing, a red mountain in front of the great white ramparts of Cathedral Mountain. Almost due west is the famous rock climb Moonlight Buttress. Turning north, one has a bird's eye view of the great Zion canyon coming together to form The Narrows.

Enjoy the view, then return the way you came.

5 Observation Point via East Mesa Trail

Type: There and back
Length: 3.4 miles (5.4 km) each way
Time: 3 to 4 hours
Altitude gain: 280 feet (85 m)
Start: East Mesa Trailhead
Cautions: Might be accused of cheating!
Shade: Most of the trail is partially shaded by ponderosa pines.

Got a vehicle? An hour drive turns an outstanding workout into a casual stroll. The road getting there, however, requires a high clearance (or rental) vehicle due to the rutted road. A wide, flat trail leads through a beautiful, sparse forest to Observation Point.

GETTING THERE: The East Mesa Trail begins on the park boundary and is accessed through the Zion Ponderosa Ranch Resort. Allow an hour driving time from Springdale.

From Springdale, take Route 9 up Pine Creek Canyon toward Mt Carmel Junction. From the East Entrance, continue 2.4 miles east, then turn Left (N) on the paved North Fork Road. Follow the winding road 5.1 miles to the Zion Ponderosa Ranch Resort—turn left into the Ranch. The following mileage points are given from the entrance.

The dirt roads from here are rough and not well signed. Please be respectful of Ponderosa residents you encounter—afoot, on ATV, on horse or in cars. You are a guest on the Ranch. A few, but not all, of the turns are marked for "Observation Point."

0.0 miles: At the entrance, go straight past a residence. Avoid going down to the main resort building to the left. Pavement ends.
0.4 miles: Y—go Right.
0.7 miles: T—go Right for Observation Point (Twin Knolls Road).
1.5 miles: T—go Right.

2.3 miles: Fir Road crosses—go straight. Road gets worse. Park here if the road is wet.
2.6 miles: Deeply rutted hill—this is the worst spot. Some 2WDs will park at the top of the hill.
2.65 miles: Pine in center of road, rough. Go right down the hill.
2.9 miles: Y—go Left
3.0 miles: End of Road at Park Boundary: Parking lot.
For those of you with GPS: UTM Nad83: 331502 mE 412942 mN

THE TRAIL: Stroll on the wide, smooth trail, 3.4 miles to Observation Point. The trail is on the mesa top with huge ponderosa pines and signs of recent fires. Pass the top of Mystery Canyon at 2.1 miles (3.4 km). Intersect with the East Rim Trail at 3.0 miles (4.9 km). Go right. A further 0.4 miles (0.6 km) finds you at a spectacular overlook.

Return the way you came, or send the driver back and hike down the Observation Point Trail to Weeping Rock, and take the park shuttle back into town.

Observation Point (either way) can be combined with Hidden Canyon or Echo Canyon (from the bottom) to make a more substantial day.

6 Middle Fork Taylor Creek

Type: There and back
Length: 3.2 miles (5.1 km) each way
Time: 2 to 4 hours
Altitude gain: 1050 feet (320 m)
Start: Middle Taylor Creek Trailhead, Kolob Canyons Section
Cautions: Trail not well marked. Carry a map. Rattlesnakes are frequently seen in the area.
Shade: First third not shaded. The rest of the hike is in a well-shaded canyon.

Orange walls soaring into a blue sky. Waterfalls and pine trees. Middle Fork Taylor Creek offers a wonderful walk up one of Zion's Kolob Finger Canyons. As a bonus, the canyon runs east-west and is shaded most of the day.

GETTING THERE: Taylor Creek is located in the Kolob Canyons section of Zion. The drive from Springdale is about one hour. From Springdale, drive 19 miles south and west on Route 9 to LaVerkin. Turn Right, and proceed 6 miles north on Highway 17 to Interstate 15. Go north on I-15 13 miles to the Kolob Canyons exit. Check in at the Visitor Center, then

Waterfall, Middle Fork Taylor Creek

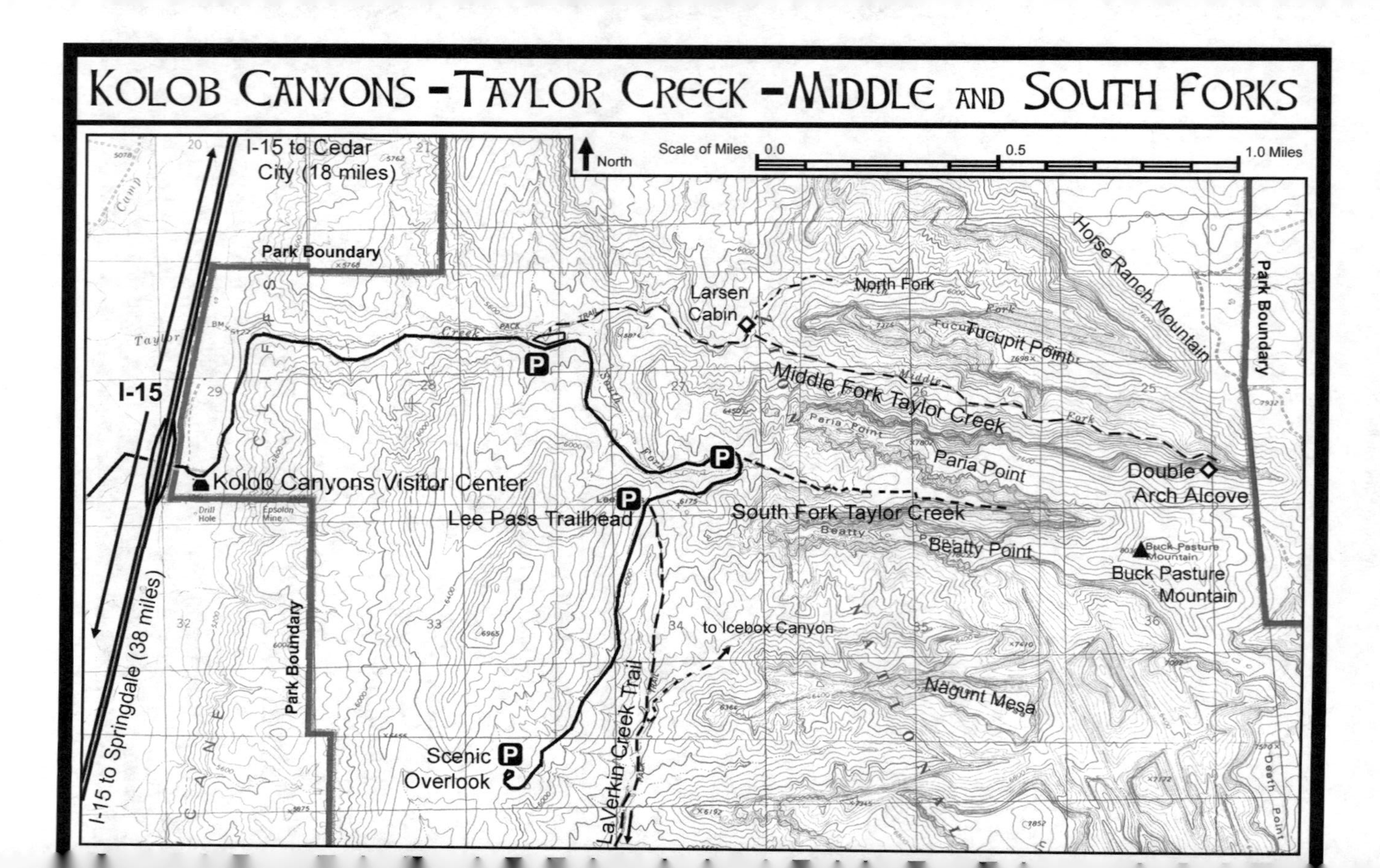

Kolob Canyons - Taylor Creek - Middle and South Forks
I-15 to Cedar City (18 miles)
North
Scale of Miles
0.0
0.5
1.0 Miles
Park Boundary
Larsen Cabin
North Fork
Tucupit Point
Horse Ranch Mountain
Park Boundary
I-15
Middle Fork Taylor Creek
Paria Point
Double Arch Alcove
Kolob Canyons Visitor Center
Lee Pass Trailhead
South Fork Taylor Creek
Beatty Point
Buck Pasture Mountain
Buck Pasture Mountain
to Icebox Canyon
Park Boundary
Nagunt Mesa
I-15 to Springdale (38 miles)
Scenic Overlook
LaVerkin Creek Trail
Death Point

drive 2.0 miles to the well-marked Middle Fork Taylor Creek Trailhead on the left.

THE TRAIL: Drop down into and across the stream and pick up the trail heading north on the other side. Take note of where the trail crosses the stream and ascends to the trailhead, for the return hike.

Follow the trail east beside the stream for 1.1 miles (1.8 km) to the Larsen Cabin, built in 1929. The Middle Fork Trail continues east, into the dramatic canyon between Tucupit Point to the north and Paria Point to the south. There is a less-well-defined trail up the North Fork.

Entering the canyon of the Middle Fork, as the trail becomes rougher, the route is dictated by the terrain. Watch for the beaten path as you travel upstream; try to stay on the main route. Too much off-trail hiking will give this canyon a worn appearance. There are several waterfalls, and the canyon is deeply shaded much of the day.

Follow the canyon upstream as the soaring walls close in. Two miles (3.2 km) past the Larsen Cabin, the trail ends at the Double Arch Alcove. An alcove and closed arch at ground level is floored with the most amazing orange sand. Five hundred feet above, a similar closed arch above a ledge creates a stunning counterpoint. The canyon walls are close together and the canyon filled with a dense forest. Wild turkeys live in the area.

What is a closed arch? While we usually think of an arch as being separate from the rock, air all around, there is another kind of arch–a closed arch. The term is used for an arch-like formation that is not fully separated from the rock near it. Another example in Zion is The Great Arch at the head of Pine Creek Canyon.

A steep landslide blocks travel further upcanyon. The more adventurous can climb the steep dirt and continue a few minutes, but most will enjoy the alcove as a fitting end to a wonderful stroll. Return the way you came.

7 West Rim Trail in a Day

Type: One Way
Length: 12.9 miles (20.7 km) or 14.2 miles (22.8 km)
Time: 6 to 12 hours
Altitude gain/loss: Gain: 500 ft (150 m). Loss: 3650 ft (1100 m)
Start: West Rim Trailhead near Lava Point.
End: The Grotto Shuttle Stop, Zion Canyon.

Cautions: A long way to go and steeply downhill at the end. Not suitable for small children, and some adults.

Shade: Hiking along the mesa plays tag with the shade of the big trees. The upper part of the descent into Zion Canyon is exposed to the full sun, with mixed sun and shade from there down.

A marvelous tour of Zion. For those with the knees for it, the West Rim Trail is a great way to see and get to know the backcountry. The first part hikes out the flat top of Horse Pasture Mesa to a small pond at Potato Hollow. A short, steep climb leads to the second part of the Mesa, where two options are available. Meeting back up at West Rim Spring, the trail then descends steeply to Zion Canyon.

GETTING THERE: The West Rim Trailhead is near Lava Point in the Kolob Terrace section of the park. A small, primitive campground is found at Lava Point—staying there encourages an early start. Drive time from Springdale is about 1.5 hours.

From Springdale, drive south and west 14 miles on Route 9 to the town of Virgin. Turn right on the Kolob Reservoir (Kolob Terrace) Road. Drive 20.0 miles to the Lava Point Road, and turn right. Follow this road 0.9 miles to a junction. The road straight ahead goes to Lava Point (great view) and the Lava Point Campground. Take the road to the left a further 1.4 miles (some rough spots) to the West Rim Trailhead. Park.

The road from the junction to the West Rim Trailhead is sometimes closed in the spring, or after storms. The "Barney Trail" leaves the back of the Lava Point Campground and makes its way down to the road, and hence to the West Rim Trailhead, adding an additional 0.75 mile. Those with delicate low-clearance vehicles might want to use this option.

The continuation of the road past the trailhead is the "MIA Road." There is a gate on the MIA Road—do not park past the gate, or blocking it.

MIA–The "Mutual Improvement Association" was a Church of Jesus Christ of Latter Day Saints program for young men and young women of the church, to school them in proper living. The MIA road leads to the MIA Camp–a church camp owned and run by a local branch of the LDS church that runs summer camp for its youth members.

THE TRAIL: Cowboy up and hit the trail. Five minutes along, the Wildcat Canyon Trail branches right. Go straight. Hike through sparse ponderosa Pine forest along the flat top of the mesa, enjoying the view out each side.

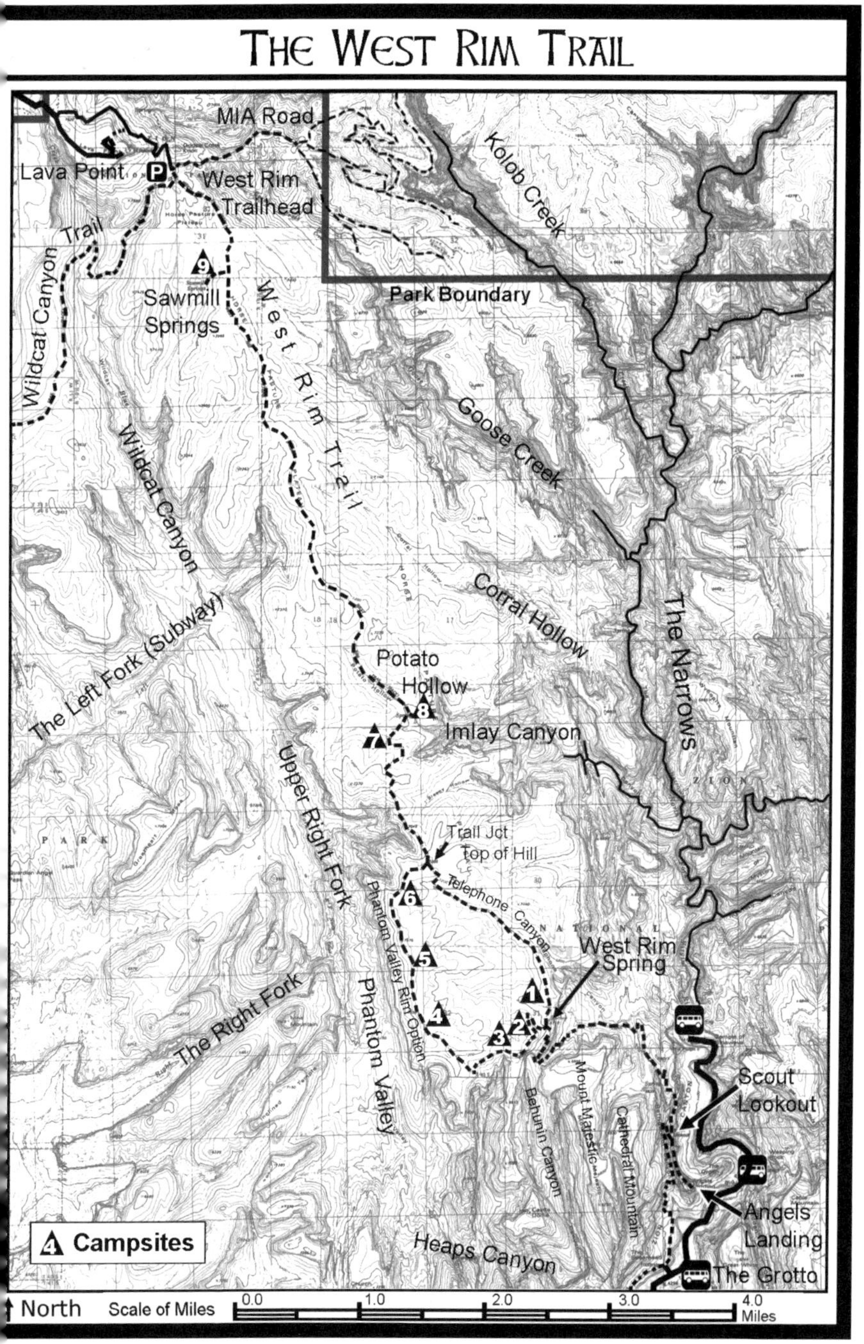

The West Rim Trail

MIA Road
Lava Point
West Rim Trailhead
Kolob Creek
Wildcat Canyon Trail
Sawmill Springs
Park Boundary
West Rim Trail
Goose Creek
Wildcat Canyon
Corral Hollow
The Narrows
The Left Fork (Subway)
Potato Hollow
Imlay Canyon
Upper Right Fork
Trail Jct Top of Hill
Telephone Canyon
Phantom Valley Rim Option
West Rim Spring
Phantom Valley
The Right Fork
Scout Lookout
Behunin Canyon
Mount Majestic
Cathedral Mountain
Angels Landing
Campsites
Heaps Canyon
The Grotto
North
Scale of Miles 0.0 1.0 2.0 3.0 4.0 Miles

The views into the Left and Right Forks of North Creek (to the right, or west) are especially spectacular. At 4.5 miles (7.2 km), the trail descends into the lush beauty of Potato Hollow. There is a pond and spring that runs dry only occasionally. Treat or filter this water before using.

The West Rim Trail makes a fine overnight hike. Campsites are assigned, and the first recommended-by-Tom campsites are here at Potato Hollow. A short stroll to the east leads to great views of Imlay Canyon.

After a little rest and relaxation, return to the trail and begin the slog up the hill on the south side. In the next 1.5 miles (2.4 km), the trail climbs 500 feet (150 m) across rough terrain with dramatic views to the west into the Right Fork of Great West Canyon. After a steep climb, the trail regains the top of the mesa and arrives at a trail junction.

OPTIONS: The West Rim Trail offers two options:

1. **Left branch, the Telephone Canyon Trail,** is the direct route to West Rim Spring taking 1.8 miles (2.9 km), all downhill.
2. **Right branch, the Rim Trail,** follows the edge of the mesa with amazing views into Phantom Valley (the upper part of Heaps Canyon), then hooks around to West Rim Spring in 3.1 miles (5.0 km), or an EXTRA 1.3 miles (2.1 km). Recommended.

Both options end up at West Rim Spring trail junction. A tiny trickle of a spring is an eighth mile down a trail to the north. This is the only reliable water on the West Rim Trail, though the trickle is small so it takes a while to collect.

Mileage Log—West Rim Trail

Landmark	Miles	Kms	Gain/Loss Feet	Gain/Loss Meters
West Rim Trailhead	0.0	0.0		
Potato Hollow	5.1	8.2	-660 ft	200 m
Trail Junction Top of Hill	6.7	10.7	+500 ft	150 m
Via Telephone Canyon Option				
West Rim Spring	8.5	13.6	-540 ft	160 m
Behunin Pass	9.0	14.4	-430 ft	130 m
Scouts Lookout	11.3	18.1	-1110 ft	340 m
The Grotto / Zion Canyon	12.9	20.7	-950 ft	290 m
Via Rim Trail				
West Rim Spring	9.7	15.7	-540 ft	160 m
Behunin Pass	10.2	16.5	-430 ft	130 m
Scouts Lookout	12.5	20.2	-1110 ft	340 m
The Grotto / Zion Canyon	14.2	22.8	-950 ft	290 m

So much for the fun stuff. From here, the West Rim Trail is steeply downhill. Take the southward-heading trail that soon comes to the edge of the slickrock. Descend on pathways cut into the rock, with great views into Behunin Canyon to the south. The trail drops 450 feet (130 m) in the first half mile (0.8 km), then continues descending less steeply as it skirts the north end of Mount Majestic. Climbing briefly to regain the ridge, the trail proceeds southward along a narrow ridge to Scout Lookout. For those who have not YET had enough, a short excursion can be made to the summit of Angels Landing. Charge down Walt's Wiggles, knees willing, and through Refrigerator Canyon, then down even more switchbacks to the floor of Zion Canyon.

OVERNIGHT HIKES

Zion has a small selection of nice, backpacker overnight hikes. Camping spots are assigned when you pick up your REQUIRED overnight permit. There are a limited number of spots available, and all sites can be taken on summer weekends. Call the backcountry desk or visit their website to find out the latest info on reserving and getting permits, and on planning your overnight trip. Permits can be obtained at either the main Visitor Center near Springdale, or at the Kolob Canyons visitor center off I-15 south of Cedar City.

8 West Rim Trail Overnight

Type: One Way
Length: 12.9 miles (20.7 km) or 14.2 miles (22.8 km)
Time: 6 to 12 hours hiking time
Altitude gain/loss: Gain: 500 ft (150 m). Loss: 3650 ft (1100 m)
Start: West Rim Trailhead near Lava Point.
End: The Grotto Shuttle Stop, Zion Canyon.
Cautions: Steeply downhill at the end. Not suitable for small children.
Water: Available at Potato Hollow (seasonally) or West Rim Spring. If not camping nearby, plan to carry enough water to dry camp.
Shade: Hiking along the mesa plays tag with the shade of the big trees. The upper part of the descent into Zion Canyon is exposed to the full sun, with mixed sun and shade from there down.

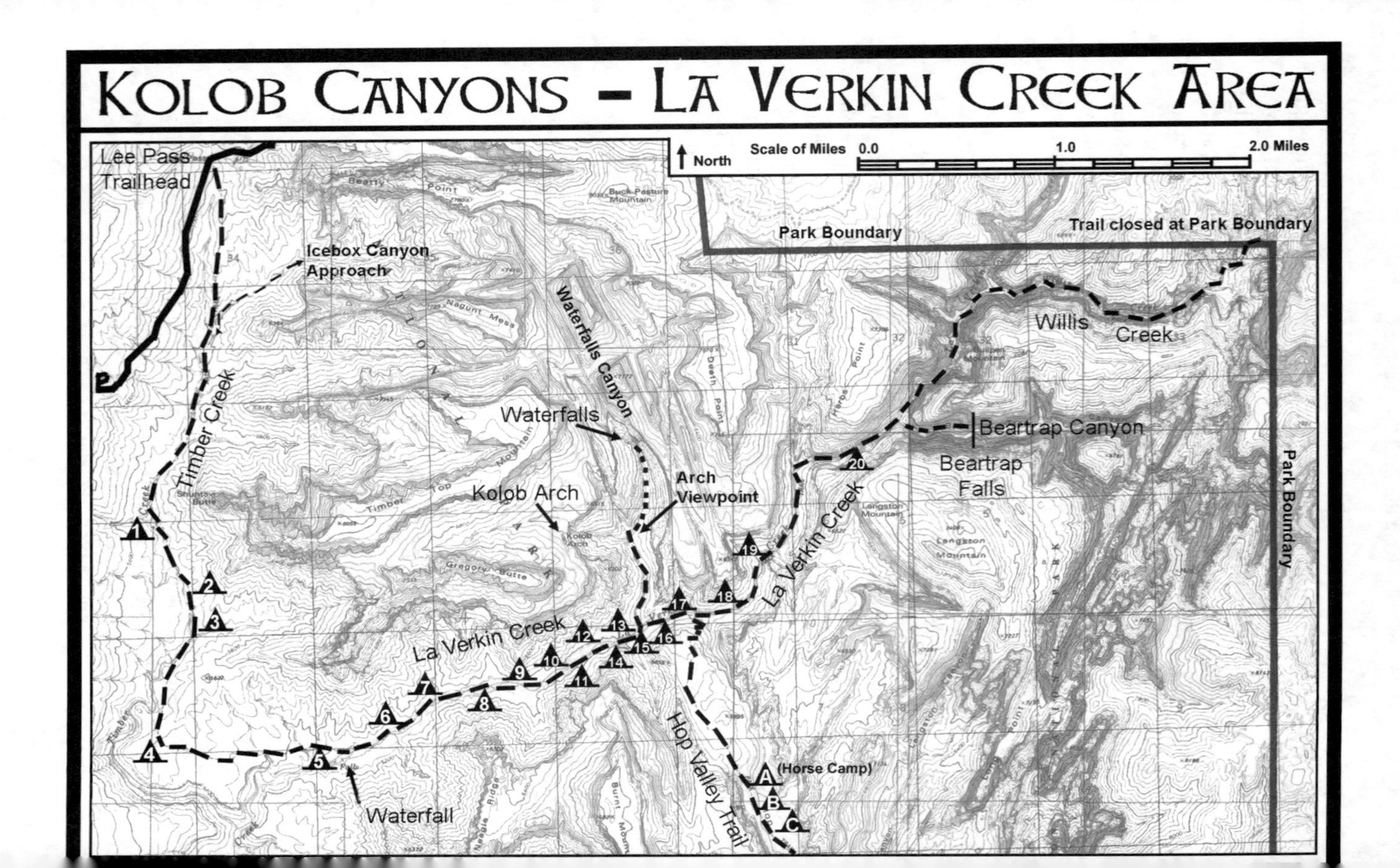
Kolob Canyons - La Verkin Creek Area
North
Scale of Miles 0.0 1.0 2.0 Miles
Lee Pass Trailhead
Timber Creek
Icebox Canyon Approach
Waterfalls Canyon
Waterfalls
Kolob Arch
Arch Viewpoint
La Verkin Creek
Waterfall
Hop Valley Trail
(Horse Camp)
Park Boundary
Trail closed at Park Boundary
Willis Creek
Beartrap Canyon
Beartrap Falls
1
2
3
4
5
6
7
8
9
10
11
12
13
14
15
16
17
18
19
20
A
B
C

While the West Rim makes a LONG one-day trip, it makes a much more casual two-day trip. Campsites are assigned. The first campsites are near the trailhead and the last ones are near West Rim Spring (Cabin Spring). One of the best campsites is number 6, overlooking Phantom Valley and Heaps Canyon. Other favorites are numbers 7 and 8 near Potato Hollow, close to water (most of the time), and the best for beating the heat–with a great sunrise.

Of the springs, West Rim Spring is small but reliable. Potato Hollow is often better, but dries up in the driest of seasons.

For description, see Trail Hike 7.

In spring, the Lava Point road can be closed. It is possible to hike from the floor of Zion Canyon and camp on the West Rim, then return the same way. In spring, the north-facing climb to the head of Behunin Canyon, an area known as Little Siberia, can be packed with snow and the trail drops steeply off one side—be careful.

9 LaVerkin Creek and Kolob Arch

Type: Out and Back
Length: At least 4.4 miles (7 km) to the first campsites. It is 6.7 miles (11 km) to the Kolob Arch viewpoint.
Time: 6 to 10 hours hiking time total
Altitude gain/loss: Descend 1070 feet (330 m) to LaVerkin Creek, then climb 320 feet (100 m) to the Kolob Arch viewpoint.
Start and end: Lee Pass Trailhead, Kolob Canyons Section.
Cautions: A steep climb to get out at the end of the trip.
Shade: Most of this trail is exposed to the full sun.

This is an unusual hike, as it starts by traveling downhill, and ends by hiking uphill. The usual objective is to get to the viewpoint of Kolob Arch. Camp along LaVerkin Creek. The canyon north of Kolob Arch, known as Waterfalls Canyon, has some cool waterfalls not far past Kolob Arch. A three-day trip allows exploring up LaVerkin Creek and to the waterfall in Beartrap Canyon. Campsites above the intersection with Waterfalls Canyon afford more privacy. Since most of the hike is in the sun, this makes a good trip in the spring.

GETTING THERE: LaVerkin Creek is located in the Kolob Canyons section of Zion. The drive from Springdale is about one hour. From Springdale, drive 19 miles south and west on Route 9 to LaVerkin. Turn Right, and proceed 6 miles north on Highway 17 to Interstate 15. Go north on I-15 13 miles to the Kolob Canyons exit. Check in at the Kolob Visitor Center, then drive 3.6 miles to the well-marked Lee Pass Trailhead on the left. (Drive another 1.5 miles to the end of the road to get a good view of Timbertop Mountain).

THE TRAIL: From Lee Pass, descend steeply down the wide trail to the bottom of Timber Creek. Cross the small drainage at the bottom and find the trail on the other side. Continue south into the main Timber Creek valley and follow along the (often dry) streambed. There are several campsites (1-4) in this area, but they are far from water in most seasons.

After a couple miles, the trail climbs away from the streambed and up through the woods. The trail is easy to lose here, so pay attention and follow the most-worn path over a shallow hill, then down into the LaVerkin Creek valley, eventually meeting the creek. LaVerkin Creek gushes with beautiful, clear water.

Campsites are found along LaVerkin Creek for several miles, from where the trail meets the creek to a few miles past where Waterfalls Canyon comes in on the left. The prettiest campsites are the furthest in.

Hike alongside LaVerkin Creek east for a couple miles to a stream coming in on the left. This is Waterfalls Canyon.

To Visit the Kolob Arch Viewpoint: Turn left and follow the trail for half a mile to where Kolob Arch can be seen to the west through the trees.

For additional fun, continue up the canyon on the right (northwest) past the Kolob Arch Viewpoint. A half-mile of slow, rough hiking takes the intrepid adventurer to the base of an un-named triple waterfall. A trail to the right may be used to reach the top of the 400-foot (120 m) waterfall system.

Return the way you came.

Additional Treats in the Area: Past Waterfalls Canyon, LaVerkin Creek and Beartrap Canyon both offer interesting exploration.

Mileage Log—LaVerkin Creek Trail

Landmark	Miles	Kms	Gain/Loss Feet	Gain/Loss Meters
Lee Pass Trailhead	0.0	0.0		
Timber Creek	0.9	1.5	-500 ft	150 m
LaVerkin Creek	4.4	7.1	-570 ft	170 m
Waterfalls Canyon Junction	6.2	9.9	+200 ft	60 m
Kolob Arch Viewpoint	6.7	10.7	+120 ft	40 m
Base of Waterfall	7.2	11.5	+350 ft	100 m
Return to Lee Pass	14.4	23.0		

Opposite: *Brian Frankle hiking in The Narrows*

PART III

OFF-TRAIL HIKING IN ZION

CHAPTER THREE

Introduction to Off-Trail Hiking

While most of Zion's off-trail terrain requires ropes and technical skills to access, there is a generous handful of canyons that are accessible to the rope-averse, and they are among Zion's gems.

Hiking off-trail requires more skill, knowledge, maturity and self-reliance than following the paved footpaths of Zion's main trails. Navigation is NOT taken care of for you. Even with accurate and thorough descriptions you should carry a topographic map, know how to use it, understand where the route goes, and exercise caution and judgment. The backcountry in Zion is ever-changing, and the descriptions here may or may not be accurate by the time you get there.

GPS units only work when a full view of the sky is available. They are no substitute for a topographic map and knowing how to read it. I find a GPS unit to be of little use in Zion.

The Hikes

Off-trail hikes in Zion range from The Narrows–which is pretty darn close to being on-trail–to scratchy bushwhacks far from civilization. I consider "hikes" those adventures that many people will not use a rope or, if a rope is employed it is only used for lowering packs or as a hand-line. For this reason, I include Orderville Canyon as a "hike," and place The Subway in the "canyoneering route" category.

Those who enjoy slot canyons MUST visit the amazing Echo Canyon (from the bottom), and persevere through that icy (or icky) pool near the bottom. For those who are truly averse to ropes, the best part of The Subway can be visited by hiking up from the bottom, although it makes for a VERY long hike on a hot summer day.

Equipment

Most off-trail hikes include some degree of wading or swimming. For these hikes, wear clothes and shoes suitable for wading. Shorts and tee-shirts should be of the synthetic, quick-drying variety. Even when

Brian Frankle in The Narrows

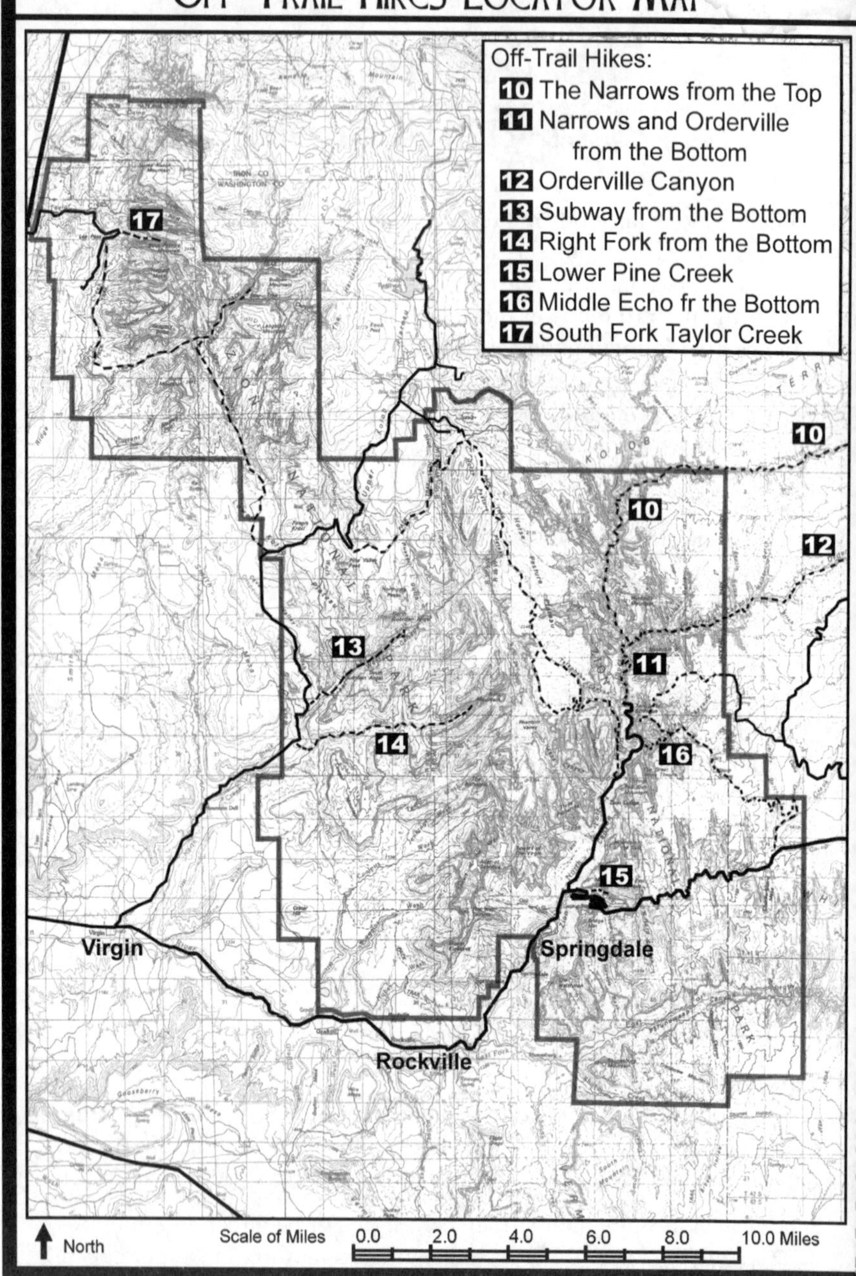
Off-Trail Hikes Locator Map
Off-Trail Hikes:
10 The Narrows from the Top
11 Narrows and Orderville from the Bottom
12 Orderville Canyon
13 Subway from the Bottom
14 Right Fork from the Bottom
15 Lower Pine Creek
16 Middle Echo fr the Bottom
17 South Fork Taylor Creek
Virgin
Springdale
Rockville
North
Scale of Miles
0.0
2.0
4.0
6.0
8.0
10.0 Miles

it is really hot in the main canyon, many of the deep, wet canyons can be cold. Bring a fleece sweater in a drybag or dry keg to wear when it gets chilly.

Specialized canyoneering shoes work best and can be rented in Springdale. However, any sturdy pair of trail-running shoes will work just fine. Those made with all synthetic materials will go in and out of water better. Wear neoprene socks, or a heavy synthetic hiking sock. Sandals are not suitable, as they provide no protection for the feet.

Poles are very useful. Aluminum trekking poles work well, but get beat up in The Narrows. Stout wooden poles last longer.

Hiking The Narrows

> *The indians call the canyon through which it runs* "Mu-koon'-tu-weap" *or Straight Canyon. Entering this, we have to wade upstream; often the water fills the entire channel, and although we travel many miles, we find no flood plain, talus, or broken piles of rock at the foot of the cliff. The walls have smooth, plain faces and are everywhere very regular and vertical for a thousand feet or more, where they seem to break back in shelving slopes to higher altitudes; and everywhere as we go along we find springs bursting out at the foot of the walls, and, passing these, the river above becomes steadily smaller; the great body of water, which runs below, bursts out from beneath this great bed of red sandstone; as we go up the canyon, it comes to be but a creek, and then a brook.*
>
> —John Wesley Powell, describing the Zion Narrows, 1872.
> From *Exploration of the Colorado River of the West and its Tributaries Explored in 1869, 1870, 1871 and 1872 under the direction of the Smithsonian Institution, Washington,* Government Printing Office, 1875.

The Narrows was first descended in 1872, but not by John Wesley Powell. Grove Karl Gilbert had that honor, on his way to becoming an important geologist of the era. Gilbert descended The Narrows on horseback as part of the Wheeler Survey of 1872, and reportedly gave it the name: "The Narrows." Exploring The Narrows on horseback was common up through the early 1960's.

The Narrows, or more formally, the narrows of the North Fork of the Virgin River, has become one of the most famous hikes in the world–for good reason. It is the hallmark hike of Zion. For beginner and intermediate hikers, it can be quite a challenging adventure. Fit, experienced hikers will be wowed by the soaring sandstone walls and the novelty of walking IN the river for miles at a time. Whether done as an overnight through-hike, from the top down as a dayhike, or from the bottom up, The Narrows is a classic hike not to be missed.

Choice of adventure is a matter of inclination, fitness level and the time of year. The weather forecast needs to be clear, and the water-level reasonably low, for a through-hike to be enjoyable. Those with ankle, knee, foot or leg problems of any kind should not attempt it top-down. The rugged nature of the hike and the hiking in the river with loose, unstable and slippery rocks underfoot conspire to make the 16 mile hike feel more like 26 miles. If you are fit enough, the through-hike is the best way to see The Narrows for the first time–nothing like it.

Seasons

May 15ish–September 15 (High Summer). High summer is the best time to through-hike The Narrows. Escaping into the deep, twisty and cool river gorge is a delight when it is hot out. Water levels are generally low, and only a spot or two of deep wading or swimming is required. First of June, the water is cold, but as the summer progresses the water becomes warmer and warmer.

High summer is, however, thunderstorm season in the desert southwest. The Monsoon pattern can set up anytime during high summer, making a trip through The Narrows dodgy at best. This is a good time to explore The Narrows from the bottom up, starting early in the morning, and keeping a careful eye on the sky. The weather forecast and flashflood warning level is posted early each morning at the Visitor Center–be sure to check it before heading out.

Even without the Monsoon, The Narrows should be hiked with a keen eye on the sky to the north. Thunderstorms occur largely in the late afternoon, so get up early and get those miles in before mid-afternoon, so you will be in a safe place during those critical hours 3:00 PM to 10:00 PM. The watershed comprises 400 square miles of terrain mostly north of The Narrows. Hard rain in any part of this watershed can cause flooding, sometimes with several hours of delay.

The top half of The Narrows can be hot and sunny, especially in July and August. Get an early start, be prepared for heat, and bring sunscreen.

September 15–November 1 (Autumn). The fall is a lovely time in Zion, and The Narrows is at its most spectacular. The slanting light can be amazing, and the colorful leaves complement the colorful walls. Fabulous.

The water level tends to be very low, and hiking in the river is at its easiest. Air and water temperatures are lower and care must be taken to be properly attired to avoid a chill. The days are shorter, early starts more difficult.

November 1–March 15 (Winter). Winter is a great time to visit The Narrows, though specialized equipment is required to stay warm. With few visitors in the lower reaches, hiking up from the bottom has a wilderness feel to it lost in the summer crowds. A dry suit and thick neoprene socks can make hiking a very reasonable proposition–equipment can be rented in Springdale.

A through-hike in the winter is difficult. The road to Chamberlain ranch is often closed in the winter, even to 4WD vehicles. The water is frigid, requiring dry suits and thick neoprene socks from the start. If the sun is out and snow is melting in the high country, the river level can rise rapidly. Ice falling off the walls can also be a hazard.

March 15–May 15ish (Spring). Spring is a great time of year in Zion, but not in The Narrows. The river is high and cold, fed by melting snow in the headwaters to the north. River levels are unpredictable–a lot depends on the upper level snowpack, and when and where the sun comes out. March and April are also the rainiest months in Utah. Toward the end of May, Zion changes over to summer conditions. Though the water is chilly, if the snow has melted out, the river gets down to a reasonable level and the hike is great.

Three Ways to Do The Narrows

1. **Overnight through-hike from the top.** For experienced backpackers, The Narrows makes a very nice one-night backpack trip. Requires stable weather. Permits can be hard to get on holiday weekends. Car spot or shuttle required.
2. **One-day through-hike from the top.** 16 miles of difficult hiking in one day? Feels like 26 miles. For the athletic, this is a fine option and makes for a fine adventure. A great introduction to Zion. Car spot or shuttle required.
3. **Day hike from the bottom.** Hike up the river as far as desired, turn around and return. Visit Orderville Canyon too, if you have the time. Makes a wonderful half-day or full-day hike with easy logistics. Good in the winter, when a through-hike is not practical. Day hiking from the bottom does not require a permit.

Permits

A permit is required for all through-hikes of The Narrows, including all overnights. Permits are obtained at the Visitor Center near Springdale, or the Kolob Canyons VC near Cedar City. The 80-person per day limit can be met on holiday weekends in the summer. Campsites are assigned for overnight visitors, and there are a limited number of sites.

Hiking from the bottom and then camping is not permitted. Hikers from the bottom are not supposed to go above Big Springs–and really, there is no real good reason to do so, as extra time is better spent enjoying Orderville Canyon.

Permits are only issued the day before the start of your hike. Reservations most likely can be made–check the backcountry info at *www.nps.gov/zion* or call the Backcountry Desk for the current procedure.

Being issued a permit does not mean The Narrows is safe. The Narrows through-hike will be closed when conditions are obviously unsafe. During spring snowmelt, when the river is high, The Narrows will be closed–usually for not more than 30 days in April and May, but in big snow years sometimes as late as July 15th. In the summer, a National Weather Service Flash Flood Warning will close The Narrows when thunderstorms are dumping rain into The Narrows, or into the headwaters 20 miles north of the park... but, the park does not "gate" The Narrows closed. During cold weather in the winter, obtaining a permit may require quite a bit of assurance on your part that you are well-equipped and know what you are doing. **Being issued a permit does not mean The Narrows is safe. The Park Service is not responsible for your safety–You are.**

Flash Floods

Flash Floods can occur any time heavy rain drops in the extensive drainage area of the North Fork. The river can rise from the normal 18" (0.5 m) deep to 6 feet (2 m) in a matter of minutes. Travel in the river is impossible during flood.

So what's a person to do?

Many people have survived flashes of The Narrows by going to high ground at the first sign of flood and staying there until it was over. "High Ground" means places more than 6 feet above water level, and preferably with mature trees. "Staying There" means waiting 24 hours for the flood cycle to complete. All of the designated campsites are in the Upper Narrows, where high ground is easily accessed. There are only occasional escapes to high ground in the Lower Narrows, below Big Spring.

If you have any doubt, WAIT. Wait, wait, and wait. You will not drown while waiting. You cannot out-run, out-swim, or out-hike flood waters. Stay put. You won't starve in 24 hours.

Do NOT expect a rescue. If you cannot get out, rescue teams cannot get in to help. Plan on taking care of yourself.

It does not have to be raining where you are for the canyon to flash.

The headwaters of The Narrows extend northward for 20 miles. A strong storm there can flood The Narrows, often with a several-hour delay.

What are signs of a coming flood? Any changes in water flow or characteristics, such as even a slight increase in flow, a change to murky, silt-laden water, a roaring sound from up-canyon, or a rapid increase in leaves and twigs on the water indicate that a flood is likely. Flash floods tend to build–they start with a modest increase in flow. A few minutes later, another increase in volume, and so on, until the gentle river has become a raging maelstrom. Don't get caught.

At the first sign, the wise hiker will find high ground to safely wait out the flood. Those who try to out-run the flood usually fail.

Equipment and Clothing

- **Poles.** A hiking staff or hiking poles are invaluable for maintaining balance while hiking in the river. Downhill ski poles work fine, but take a beating.
- **Footwear.** Imagine walking through knee-deep murky water with a bunch of roughed-up bowling balls hidden in the murk. This is what hiking The Narrows is like, and sandals, even Tevas or Keenes, do not provide protection for the feet. Specialized water shoes such as Five Ten Canyoneers and La Sportiva Exum Rivers are by far the best, but any sturdy sneaker or light hiking boot that is made from 100% synthetic materials will work fine. Neoprene socks or synthetic hiking socks work well. Neoprene socks provide warmth and padding, AND keep fine sand away from your feet. Canyoneers and Exum Rivers can be rented in Springdale.
- **Shorts.** Long pants are never in fashion in The Narrows. Get yourself a nice pair of quick-drying, synthetic hiking shorts and you will be happy. Any trip through The Narrows is likely to include wading to at least waist deep and your shorts will get wet.
- **Shirts and Sweaters.** Some people find the classic cotton T-shirt works well in the middle of the summer, but most times of the year, hikers will enjoy a quick-drying, lightweight synthetic top such as those made from Patagonia's Capilene. All hikers should bring a synthetic sweater to ward off the chill. Even in the hottest weather, it is cool and damp in The Narrows and a bit of warmth can be very welcome. Through hikers will want to carry a warm hat.
- **Keeping Stuff Dry.** Anything valuable–wallet, camera, car keys–ought to be fully protected from immersion, as even the most nimble hiker can trip and fall into the river at any time. Those with a river-running background will have drybags or Dry Kegs to use, or these can be purchased for about $25 at many outdoor stores, including those in

Springdale. The frugal hiker can make do with large plastic bags–use the thicker, trash-compactor bags–double sealed. When using plastic bags, it is important to get everything INSIDE the pack–plastic bags on the outside quickly spring leaks.

- **Pack Light.** For all Narrows trips, keep the pack as light as possible. The rugged terrain and in-stream hiking exact a toll on the over-burdened. A tent is not necessary, nor is excess camping gear like camp chairs. There are a few campsites that have a few mosquitoes–bring a bit of repellant, rather than a tent. A pair of cheap flip-flops are nice for loafing around camp and letting your shoes dry out.
- **Winter Wear.** In winter, a dry suit and thick neoprene socks are a necessity. These can be rented in Springdale, but call ahead as outfitters may not keep regular hours in the off-season.

Hygiene and Safety

Poo. The Narrows is a heavily-used camping area, and thus has a fecal impact problem. The river corridor is narrow and after the first two miles, provides no ecologically sound place to leave your crap. The Backcountry Desk will supply you with a "Rest Stop" system for capturing and carrying out your poop, and these work surprisingly well. A gel inside the bag absorbs all moisture, and chemicals significantly reduce the odor. These work great–use them!

Pee. Whenever possible, pee directly into the flowing water of the river. The smell of your urine, on land, will persist for months. At the very least, carry a Ziploc bag to pack out your toilet paper.

Water. there is reasonable water for drinking almost every step of The Narrows–literally. However, the water in the North Fork is often silty and clogs filters rapidly. North Fork water itself is contaminated from cows grazing above, and from the less-socially-conscious hikers that preceded you. From place to place, there are better places to get water including: Deep Creek, Goose Creek and Big Springs. Below Big Springs, there are many small springs to the side that provide silt-free water. All water should be filtered or treated before drinking. Use a coffee pre-filter to keep your pump from clogging. Watch out for poison ivy at Big Springs.

Challenging Water Levels. Deep Creek enters the North Fork nine miles from Chamberlain Ranch, near campsite number 2, about half way through the hike. Deep Creek at least doubles, and usually triples, the flow of the North Fork. If the depth or strength of the flow has been challenging for you to this point, turn around and hike back out to Chamberlain. The canyon narrows and difficulties with the flow only increase from Deep Creek onward.

10 The Narrows from the Top

Type: One way
Length: 15.7 miles (25.1 km)
Time: 8 to 14 hours
Altitude loss: 1500 feet (450 m)
Start: Chamberlain Ranch
End: Temple of Sinawava
Cautions: Strenuous. Subject to flash floods
Shade: Only first 2 to 4 hours not shaded

GETTING TO THE START. The start is Chamberlain Ranch–a small ranch on the North Fork of the Virgin River managed by the Chamberlain family, where they still run a few cows during the summer. It is about an hour and a half drive from Springdale to Chamberlain, on a dirt road that is often heavily wash-boarded. Folks in passenger cars unused to driving dirt roads will find this challenging, and might take quite a bit longer to drive this stretch. The dirt road crosses clay soils and is impassible after rain or snow–even for 4WD vehicles. Paid shuttles to Chamberlain Ranch are available through outfitters in Springdale. Remembering that it takes 3 hours to fetch the car at the end of a through hike can make the cost of a paid shuttle seem much more reasonable.

DRIVING DIRECTIONS TO CHAMBERLAIN RANCH. From Springdale, drive north into the park, then east through the Mt. Carmel tunnel to the East Entrance of the park. Continue on Highway 9 2.3 miles east of the East Entrance, turn left (N) on the North Fork Road. This road is initially paved but turns to dirt at the Ponderosa Ranch, at 5.4 miles. Continue on the dirt road another 11.4 miles to the only bridge crossing a river. (Total mileage from Highway 9 is 16.8 miles). Turn left at the T, then left again and follow ¼ mile to the Chamberlain Ranch main gate. Enter and close the gate. Continue down the road, then follow the posted instructions for parking. See map on page 19.

THE HIKE (FROM THE TOP). Follow the small dirt road across the river and then west along the river. The North Fork is small here, and perhaps

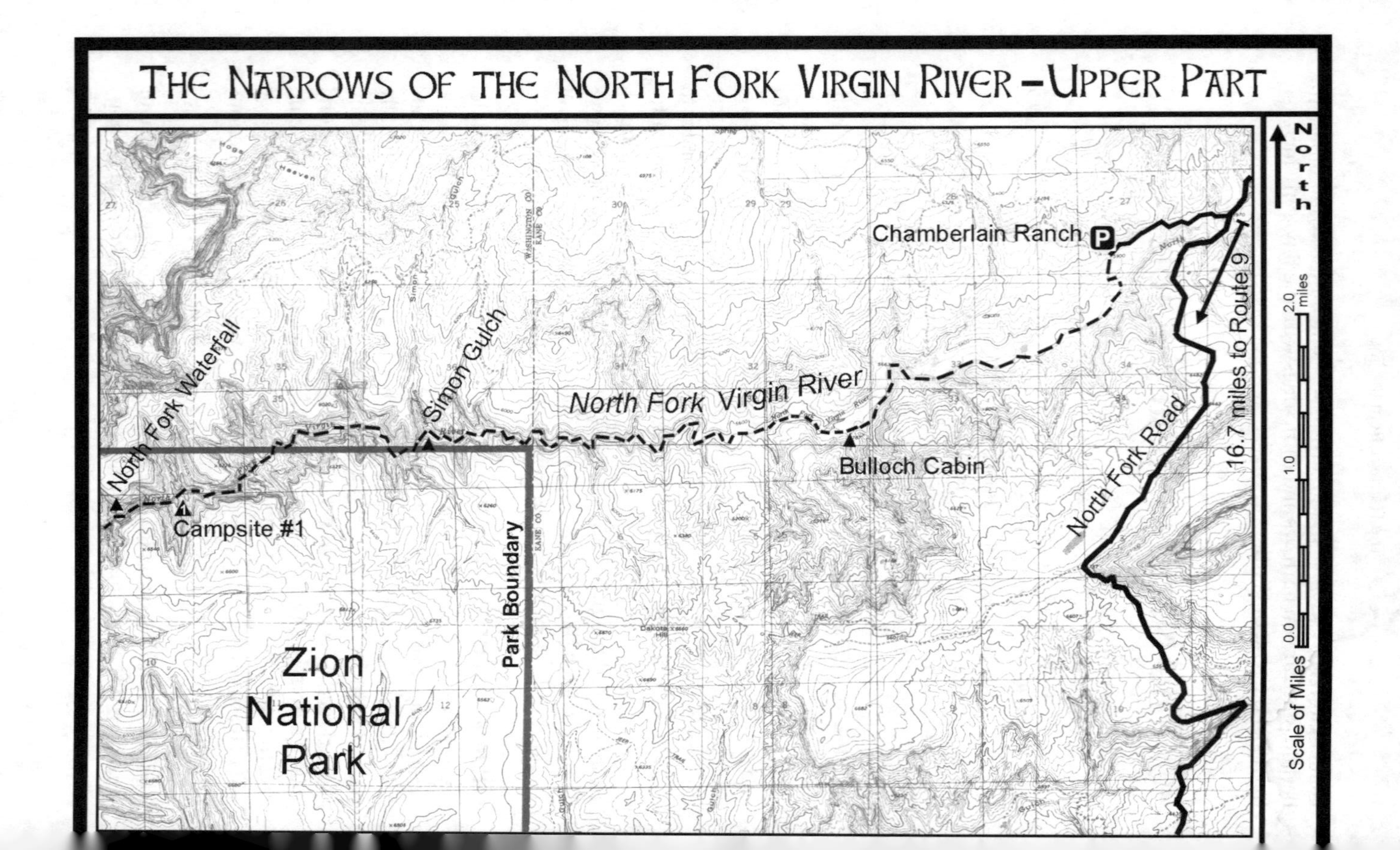
The Narrows of the North Fork Virgin River – Upper Part
North
Scale of Miles
0.0
1.0
2.0
miles
Chamberlain Ranch
16.7 miles to Route 9
North Fork Road
North Fork Virgin River
Bulloch Cabin
Simon Gulch
North Fork Waterfall
Campsite #1
Park Boundary
Zion
National
Park

is better referred to as a stream. You are a guest on the Chamberlain Ranch–please stay on the trail and don't harass the cows. In an hour, the collapsing Bulloch Cabin is passed and the road ends as the canyon becomes a gorge.

The Bulloch Cabin was built in the 1890's, when the head of the North Fork was farmed in the summer by several families, and trees were logged and milled for delivery in the region. The families wintered over in Cedar City.

From here, the second of many stream crossings is made–the water is quite nippy early on a summer morning. Continue down the canyon, frequently crossing the stream, as the canyon becomes deeper and more interesting. This part of the hike can be quite hot in summer, so an early start is recommended. Another hour of hiking takes one to Simon Gulch coming in from the north, and the first real narrows section. An hour or less past Simon Gulch, the first designated campsite appears. Campsites are discretely marked by Carsonite posts with decaled numbers.

What is a narrows? There is no formal definition, but usually any canyon with vertical rock walls that are at least twice as high as the canyon is wide is a *narrows*. If the walls are close enough to be both touched at the same time (about 5 feet), then it is a *slot canyon*.

Shortly afterwards, the mighty North Fork Waterfall is found, where rocks and trees have dammed the river, creating a twelve foot (4 meter) waterfall. There is an easy slot to the left (left looking down-canyon) that bypasses the waterfall. Do not be tempted to jump the waterfall–while the pool downstream from the falls is 6 feet deep, the water directly below the falls is only about a foot deep. More than one leg has been broken at this spot.

Deep Creek

Continuing downcanyon, the hiker arrives at the confluence with Deep Creek in about 45 minutes. This is a major confluence, and hard to miss. The water of Deep Creek usually runs clear, and this is a good place to filter water for the journey ahead. Campsite 2 is tucked in the woods nearby. Ten more campsites are carefully sited in the next 2.5 miles from here to Big Springs. Prior to arriving at Deep Creek, the hiking is relatively easy, and a good pace can be kept. Below Deep Creek, much of the hiking is in the river, and picks its way around and through obstacles–so the pace slows considerably–for some, almost to a crawl.

THE NARROWS — MIDDLE PART

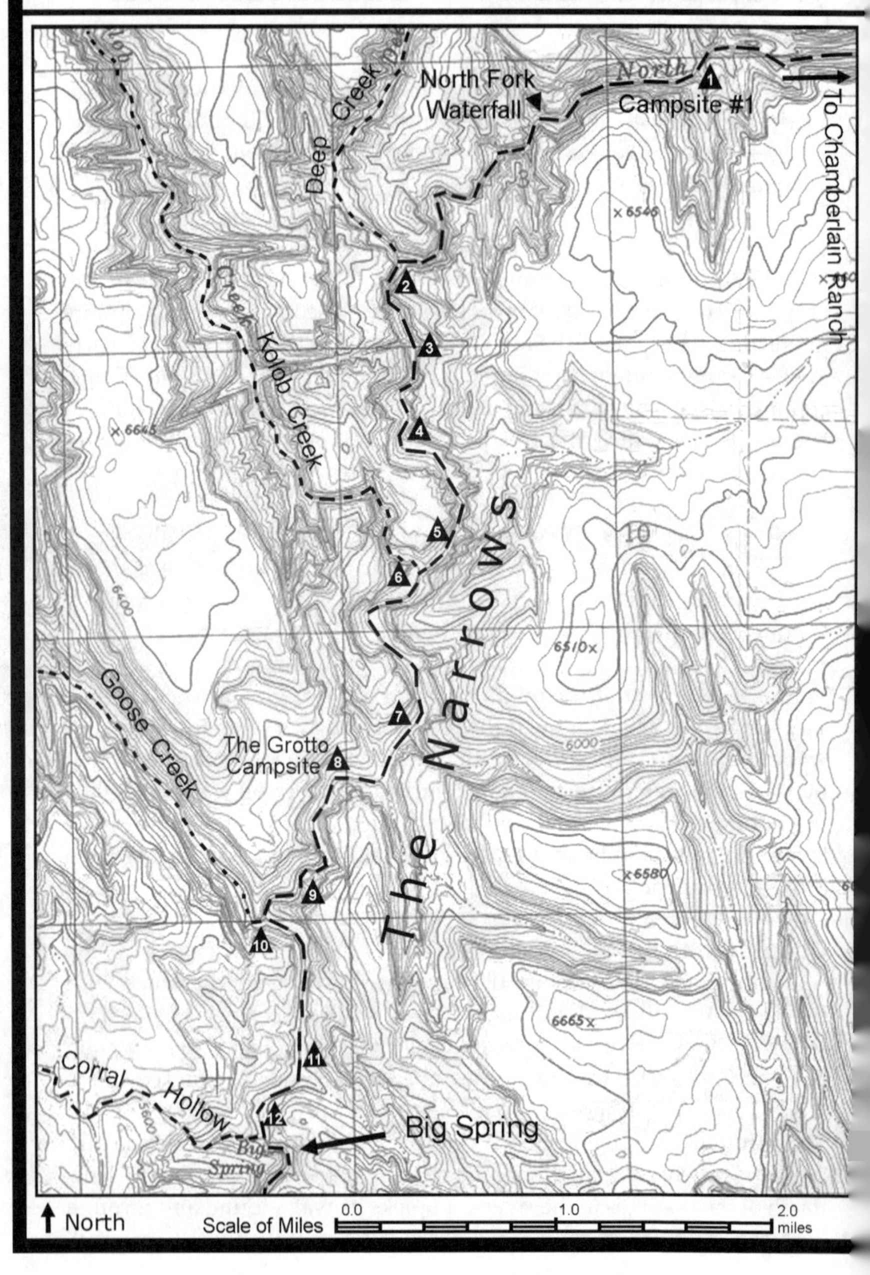

Travel times are given for the average fit hiker–many people will not be able to go this fast.

The river dominates and the gorge becomes more intense. Short sections of narrows are interspersed with pocket forests on one or both sides of the river. Pick your way downcanyon, staying on established paths when possible, or wading the edges of the river. Forty-five minutes below Deep Creek, Kolob Canyon comes in on the right, usually dry. A brief trip up the canyon makes for an interesting side-trip, but the really nice stuff is several hours up Kolob.

From Kolob, it is about an hour to the next major canyon coming in on the right, Goose Creek. A lovely sand-floored alcove on the right–The

Big Spring—The Narrows

Grotto, campsite number 8–is about halfway through this section, and is one of the nicest campsites.

Of the several options for side-canyon exploration, Goose is the most interesting side trip in the Upper Narrows. It comes in as a narrow, swampy canyon with a small flow, and is easily missed. Hiking upcanyon, the source of flow is found in about 20 minutes, and interesting narrows continue upcanyon a ways. Travel up the canyon is blocked by a 60-foot dryfall after about an hour's walk. The light in the afternoon can be remarkable. Watch out for quicksand.

Goose Creek is designated as a Research Natural Area, and even the easily accessible lower section might be restricted in the future.

Big Spring

A half-hour below Goose Creek, Big Spring bursts out of the wall on the right. There may be poison ivy on either side of the canyon in this area–keep watch. Big Spring marks the end of the Upper Narrows, and this is a good place to water up. Just up-stream from Big Springs is a short, pretty slot canyon called Corral Hollow. It makes for a nice, 10-minute side trip.

The section of Narrows below Big Spring is the most spectacular and continuous in the entire canyon, running almost uninterrupted for two

---

In the following table, times are meant to be conservative, representing a casual pace for experienced hikers in normal water conditions. Use these times to gauge your own pace.

Time and Distance Table—Narrows From the Top

Landmark	hours	hours total	miles (km)	miles (km) total
Chamberlain Ranch	0:00	0.0	0.0	
Bulloch Cabin	1:00	1:00	2.3 (3.7)	2.3 (3.7)
Simon Gulch	1:45	2:45	3.3 (5.2)	5.6 (8.9)
N Fork Waterfall	1:30	4:15	2.4 (3.8)	8.0 (12.8)
Deep Creek	0:45	5:00	0.6 (1.0)	8.6 (13.7)
Kolob Creek	0:45	5:45	0.8 (1.3)	9.4 (15.0)
Goose Creek	1:00	6:45	1.1 (1.8)	10.5 (16.8)
Big Spring	0:45	7:30	0.6 (1.0)	11.1 (17.7)
Orderville	2:30	10:00	2.0 (3.2)	13.1 (20.9)
Mystery Falls	1:15	11:15	1.3 (2.1)	14.4 (23.0)
Paved Trail	0:15	11:30	0.3 (0.5)	14.7 (23.5)
Temple of Sinawava	0:30	12:00	1.0 (1.6)	15.7 (25.1)

Hikers in The Narrows below Orderville

miles. All campsites are above Big Spring for good reason–this long section of narrows offers no escape. Overnight hikers enter this section–the most dangerous in flashfloods–in the morning of their second day, when thunderstorms are least likely to strike.

Hiking is mostly in the river from this point onward. Murky water allows seeing only a few inches into the flow–ski poles or walking sticks can come in real handy. Continuing downcanyon, the intrepid canyoneer starts to meet dayhikers coming up from the Temple of Sinawava. The next landmark is more than two hours downcanyon.

Orderville Canyon

Orderville enters as a spectacular twisting corridor on the left. It often has a stream coming out of it, sometimes muddy, sometimes aromatic. Orderville is a great side-canyon to explore as far as time allows. It offers a couple sunny spots, and respite from the rushing-water sound of the North Fork in The Narrows. Many parties will want to walk a few minutes up Orderville to have lunch.

From Orderville down, the crowds thicken and The Narrows become less continuous. The canyon twists and turns, creating marvelous alcoves. The through-hiker will notice the canyon shows considerable wear and tear, where the heavily-used hiker trails have torn up the fragile desert environment. All the more reason to stay on trails close to the waterline, rather than climbing over the hills and contributing to the erosion.

After a few turns of the canyon, a lovely 120 foot (40 meter) waterfall marks the mouth of Mystery Canyon. This is Mystery Falls, the marker that says the end is near. Another 15 minutes, and a stone veranda appears on the left, along with trappings of civilization such as signs, a pile of hiking sticks and a paved trail. Hike one mile (1.4 km) on the paved trail to the Temple of Sinawava, bathrooms, benches, trash cans, and the shuttle bus stop.

Now you can reflect on Major Powell's purple prose that opened this chapter. Do you think the Major hiked far up The Narrows?

11 The Narrows and Orderville Canyon from the Bottom

Type: Up and Back
Length: Up to 14.2 miles (22.7 km)
Time: 4 to 10 hours
Altitude gain/loss: Up to 400 feet (120 m)
Start: Temple of Sinawava
Cautions: Strenuous. Subject to flash floods
Shade: Yes

The hike UP The Narrows from the Temple of Sinawava, often with a visit to Orderville Canyon, is a wonderful hike, perhaps the third best hike in the park. The logistics are simple, and it can be a couple-of-hours thing, a half-day hike, or a full-day adventure. In winter, The Narrows can be an extraordinary place, with beautiful ice sculptures from the springs and intersecting canyons.

Gear

See *Gear* under "The Narrows From the Top." Poles are very useful, good footwear essential, and carry a sweater, even when it is hot.

Getting Started

Take the shuttle (in-season) or drive your car (off-season) to the Temple of Sinawava. Complete any unfinished business in the bathroom, then

Lower Narrows and Orderville Canyon

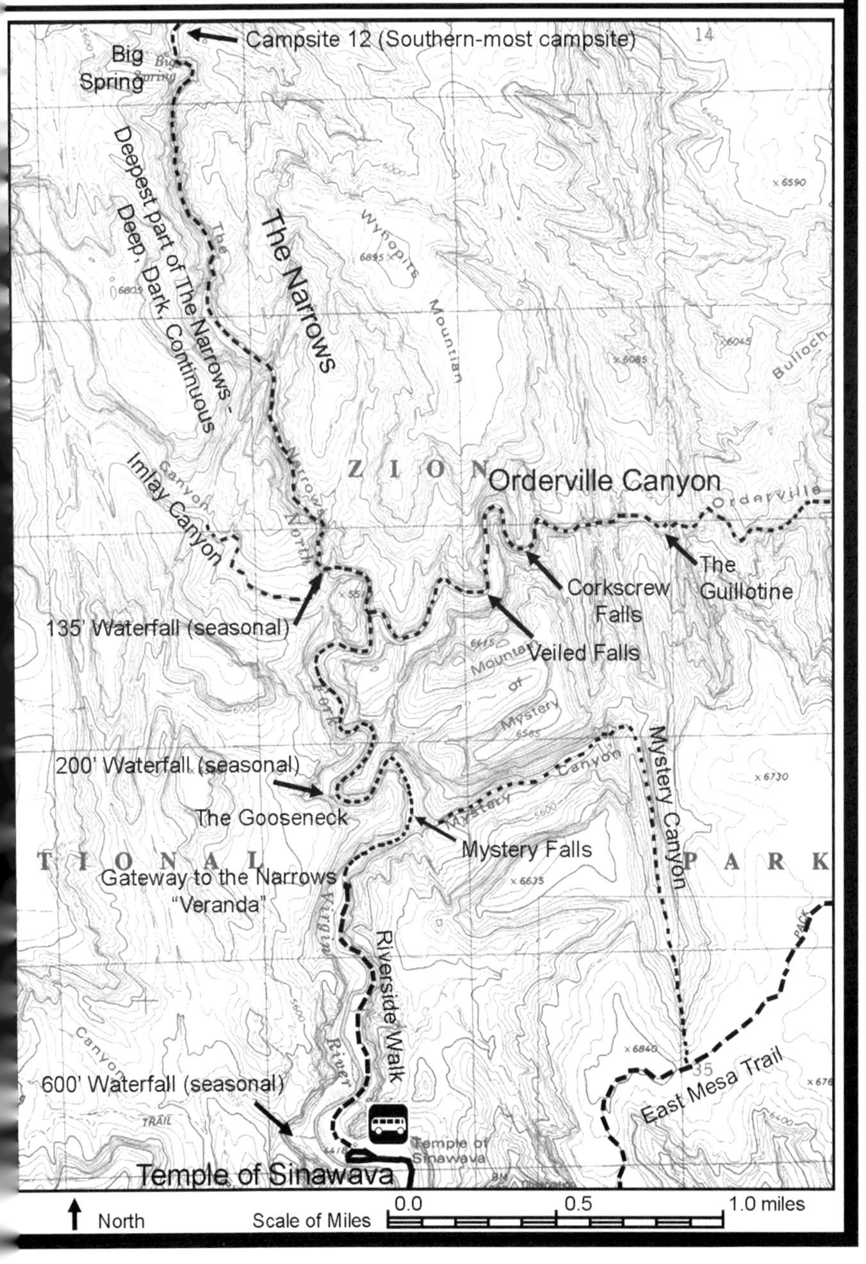

head up the Riverside Walk, built in 1925. After one mile the trail ends at a lovely stone veranda. From there, the path is up the river.

Hiking up The Narrows

Wade on in and go to it. The river is initially shallow, with no wades above waist-deep for an hour or so. Except sometimes, when there are. Work your way up the river. About 15 minutes upcanyon, Mystery Falls slides 120 feet (40 m) down a slab on the right. Makes for a good "shampoo commercial" photo.

The river winds its way through the stone, with walls soaring 800 feet into the air. Please walk in the river or on established trails next to the water. There are many unnecessary and sadly destructive hiker-made trails up hills and over dales–don't use these.

A bit further upstream, the river turns sharply to the left, the start of a gooseneck. In the next four-tenths of a mile, the river will swing back to the right and end up a mere 400 feet from the start. The gooseneck (and the meandering course of the entrenched river) indicates that the river established a windy course on a relatively flat valley before the uplift came along and lifted the land, the river working hard to stay where it was.

Not far past the gooseneck, the river takes a big sweeping turn to the right, forming a deep, dark alcove on the left. The seeping walls and rushing river combine with outstanding light at certain times of the year (and day) to produce one of the most-photographed places in The Narrows. The light and conditions challenge the photographer to capture the essence of The Narrows.

Orderville Junction

Not far past the alcove, Orderville canyon enters The Narrows on the right as a 20-foot wide, twisty slot with high walls and a small stream flowing in the bottom. The intrepid hiker is faced with a choice here–continue up The Narrows, or visit Orderville–or both. If you can only do one, hike up Orderville to experience a wider variety of canyon scenery. But first, let's finish hiking up The Narrows.

The Narrows above Orderville

Below Orderville, The Narrows is a windy river with frequent pocket forests on the sides, bits of sunlight, lots of people and short sections of tall, intense narrows. Above Orderville, the walls soar upward, the crowds thin out and the sun hides behind the walls. The 2 miles (3.2 km) to Big Spring is the most impressive and continuous section of The Narrows. In winter, numerous seeps and small waterfalls are highlighted

Hiking in The Upper Narrows

by the ice sculptures they form. A couple spots may require deep wading or short swims.

Big Spring is easily identified. Beautiful clear water gushes from the canyon wall, flowing 20 feet through lush greenery before dropping into the river. Watch out for poison ivy in the area.

The canyon changes nature at Big Spring, opening up and regaining pocket forests on each side, and becoming rougher as giant boulders often block easy hiking upcanyon. Up-canyon hikers are not permitted by the park to hike above Big Springs.

Orderville Canyon from Orderville Junction

Orderville is cool, Orderville is fun! While The Narrows soar, somber and awe-inspiring, Orderville is more playful. Hiking up The Narrows, you are, well, hiking. Charging up Orderville involves swimming, wading, scrambling, splashing through water and climbing over obstacles.

The first part of Orderville is a narrow, soaring slot almost like an alley between two buildings. Look up to see the marvelous light bouncing off the walls. A small stream runs in the bottom, often carrying silt and sometimes malodorous. Rain washes silt, pine needles and leaves into the canyon higher up. The leaves and pine needles rot, producing aromatic matter carried into the stream. The silt can make the canyon slippery and swimming the pools a down-and-dirty proposition.

Ten minutes up Orderville, the character changes again as the canyon opens up briefly. A multi-colored wall on the right can be seen rising 1000 feet in several tiers. Soon, a deep pool is encountered that often requires

Times and Distance Table—The Narrows and Orderville from the Bottom

Landmark	hours	hrs total	miles	miles total	km	km total
Temple of Sinawava (TS)	0:00	0:00	0.0			
End of Paved Trail	0:30	0:30	1.0	1.0	1.6	1.6
Mystery Falls	0:15	0:45	0.3	1.3	0.5	2.1
Gooseneck	0:15	1:00	0.3	1.6	0.5	2.6
Alcove	0:30	1:30	0.5	2.1	0.8	3.4
Orderville Junction	0:30	2:00	0.5	2.6	0.8	4.2
Return from Orderville Junction	1:30	3:30	2.6	5.2	4.2	8.3
Orderville Junction	0:00	0:00	0.0	0.0	0.0	0.0
Up Narrows, Big Springs	2:00	2:00	2.0	2.0	3.2	3.2
Return to Orderville Junction	1:30	3:30	2.0	4.0	3.2	6.4
Orderville Junction	0:00	0:00	0.0	0.0	0.0	0.0
Up Orderville, Veiled Falls	0:20	0:20	0.5	0.5	0.8	0.8
Corkscrew Falls	0:20	0:40	0.5	1.0	0.8	1.6
The Guillotine	0:30	1:10	0.5	1.5	0.8	2.4
Canyon becomes dry	0:45	1:55	1.0	2.5	1.6	4.0
Return to Orderville Junction	1:15	3:10	2.5	5.0	4.0	8.0
Total, TS/Big Springs/TS		7:00		9.2		14.7
Total, TS/Orderville/TS		6:40		10.2		16.3
Total, TS/BigS/Order/TS		10:10		14.2		22.7

a short swim or deep wade. Cross the pool, and clamber up the logs and rocks on the other side.

Next up is Veiled Falls, where a short waterfall drops into a slot. Moki steps on the right allow passage around the waterfall.

This is a good place for Tom's Safety Talk on Jumping. It is amazing how many people each year jump into a shallow pool when they cannot see the bottom, and are surprised to hear their bones break. Jumping is fun, but breaking bones is not. There are very few places in Zion where jumping is safe, and none of them are in Orderville. The murky water is very successful at hiding the bottom. Don't jump.

Above Veiled Falls, about 45 minutes from The Narrows, is the next fun spot, Corkscrew Falls. This is also the first spot that can be a challenge to get up. As you continue upcanyon past this and other obstacles, remember that it is harder to climb down than it is to climb up. **Don't climb up obstacles you cannot climb down**.

There are many more fun spots. The next landmark is The Guillotine, where a very large block hangs wedged between the canyon walls. About 45 minutes above the Guillotine, the canyon becomes dry and the scenery less impressive.

Returning to Civilization

Return the way you came. Hiking back down Orderville and The Narrows takes less time than it took to hike up. Hiking in the river in the dark is extremely challenging and extremely slow, so plan to complete your hike during daylight hours.

12 Orderville Canyon

Orderville is a wonderfully fun canyon. With two short obstacles where ropes are often used, it is the easiest technical canyon in this book, or the hardest off-trail hike. Due to the clay soils in its headwaters, Orderville can be exceptionally slippery, so the experienced Ordervillean brings a short rope on all trips. Orderville changes from trip-to-trip more than most canyons, and the washing away of a log or filling of a pool could make that easy move last trip difficult and dangerous. Bring a rope to use as a handline, and the skills required for using it safely.

ORDERVILLE - BIRCH HOLLOW - ENGLESTEAD

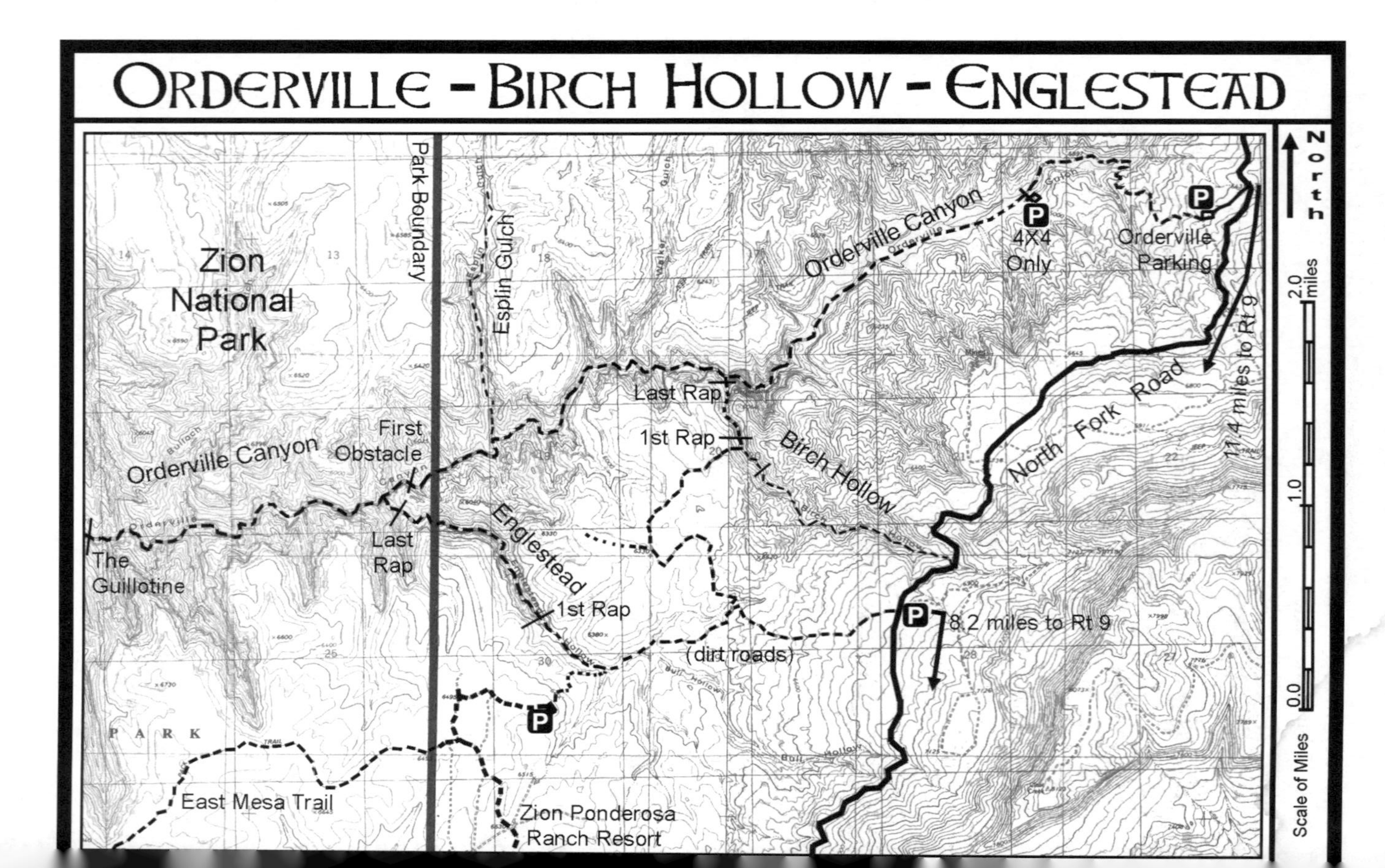

Orderville Canyon is named for the town of Orderville, founded in 1875 by the pioneers in Mount Carmel who enrolled in The United Order of Enoch. Orderville became the most successful expression of the communal United Order movement, and included Zion luminaries Isaac Behunin and William Heaps. It expanded to 546 people by 1877. Interest in the communal life waned and the town returned to ordinary capitalism about 1883.

Orderville Canyon sees quite a few accidents. Jumping into shallow pools tends to break ankles and lower legs. Rescue is slow and difficult. **Don't jump.**

The start of Orderville includes a fair amount of hiking in the full sun. In summer, an early start is highly recommended. The short spur road down to the floor of Orderville is a high-clearance 4WD road, and should only be attempted by experienced jeepers. Once started down this road, turning a vehicle around is impossible.

The bottom half of Orderville is wet—great fun when it is hot out. A backcountry water-park. Water protection for cameras and anything else you want to keep dry is essential. The footing can be uncertain, and the technical difficulties are few, so ski or trekking poles, or a hiking staff, are useful.

Type: Through-hike
Length: 12.3 miles (19.6 km)
Time: 6 to 10 hours
Longest rappel: 15 feet (3 m)
Number of rappels: 2
Start: Orderville Trailhead off North Fork Road.
End: Temple of Sinawava
Season: Summer and Fall. Wetsuit recommended if not really hot out.
Permit: Required for the through hike.

LOGISTICS: Starts off the North Fork Road, ends at Temple of Sinawava. Self-shuttle with 2 cars, or shuttles are available for a modest fee from the outfitters in Springdale. Though a through-trip is preferred, the best parts of Orderville can be visited from the bottom. See "Narrows and Orderville from the Bottom."

GETTING TO Start: Orderville starts off the North Fork Road. The road can be impassable when wet, even for 4WD vehicles. From Springdale, take Utah Route 9 through the park. 2.3 miles past the East Entrance, turn left (N) on the North Fork Road, initially paved, but soon turning to dirt. Follow this 11.4 miles to a field and dirt road on the left, signed for Orderville Canyon ORV Area. Follow the road 0.1 miles across the field to a corral, and park among some trees. Those with a true 4WD vehicle can continue down the steep, rutted road another 2.2 miles.

APPROACH: Follow the rutted dirt road steeply downward, pondering how Mom's Subaru would look stuck on it. At the bottom, follow the dirt road beside the creek downcanyon. After about an hour, the burly-vehicle carpark appears. A few minutes walk beyond this, the canyon drops dramatically in a dryfall. Follow trails left, then down steep, loose shale to the canyon floor. These Carmel-formation silts are the source of the super-slippery clays that make Orderville so slippery after a good rain.

THE CANYON: Stroll downcanyon. At first, the canyon is open with large trees, punctuated by short sections of interesting narrows. The narrow sections become longer and more frequent, the terrain providing a wide variety of scenery. Numerous canyons come in from the north and south, including Esplin Gulch, named for Lynn Esplin, who made the first descent in 1947 while looking for missing sheep. Unfortunately, he did not survive his descent. Other drainages dropping into Orderville are named for pioneers that farmed in Orderville Canyon and ran livestock on the high ground to the north and south.

About an hour downcanyon from the mudslide, the hearty canyoneer arrives at the first obstacle. A large boulder blocks the canyon, with a bolt anchor on the right wall. Youth groups and others not concerned with human frailty slide down the rock and jump to the ground below, but more mature individuals will wish to use a rope to rappel, or as a handline for downclimbing the chimney below the anchor. Slippery clays can make this treacherous–use caution.

Further downcanyon, the narrows become more continuous. A few small springs provide water and a small flow starts. A log dam often backs up a shallow pool, and another one requires a short downclimb next to a waterfall. Stay in the watercourse in these areas and avoid using trails to the side that contribute to erosion.

The second obstacle is reached about an hour and a quarter past the first obstacle. A large boulder blocks the canyon. Thirty feet above the canyon floor, an even larger block spans the width of the canyon as a chockstone, and has been there long enough to have a lush growth of vegetation on its top. This is The Guillotine. Bolts and slings on the left side overlook a steep V-slot. This downclimb is especially slippery because the rock is polished and practically frictionless. Use the rope to rappel, or as a hand-line to assist and protect the downclimb. If there is water at the bottom, it is likely shallow.

A half-hour past this, another boulder blocks the width of the canyon. A scary-looking V-slot downclimb on the left looks like the obvious path, but following the water down a short fall on the right is easier and safer. This is Corkscrew Falls.

Numerous interesting obstacles make for fun splashing in the water. In another half-hour, Veiled Falls is passed on the left using some shallow moki-steps. This is a popular destination for folks hiking upriver, so don't be surprised to find a crowd. A couple of downclimbs past logs might require a short swim. About an hour past The Guillotine, the final narrows section soars spectacularly skyward. Just beyond, Orderville joins The Narrows. Turn left and hike downstream about an hour to the Veranda at the end of the paved path leading 1 mile to the Temple of Sinawava.

Times and Distance Table—Orderville Canyon

Landmark	hours	hrs total	miles	miles total	km	km total
Carpark, Trailhead	0:00	0.0	0.0			
End of Jeep Trail	0:45	0:45	1.5	1.5	2.4	2.4
Dryfall, Mudslide	0:45	1:30	1.4	2.9	2.2	4.6
First Obstacle, Park Boundary	1:30	3:00	3.3	6.2	5.2	9.9
Guillotine	1:00	4:00	2.0	8.2	3.2	13.1
Corkscrew Falls	0:30	4:30	0.5	8.7	0.8	13.9
Veiled Falls	0:20	4:50	0.5	9.2	0.8	14.7
Orderville Junction	0:20	5:10	0.5	9.7	0.8	15.5
End of Paved Trail	1:30	6:40	1.6	11.3	2.6	18.0
Temple of Sinawava	0:30	7:10	1.0	12.3	1.6	19.6

13 The Subway from the Bottom

The Subway is one of the best routes in the park, and hiking up from the bottom gets to the best stuff without ropes and swimming. If you're carrying camera gear, it is winter, or you are averse to ropes and swims, it is a great way to see The Subway.

The short version goes like this: Hike down a 400-foot (120 m) steep, loose gully. Pick your way up a rugged streambed for two hours. Enjoy some really nice scenery. Hike back down the streambed for two hours, then up the 400-foot steep, loose gully. If it is at all hot out, hiking in the streambed is hot, hot, hot. Bad hot, not good hot. Save energy for the strenuous up-hike to get back to the car.

"The Subway" is a short, spectacular section of the Left Fork of North Creek. The canyon itself is called Great West Canyon. The Subway section is not marked on most maps, but is where the Left Fork tightens up and twists sharply, between North Guardian Angel and Guardian Angel Pass. The hike is also known as "The Left Fork."

Due to its popularity, The Subway is managed under a quota system. Reservations are distributed by lottery several months in advance and are highly recommended. Call the Backcountry Desk (435-772-0170) or use the Internet (*www.nps.gov/zion*). If you do not have reservations, don't fret—permits are available either the day before or early on the day of your hike at the Main and Kolob Canyons Visitor Centers. Be flexible and plan ahead to avoid being denied. A permit is required for hiking The Subway from the bottom or from the top. Group size limit is 12.

Type: There and back
Length: 3.5 rugged miles (5.3 km) each way
Time: 6 to 10 hours
Altitude gain: 1000 feet (300 m)
Start: Left Fork Trailhead, Kolob Reservoir road.
Shade: Most of the hike is in the full sun.

GETTING THERE: From Springdale, drive south and west 14 miles to the town of Virgin. Turn right on the Kolob Reservoir Road (KR road, sometimes called the Kolob Terrace (KT) road). The paved KR road winds through town, then climbs a dramatic ridge in making its way to Kolob Terrace. Six and a half miles from Virgin, the road enters the park and three trailheads are soon encountered–the Right Fork, Grapevine Springs, then the Left Fork. Park at the Left Fork Trailhead. The trailhead is not shown on many maps, but is close to the Bench Mark labeled BM 5248. Mileage from the town of Virgin is 8.6 miles. Driving time from Springdale is 45 minutes.

THE TRAIL: Follow the trail into the woods. In 15 minutes, the trail comes out on the rim of the canyon, with a great view of the Left Fork and the Guardian Angels standing proud to the east. Follow the trail left along the rim to where it drops into the canyon. Take great care to stay on the path as it descends steeply to the canyon floor. The trail is steep and

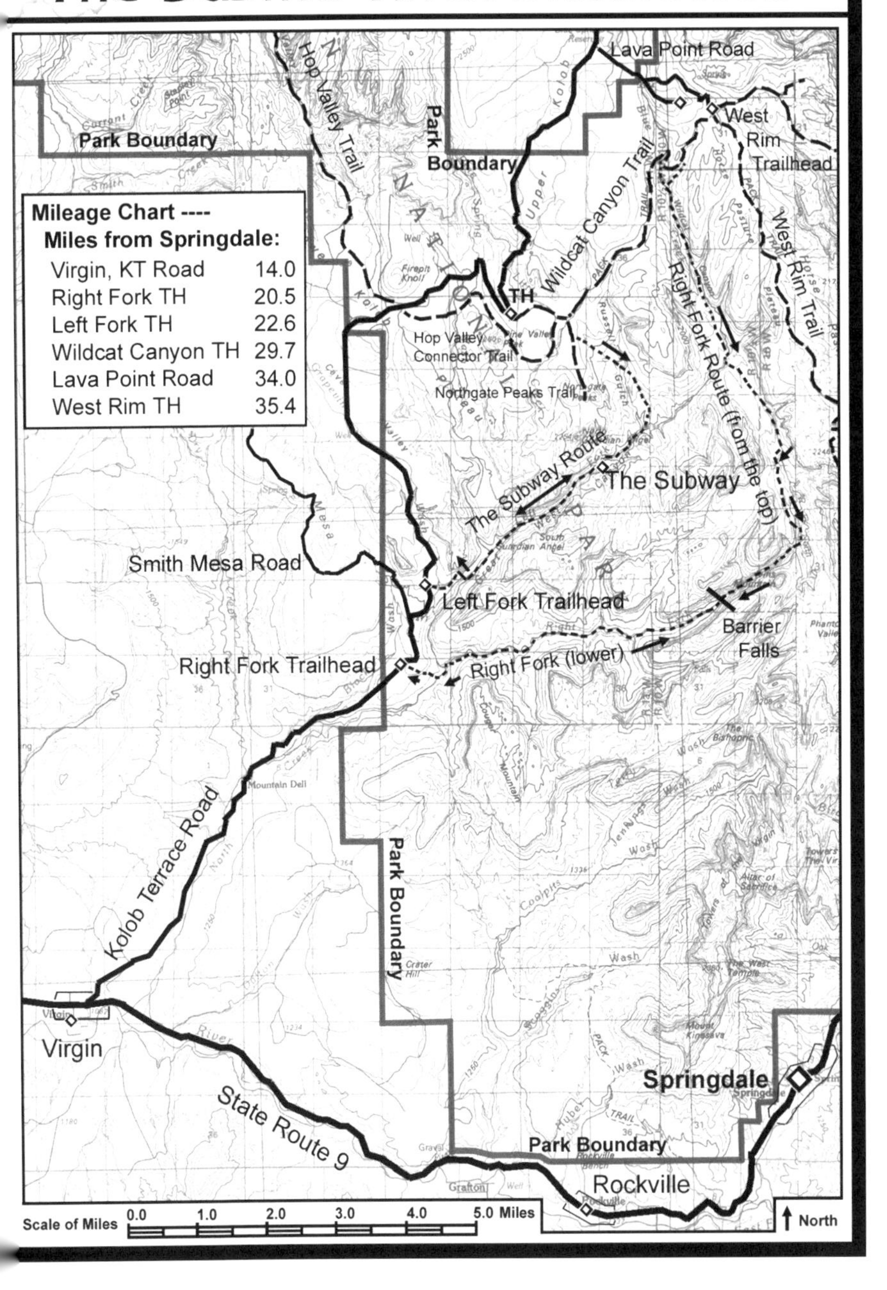

THE SUBWAY AREA DRIVING MAP
Mileage Chart ----
Miles from Springdale:
Virgin, KT Road 14.0
Right Fork TH 20.5
Left Fork TH 22.6
Wildcat Canyon TH 29.7
Lava Point Road 34.0
West Rim TH 35.4
Park Boundary
Hop Valley Trail
Park Boundary
Lava Point Road
West Rim Trailhead
Wildcat Canyon Trail
TH
Hop Valley Connector Trail
Northgate Peaks Trail
Right Fork Route (from the top)
West Rim Trail
The Subway Route
The Subway
Smith Mesa Road
Left Fork Trailhead
Barrier Falls
Right Fork Trailhead
Right Fork (lower)
Kolob Terrace Road
Park Boundary
Virgin
State Route 9
Springdale
Park Boundary
Rockville
Scale of Miles
0.0
1.0
2.0
3.0
4.0
5.0 Miles
North

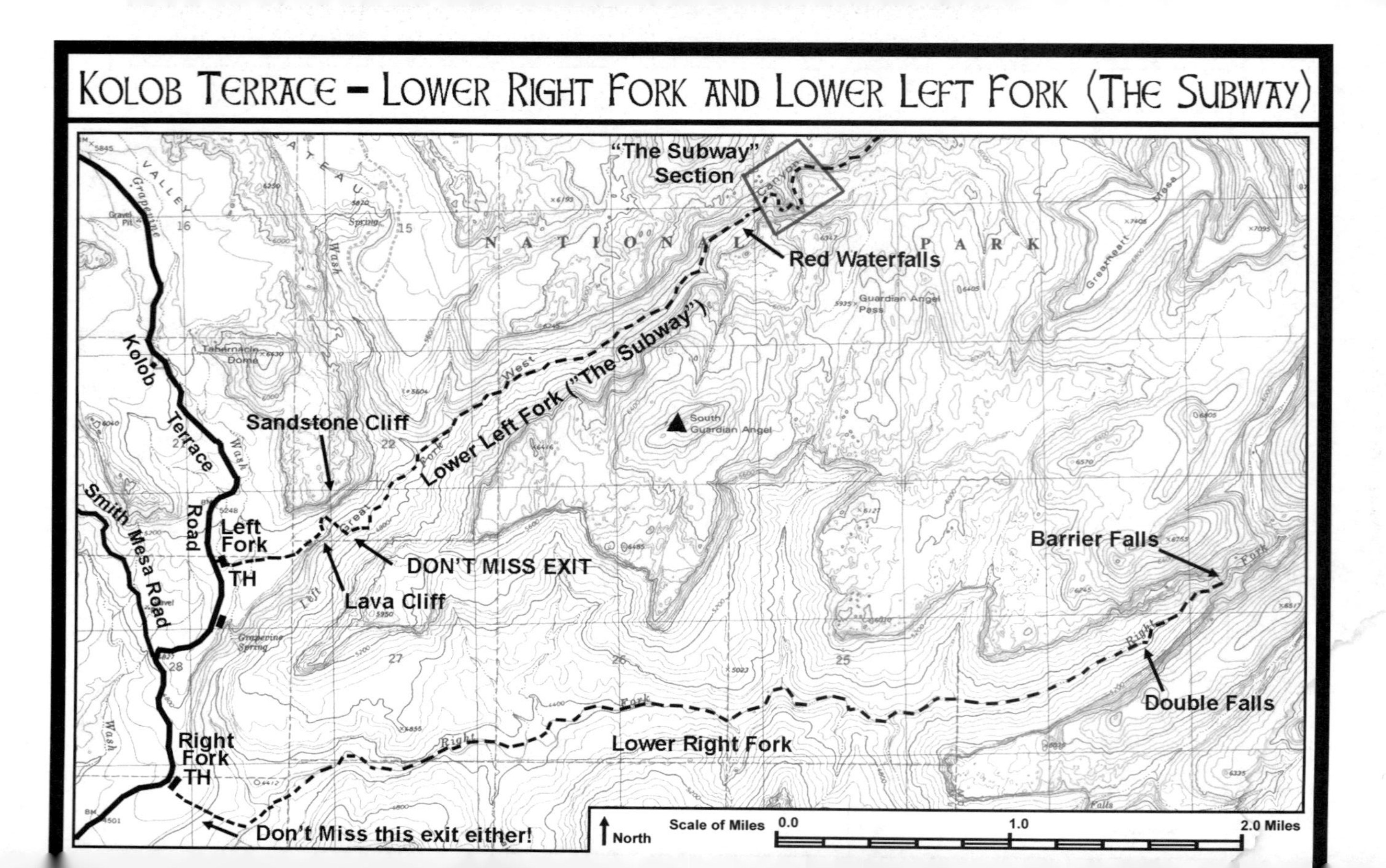
Kolob Terrace – Lower Right Fork and Lower Left Fork (The Subway)
"The Subway" Section
Red Waterfalls
Lower Left Fork ("The Subway")
Sandstone Cliff
Lava Cliff
DON'T MISS EXIT
Left Fork TH
Right Fork TH
Don't Miss this exit either!
Kolob Terrace Road
Smith Mesa Road
Kolob
South Guardian Angel
Guardian Angel Pass
Barrier Falls
Double Falls
Lower Right Fork
NATIONAL PARK
Tabernacle Dome
Grapevine Spring
North
Scale of Miles
0.0
1.0
2.0 Miles

loose. At least one person has died here when they strayed from the trail and fell.

THE CANYON FLOOR: At the bottom, turn around and make a careful mental note of where the trail up starts. You do NOT want to miss this on the way out. Cross the stream and turn left. This is a backcountry, off-trail route, so there is no official path, though well-established social trails provide easy passage for much of the canyon. Follow social trails up the main canyon, crossing the stream numerous times, for about two

Jim Schnepel, Denise Manweiler and Eric Godfrey enjoying a pool in The Subway

hours. The canyon starts wide and gradually narrows as it approaches The Subway.

Close to The Subway, the stream gets more rugged and travel becomes slower and more difficult. Picking through a series of boulders and splashing up the stream, the intrepid Subway hiker finally comes to a series of Red Waterfalls, where the stream flows down slabs of dark red Kayenta sandstone. Hike up the slabs, then turn the corner and you are at the mouth of The Subway.

THE SUBWAY: "The Good Stuff" is a series of slots, alcoves, pools and waterfalls of marvelous beauty, about a third of which can be easily reached from the bottom. With a little swimming and climbing, all of the good stuff can be reached.

From the bottom, it starts with the namesake tunnel-like formation. The top is not closed over to form a true tunnel, but it almost feels like it is. The bulgy, round tunnel at the bottom of a slot curves into the rock, with the solid red floor spotted with pools, slots and flowing water. Be careful of your footing here, the rock can be very slippery. The pools are filled with clear, clean water and are only a few feet deep. In the fall, red and orange maple leaves accent the red rock and make the place almost psychedelic.

Around the corner, the canyon opens up a bit and larger pools block progress upcanyon. Swim the pools and explore the slot beyond. Be sure to step through the waterfall at the end and visit the waterfall-room behind the curtain. Those who are athletically inclined can boulder up to a ledge, then climb right on a series of ramps to gain access to more good stuff above this obstacle. A 60-foot (20 m) rope may be useful for

Times and Distance Table—The Subway from the Bottom

Landmark	hours	hours total	miles	miles total	km	km total
Left Fork Trailhead	0:00	0.0	0.0			
Top of Steep Slope	0:15	0:15	0.6	0.6	1.0	1.0
Bottom of Canyon	0:15	0:30	0.1	0.7	0.2	1.2
Start of Red Falls	2:00	2:30	2.0	2.7	3.2	4.4
Start of Subway	0:15	2:45	0.4	3.1	0.6	5.0
Play at The Subway	1:00	3:45	0.4	3.5	0.6	5.7
Return to Start of Steep Slope	1:45	5:30	2.4	6.0	3.9	9.6
Climb Steep Slope	0:20	5:50	0.1	6.1	0.2	9.8
Stroll to Carpark	0:20	6:10	0.6	6.7	1.0	10.7

belaying members of your party. Further up is the famous "Log in The Subway," plus a marvelous long corridor and Keyhole Falls.

THE SIESTA: If it is really hot out, a siesta in the cool area at the start of The Subway might be in order. Be sure to leave enough time to get ALL the way out before dark.

THE WALK OUT: Return the way you came. It takes parties two to four hours for the hike out. About halfway downcanyon, look for two large tumbledown boulders close to the water on the right. Their flat, gray faces hold many dinosaur tracks. This is a good place to stop for a snack and rest. Do NOT actually touch the dino tracks–they are in a soft layer of rock that is easily damaged.

Another hour downcanyon and it's time for the steep climb up to the road. Missing the exit is easy, so make sure you pay attention. Two streams come into the Left Fork from the north (right). One-third of a mile (0.5 km) past the second stream, the exit gully will be in front of you. The north (right) wall of the canyon is a 400-foot (120 m), steep, tree-covered talus slope with 400-foot (120 m) vertical sandstone wall above. Downstream, the sandstone at the top ends and a black lava cliff replaces the steep talus. The trail out climbs the crease below the left edge of the vertical sandstone where it meets the lava flow.

The climb out is extremely hot—the black rock traps the heat. Take a final dip in the stream before starting the steep, 400-foot climb. Find a well-established trail on the right side of the creek that starts up a gully. Do not begin the climb without finding the trail. At the top of the slope, the trail traverses left to the top of the lava flow and works its way left through ledges to the mesa top. Follow the trail through the piñon-juniper forest 0.5 mile (800 m) to the parking area. Enjoy the ice-cold beverages you left in your cooler.

14 The Right Fork from the Bottom

The Right Fork is a beautiful canyon, though it takes considerable effort to get to the best parts. While the Left Fork requires 2 miles of rugged hiking up a streambed to get to The Subway, the Right Fork takes about twice as much effort to get to the first waterfall. Once you get there, the Right Fork offers several nice waterfalls and a really interesting section of canyon.

The Right Fork from the Bottom makes a good off-trail backpack trip. The Right Fork through-hike is a wonderful, two-day canyoneering route requiring rappels and swims.

There is a great deal of poison ivy in the Right Fork. Fresh flowing water is available the full length of this hike, and requires filtering.

Type: There and back
Length: 5.3 miles (8.5 km) each way
Time: 8 to 12 hours
Altitude gain: 1000 feet (300 m)
Start: Right Fork Trailhead, Kolob Reservoir road.
Shade: Most of the hike is in the full sun.

GETTING THERE: From Springdale, drive south and west 14 miles to the town of Virgin. Turn right on the Kolob Reservoir (KR) road. The paved KR road winds through town, then climbs a dramatic ridge in making its way to Kolob Terrace. Six and a half miles from Virgin, the road enters the park and three trailheads are soon encountered—Right Fork being the first. Park at the Right Fork Trailhead, 7.0 miles from the town of Virgin. The trailhead is not shown on many maps, but is close to the Bench Mark labeled BM 4501. Driving time from Springdale is 45 minutes.

THE HIKE: From the Trailhead, follow the trail southeast through the Piñon-Juniper woods to the rim of the canyon. The map does not show the steepness of the rim. Carefully descend the trail through lava cliffs and down to the stream. Make a very careful mental note of where the trail cuts back up to the rim. It can be hard to find at the end of the day, and getting back to the rim without the trail is dangerous.

Turn left (upstream, northeast) at the stream and proceed upcanyon 0.25 mile (400 m). The stream forks–take the right fork east into the wide canyon. Rugged hiking along the stream for several hours eventually leads to the nice part of the canyon. Working upstream, the hike soon comes to Double Falls. A trail on the right cuts around the falls, and allows access to the next waterfall, then to the fall above that–Barrier Falls. Getting past Barrier Falls requires technical rock climbing on bad rock and is not recommended.

Return the way you came.

15 Lower Pine Creek

This is a quick little stroll to a charming waterfall and a couple of shallow pools. The hiking is on a flat social trail, and involves a little boulder hopping and possibly wading to get to the waterfall itself. The pool is

Log in The Subway

Pool in The Subway

Rock in The Narrows

The Narrows near Orderville Canyon

Lower Emerald Pools Trail

Mel Brown in the Grand Alcove, Right Fork of North Creek

Double Falls, Right Fork of North Creek

Felicia Bicknell rapping the Great Cathedral, Pine Creek

Crossing a pool in Spry Canyon

Jason Robertson on the second rap, Englestead Canyon

Hank Moon rapping South Fork Oak Creek

Kolob Creek—Lin Alder on rappel

Balanced rappel in Imlay Canyon

Doug Noel crossing a pothole in Imlay Canyon

Denise Manweiler rapping into The Narrows, Imlay Canyon

The last rap in Heaps

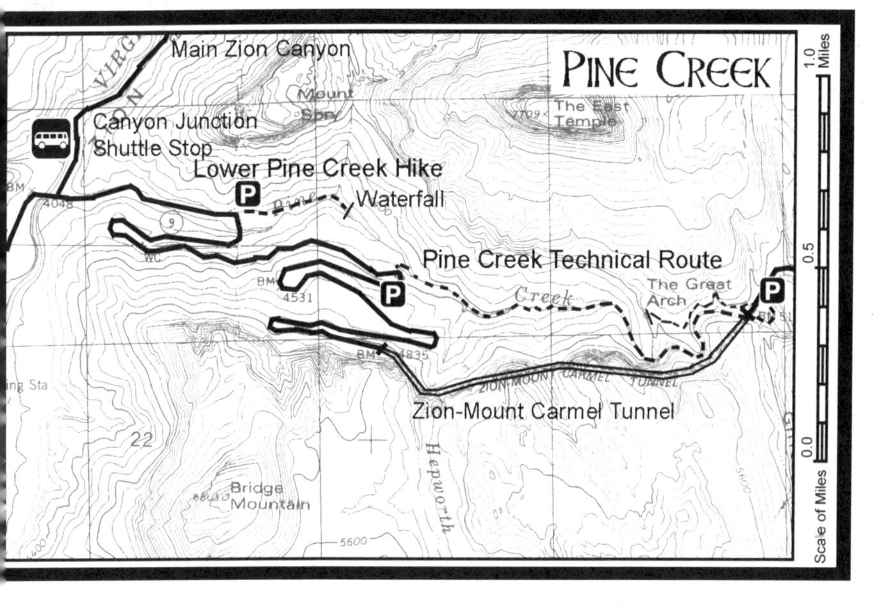

not deep enough to swim in, though deeper pools can be found further up-canyon.

Type:	There and back
Length:	0.3 miles (0.5 km) each way
Time:	1 to 2 hours
Altitude gain:	none
Start:	Pine Creek Bridge.
Shade:	Mostly in the full sun.

GETTING THERE: The trail starts at the Pine Creek Bridge, a half mile east of the Canyon Junction shuttle stop. Park on the wide shoulder of the road before the bridge.

The Pine Creek Bridge was completed July 10, 1930, six days after the Zion-Mount Carmel tunnel and highway were dedicated. The stonework includes blocks from all areas of Zion.

THE TRAIL: Hike east on the obvious trail up the canyon. Please stay on the established path. Follow into the gorge of the canyon, then boulder-hop to get to the waterfall and pools.

The gorge is formed by the Springdale Member of the Moenave formation. This 100-foot layer of hard sandstone can be seen in most of lower Zion canyon, and above the town of Springdale.

There are more waterfalls and pools upcanyon, including some deep enough for swimming. To access the higher canyon, backtrack a hundred yards or so from the waterfall, and follow a climbing route up the layers on the right (north side) of the canyon to the bench. Follow a small trail along the edge of the gorge upcanyon, then boulder-hop up the creek. A trail from the biggest swimming hole leads up to the second switchback on the Pine Creek road.

Return the way you came.

16 Middle Echo Canyon from the Bottom

Technical canyoneers revel in the coolness of the places they get to visit. This non-technical canyon exploration visits one of the coolest places in Zion, and makes a great introduction to Zion's off-trail backcountry. The price for this? You have to wade a few ice-cold pools and clamber up some boulder piles.

Middle Echo can be combined with a visit to Hidden Canyon to make a fuller day; or it makes a fine treat on the way down from hiking Observation Point.

Echo Canyon holds snow and ice long into the spring. Exploring in April and May can be treacherous due to snow and ice. Turn around if there are dangerous snowdrifts.

Middle Echo Canyon also makes a fine moderate technical canyon route. See *Technical Canyoneering Routes*.

Type: There and back
Length: 1.5 miles (2.4 km) each way
Time: 3 to 5 hours
Altitude gain: 1200 feet (350 m)
Start: Weeping Rock Shuttle Stop (bathrooms)
Cautions: Off-Trail. Includes wading or swimming and some short climbs.
Shade: Lower part shaded in the morning. The canyon itself is shaded all day. Very shaded.

GETTING THERE: The Echo Canyon/East Rim Trail starts at the Weeping Rock shuttle stop, in the Main Canyon. Bathrooms available.

THE TRAIL: Ascend the East Rim Trail on the painfully obvious switch-

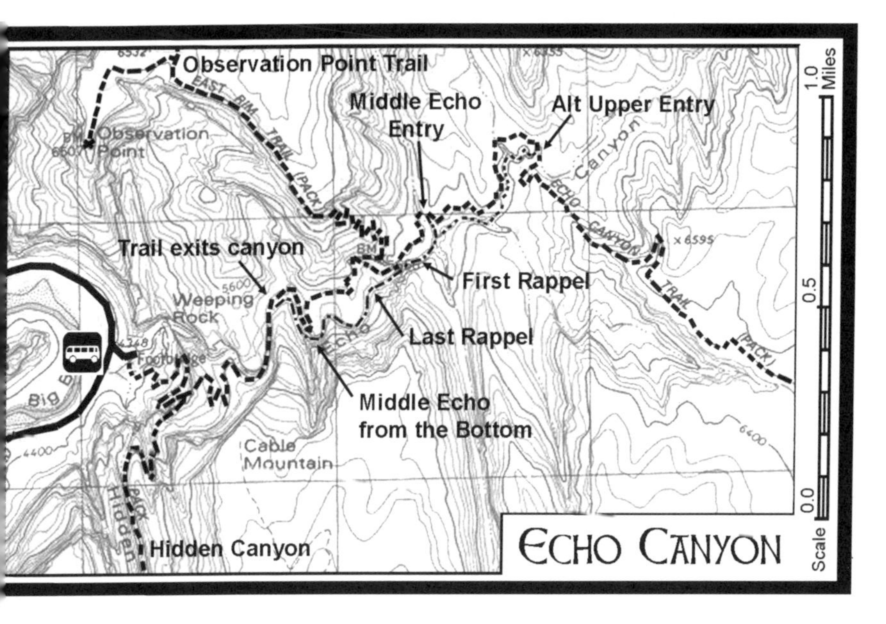

backs for 0.66 mile (1 km), gaining 600 feet (180 m). The signed Hidden Canyon Trail branches right. Continue up the East Rim Trail, passing under the impressive, smooth face of Cable Mountain and into Echo Canyon. Total distance to the start of the canyon is 0.9 mile (1350 m), with a gain of 1200 feet (400 m). Allow 45 minutes.

In summer, this portion of trail is shaded in the morning, so try to get an early start.

THE CANYON: Where the trail exits the canyon bottom, continue in the canyon through a couple of pools and over a small check dam. After five minutes, the canyon opens again, and the hiking trail can be accessed up slickrock to the left.

Continue up the canyon, wading or swimming pools, and clambering over boulders. There are a couple of pools to wade or swim, all right at the beginning. Persist. After fifteen minutes, the canyon cuts left into the rock, the floor becomes smoother, the pools disappear and the walls soar upward dramatically. Very cool. It is shady in the canyon–a great place to be on a hot day.

Work your way up-canyon as far as temperament and temperature allow. About an hour up, a very cool place is found–the Echo Chamber. This huge, curving, slanted chamber has marvelous acoustic properties. Another 15 to 20 minutes up, a pool and 10-foot pourover mark the end of up-canyon exploration. Return the way you came.

17 South Fork Taylor Creek

South Fork Taylor Creek is a delightful canyon that makes a wonderful diversion. Soaring sandstone walls enclose beautiful meadows, and easy walking leads deep into the sandstone. The South Fork is between Paria Point and Beatty Point, two jutting ridges of sandstone.

Type: There and back
Length: 1.2 miles (1.9 km) each way
Time: 1 to 3 hours
Altitude gain: 400 feet (120 m)
Start: Hairpin turn on Kolob Canyons road.
Cautions: Off-Trail.
Shade: The start is in the sun, the depth of the canyon is in the shade. Very nice at sunset.

GETTING THERE: Taylor Creek is located in the Kolob Canyons section of Zion. The drive from Springdale is about one and a quarter hours. From Springdale, drive 19 miles south and west on Route 9 to LaVerkin. Turn right, and proceed 6 miles north on Highway 17 to Interstate 15. Go north on I-15 13 miles to the Kolob Canyons exit. Show your entrance pass at the Visitor Center, then drive 3.2 miles to where the road makes a hairpin turn right. There is a large parking lot inside the hairpin turn.

THE HIKE: Pick up a social trail heading east upcanyon from the apex of the turn. Follow the trail down, through some vegetation, then in and out of a few small washes. The trail climbs away from the bottom of the canyon and up steep dirt, then through scrub oak to the top of a hill. Ah, a half-hour of effort, and you are there. The scrub oak fades and you are left with ponderosa pines, dry fields and spectacular smooth sandstone walls. To proceed upcanyon, cut right (south) to the canyon wall, and walk easily along the wall. It is possible to hike about fifteen minutes up the canyon, to a steep, impassable rockfall. Return the way you came. See map on page 69.

Opposite: *Sharon Lake, first rappel in Behunin*

PART IV

TECHNICAL CANYONEERING IN ZION

CHAPTER FOUR

Introduction to Technical Canyoneering

Zion is a wild place. Soaring walls and deeply cut canyons make at least half of Zion's terrain inaccessible to the hiker. Combining hiking, swimming, climbing, rappelling and adding a few of its own techniques, Technical Canyoneering is the "sport" of visiting the incredibly beautiful places hidden in the backcountry.

Is Canyoneering, Like, an Extreme Sport, Dhhude?

No. While canyoneering is not just hiking with ropes, it is not particularly risky or dangerous for those with adequate skills and training. Canyoneering does not emphasize risk as an important aspect of the sport. Like technical rock climbing, canyoneering leads us through technical terrain (terrain requiring technique and equipment to access). Unlike rock climbing, there is little emphasis on difficulty, and while a certain level of fitness, a certain set of skills and the right equipment are required to canyoneer safely, the sport is not ABOUT difficulty. It is about aesthetics–about what is around the next corner, about being continually amazed by the variety and beauty found there.

It is also not just a walk in the park. While not difficult like high-standard rock climbing, technical canyoneering requires judgment, experience and a certain set of technical skills, some of which are shared with rock-climbing, and some of which are not. People who venture into the canyons without the proper skills are not "bold," "brave" or "extreme"; they are just darn fools.

The biggest surprise to many new canyoneers is the amount of shockingly cold water hidden in the depths of the canyons. In the heat of summer, some canyons can be descended without special protective clothing, but many require neoprene wetsuits or water-tight dry-suits for protection from the continuous exposure to cold water. On many days, a careful judging of the weather, recent thunderstorm activity, and information about the canyon is required to make an informed decision about how much protective clothing is required. Choosing too little warmth

Opposite: *Chris Avery on the last rappel in Kolob Creek*

will mean, at the least, that much of the canyon's charm will be lost to the canyoneer who is focused on getting through the canyon fast; at the most it can mean serious hypothermia with its associated loss of judgment and muscle strength–very dangerous and potentially deadly.

Conditions in canyons are constantly changing. That is part of the experience, and part of the fun. Wise canyoneers will anticipate changes and carry equipment and have skills for dealing with them. Anchors will come and go; webbing may be damaged by flash floods; and new obstacles or swims may appear. Be prepared to re-rig and re-engineer anchors as required.

Zion is unique as a canyoneering venue in the United States, as it packs a large number of interesting canyons into a small area. Quite a variety of canyons are available, ranging from "moderate" (requiring only a few technical skills) to "fairly difficult and demanding" (requiring substantial skills and judgment). Folks new to canyoneering should start with the

Felicia Bicknell on the first rappel, Pine Creek

easy and moderate canyons until they develop the skills and experience necessary to tackle the more challenging canyons.

Unfortunately, descending classic moderate canyons in Zion will teach you very little about the more advanced skills required for the more advanced canyons. Canyoneers should develop these skills by canyoning with other, more skilled canyoneers, by taking classes and by practicing in safe places.

The classic moderate canyons described in detail in this book are good places to start. For the most part, they are popular, well traveled and use mostly fixed anchors (bolts). Rock-climbers will find that their skills cross-over well in these canyons. More advanced canyons require the use and building of natural anchors, pothole escape tricks, continuous cold-water immersion management and other, canyoneering-specific skills. Descriptions for these canyons are considerably more abbreviated.

That's the plain English version–here's the lawyer-speak version:

WARNING

Canyoneering is a sport where you may be seriously injured or die!

Canyoneering is a technical activity that uses judgment, technique and equipment to traverse hazardous terrain. Canyoneers subject themselves to many hazards, none of which this book will protect you from. Enter the canyons of Zion respecting their ever-changing nature and their ability to kill you when you exercise poor judgment, and you are more likely to survive and have a good time.

USE A MAP! There are few adventures in this book where enough information is provided to get to the canyon without a map. Always use a map and know how to use it. Figure out where the route goes, then use your judgment in the field to make CERTAIN you are in the right place.

The information in this guide was compiled over many descents, and was most likely accurate at the time of publication. However, **canyon conditions change continuously and the wise canyoneer expects the unexpected, and is prepared to find or create anchors as needed. Where reality and this book disagree, make decisions based on reality.**

Clothing and warmth recommendations in this book are for the SUMMER season. Exercise caution when descending canyons in the spring, fall or winter, and carry more protection from cold water. Even in summer, cold water can be a problem in many canyons. Hypothermia, technical activity and swimming are a bad combination that can quickly lead to death.

The canyon environment is especially unforgiving of incompetence.

Canyoneering is NOT an extreme sport—don't make it one.

GET SOME SKILLS: While many of the introductory canyons require only a minimal skill set, the next level up is a big jump. Don't fool yourself! There are specific canyoneering skills required to safely descend these canyons—learn them before you need them.

The following are some ways to make your use of this book and your visit to Zion safer:

- CONSULT: You should consult with other canyoneers and park staff about current conditions in the canyons, especially regarding water levels and protective clothing needs. Also ask what canyons would be appropriate for your skill level.
- INSTRUCTION is available and recommended. The skills required in Zion's canyons are not the same as those required for rock climbing, big wall climbing or European-style canyoning. Even experienced canyoneers and climbers should start with easier canyons while developing the skills required for Zion's canyons.
- FIXED ANCHORS should ALWAYS be treated with suspicion, and backed up whenever possible. Bolts and drilled pitons can have a short life in the soft Zion sandstone, and can fail with no outward signs of weakness. Many bolts are placed in canyons by people who have little or no idea of what they are doing. Canyons are a dynamic environment, and even large chockstones and logs can become unstable and dangerous as anchors.

  Be aware of the following specific hazards that could arise when using this book.
- ERRONEOUS DESCRIPTIONS OF ROUTES: Use a map and exercise judgment when descending canyons. There are mistakes in this book, and canyons are constantly changing. Anchors change, rocks fall and logs move. Potholes will change depth with the washing in or out of sand. Be prepared for the route to be different than described.

Staying Alive

The best climber is the one who's having the most fun.

—Alex Lowe

There have been joys too great to be described in words, and there have been griefs upon which I have not dared to dwell, and with these in mind I say, climb if you will, but remember that courage and strength are naught without prudence, and that a momentary negligence may destroy the happiness of a lifetime. Do nothing in haste, look well to each step, and from the beginning think what may be the end.

—Edward Whymper

Security is mostly a superstition. It does not exist in nature, nor do the children of men as a whole experience it. Avoiding danger is no safer in the long run than outright exposure. Life is either a daring adventure, or nothing. To keep our faces toward change and behave like free spirits in the presence of fate is strength undefeatable.

—Helen Keller

Canyons present a variety of opportunities for people to hurt or kill themselves. Unlike climbing, which requires a certain amount of competence to get high enough to get into trouble, any darn fool can wander down a technical canyon and get into big time trouble. Once you pull the ropes on that first rappel, the die is cast and you are committed to descending the canyon, come heck or high water.

Some Recommendations On How To Not Get Killed:

For Everyone:

- Respect the ever-changing nature of Zion's canyons. They can change a lot, in a short period of time. Carry extra gear, like extra rope, slings, food, ascenders, headlamps, a fleece jacket (etc.). Be prepared for each canyon to be different than described, or different than the last time you went through. Bring along the common sense.

For Beginners:

- **Don't be a beginner, led by a beginner.** The majority of accidents occur to people doing their first or second canyon; people who are unfamiliar with canyoneering and the skills required, often in large groups, led by someone who has only a vague idea of what they are doing. Don't do this. Instead, hook up with experienced canyoneers who can show you how this stuff is done.
- **Don't train people in the canyon.** People who don't know how to rappel should be trained in a safe, comfortable environment—not in a canyon. There are numerous places in the park where a rope can be set up down a slab. Use these places for teaching–not canyons.
- **Know before you go**. You'd be surprised how many people start down a canyon with very little idea of what they will encounter.

Read this book, but also verify the information with other sources. Ask at the Backcountry Desk about the latest conditions. Pine Creek, in particular, changes nature dramatically depending on the water level. What was a delightful romp the week before could be a desperate struggle against hypothermia the next Saturday when you bring Uncle Bob and his ten kids in blue jeans and T-shirts into its watery maw.

- **Do the right thing.** Some of the adventures in this book are appropriate for beginners—many are not. Choose your route based on your skills and the skills of your group. This is no contest—if you are in it for the challenge and adrenaline, you are in the wrong sport—take up sport climbing or motocross.
- **Bring the right stuff.** Skimping on gear is not a good idea. Everyone should have a helmet–and everyone should have his or her own harness and his or her own rappel device—everyone should have a wet suit or dry suit when it is required. Everyone should be prepared and practiced for rappelling on the chosen rope size with the gear that they have.
- **Get some skills.** Canyoneering requires specific skills—learn them, either by taking a course or by hanging out with more experienced canyoneers. Safety, efficiency and enjoyment will be your companions when you attain proper experience and skills.
- **Wear a helmet.** Sure, they are not real cool looking. But you'll look even worse lying in a hospital bed being fed through tubes.

For Experienced Climbers:

- **Wear a helmet.**
- **Avoid hubris.** Good traditional climbing skills are the basis for good canyoneering skills, but there's more stuff to learn. Don't kid yourself. The easy canyons are very straightforward and will teach you little about more advanced skills. Canyoning with experienced canyoneers is your best bet.
- **Don't stick the rope.** Consider every rappel carefully. Wet ropes are often much more difficult to pull. Canyoneering rappels are often much more difficult to pull than climbing rappels. If you have doubts, do a test pull before the last person comes down. Rappel single strand to keep the ropes untwisted.
- **Keep your eyes open.** There are often multiple anchors available at a drop—consider all options before committing to one or the other. Just as lost hikers leave cairns, canyoneers who make bad choices also leave slings in the wrong places.
- **Check the anchors.** Folks with poor skills descend canyons, which leads to poorly chosen, poorly placed and poorly rigged anchors.

Check anchors and rigging before using them, re-rig when needed, and remove worn and old slings.

For Experienced Canyoneers:

- Zion canyons are unlike canyons elsewhere in the world, even elsewhere in Utah. Take it easy and get a feel for the lay of the land before charging off to do the hard ones.

Canyon Rating System

The American Canyoneering Association (ACA) Canyon Rating System was developed to give a general idea of the difficulties canyoneers can expect in a canyon. All ratings are estimates for fit adults in small groups, with proper gear and in normal conditions. The difficulty encountered will likely be higher in the off-season, after rain, and possibly after extended drought.

We have ratings so that you may match ventures to your abilities and proclivities. The ratings also indicate the seriousness of the canyon, and provide guidance on what gear to bring. The wise adventurer will choose companions for which the canyon is also appropriate, thus extending, rather than shortening, friendships.

The rating is divided into four parts: The Technical Class, which indicates the technicality of the terrain and the type of ropework required; the Water Rating, which indicates the complications due to flowing or still water; the Risk Rating which indicates the presence of more risk factors; and the Time or Grade, which indicates the length of the adventure.

Technical Classification

1 **Canyon Hiking**: Non-technical. No rope is required. See the route description for difficulties.

2 **Basic Canyoneering**: Scrambling, easy climbing or downclimbing. A rope may be handy for handlines, belays, lowering packs and emergency use. Exit or retreat possible upcanyon without fixed ropes.

3 **Intermediate Canyoneering**: Rappels or technical climbing and/or downclimbing. A rope is required for belays and single pitch rappels. Retreat upcanyon would require fixing ropes.

4 **Advanced Canyoneering**: Aid climbing, multi-pitch rappels and/or complex rope work (such as re-belays and guided rappels) may be required. Might also require difficult pothole escapes, serious squeezing, or extensive high-risk downclimbing.

Water Rating

- **A** Normally dry or with little water. Wading to waist deep.
- **B** Water with no current or light current. Still pools. Falls are normally dry or running at a trickle. Swimming expected.
- **C** Water with strong current. Waterfalls. Wet-canyon rope techniques required.

Risk/Seriousness

(no rating)—Normal risk factors are present on this adventure.

- **R** Risky: One or more extraordinary risk factors exist that will complicate the descent. Solid technical skills and sound judgment required. Not appropriate for beginners, even in competent company.
- **X** Extreme: Multiple risk factors exist that will complicate the descent. Errors in technique or judgment will likely result in serious injury or death. Descent should be attempted by expert canyoneers only.

The presence of an R or X in the rating suggests the canyon will involve risks over and above the many risk factors found in canyons normally. Some examples of additional risks: Long and/or difficult rappels, station to station rappels, exposed climbing or traversing, extensive 4th or 5th class climbing unroped, difficult to establish natural anchors, sections of loose or dangerous rock, difficult or committing route finding, prolonged immersion or extensive swimming. Specific factors should be addressed in the route description.

Grade—Time Required and Seriousness

- **I** Short. A couple of hours.
- **II** Requires about a half day.
- **III** Normally requires most of a day.
- **IV** Expected to take a long day. Get up early, bring a headlamp. Possible bivy.
- **V** More than one day. Normally done in two days.
- **VI** Two full days or more.

The rating does not tell you how difficult the canyon you are about to do IS, it only tells you how difficult it is in NORMAL conditions. You must apply common sense and your knowledge of recent weather and conditions to make a rational estimate of the difficulties ahead of you. Be prepared for the canyon to be a fair amount harder than stated.

All adventures require map-reading skills and a map. Careful analysis of the route description should indicate the difficulty of getting there

and back, but the route descriptions do not replace carrying and using a good map.

Who Will Like What

Hikers of Reasonable Fitness and Skills will like 1A, 1B, 2A and 2B adventures. They may like the easier 3A and 3B routes, if possessing a little climbing experience or accompanied by a climber. Carefully read the 3A and 3B route descriptions to make sure you are up to the technical obstacles involved.

Climbers will generally enjoy 3A and 3B routes. The set of skills required for technical routes has little to do with yanking your way up the local sport route, and everything to do with good ropework, judgment and experience. It is essential to have the right gear and know how to use it. Creative natural anchor skills are developed by getting out with experienced canyoneers.

Climbers will want to have at least five or six 3A and 3B routes under their belts before taking on 4A and 4B canyons, or any canyon with an R or X rating.

Experienced Canyoneers will understand that flowing water has its own risks and techniques that require special training. Class 3C and 4C canyons should only be attempted by trained, well-equipped canyoneers.

Large Groups

Leading large groups should be done with extreme caution. Especially in wet canyons, things can get out of control very quickly. It is not uncommon to see a large group of non-climbers being led by one novice climber in a technical canyon like Pine Creek, making poor decisions, and putting innocent people at risk. Don't do this.

I am not fond of large groups in our canyons. If you do bring a large group (larger than 6 persons), here are some suggestions:

- **Break It Up**: Take your group down in smaller groups of about 6. If you don't have enough competent leadership to break into groups, you don't have enough to manage the larger group.
- **Respect Your Fellow Travelers**: Large groups can be obnoxious to other groups. Play well with others by giving them ample space, and keeping the raucous laughter and social chitchat to a minimum. That touch-football game can wait until you are back in camp.
- **Let Others Play Through**: Your large group moves slowly–show respect for others by letting them pass you as soon as possible. Let them rappel on your ropes.

- **Carry Extra Gear**: Given the carrying power of all those people, you should bring a spare set of ropes, plus ascenders and a spare rappel device. In case of injury, one group can go for help without stranding those who stay behind.

Gear for Technical Canyoneering

Each canyon will, of course, require somewhat different gear for safe passage. This discussion is of the "standard kit" for canyoneering in Zion–add or subtract as required for each adventure. Though most people will want to own their own gear, many items can be rented at several outfitters in Springdale.

Personal Gear

Each person in the party should have, at a minimum:

- **Helmet**. A helmet protects your head from falling objects, and you from banging your head against the canyon walls. You probably don't do that on purpose anymore, but the slippery environment found in canyons, and the many awkward starts to rappels, makes wearing a helmet mandatory. A climbing or mountaineering helmet is preferred, but a bicycle or kayaking helmet is better than nothing.
- **Harness**. Each member of the party should have their own harness. Climbing shops offer a wide variety of harnesses, the nuances of which escape notice while slogging around in a wet suit. For canyons, a sturdy, moderately-priced harness with gear loops, a belay loop and adjustable leg loops is the best choice.
- **Rappel Device and Locking Carabiner.** Each party member should have their own rappel device and locking 'biners. A wide variety of rappel devices are available, each with benefits and liabilities. What is most important is that the person using the device knows how to use it on the ropes in use, and be able to add or subtract friction as needed. My favorite device is the Black Diamond ATC-XP, which works well on small diameter (8 mm to 10 mm) ropes.

  A rappel device is used with one or two locking 'biners. In Zion's canyons, springloaded auto-locking lockers quickly clog with sand, so the simpler, cheaper screw-gate locking 'biners are vastly preferred. I especially like small-HMS-Screwlock 'biners like the Petzl Attache.
- **Gloves.** Gloves are the secret weapon of the canyon rappeller. A sturdy leather or synthetic-leather glove on the brake hand adds vastly to the control and safety of the rappeller. Good artificial leather does not funk out in water like the real animal hide, but can burn through

on long or fast rappels. Cloth or thin leather gloves are worse than nothing and should be avoided. GLOVES ARE NOT A SUBSTITUTE FOR SETTING UP YOUR RAPPEL WITH ENOUGH FRICTION IN THE FIRST PLACE.

- **Slings, Biners, Extras**. Each canyoneer should carry four to six over-the-shoulder slings (24″ slings) and four to six locking carabiners. Use these for clipping into anchors and safety lines, and for managing your pack while rappelling and downclimbing. Many people bring Prusik cords so they can deal with an emergency quickly while on rappel.
- **Food**. Days in the canyon are unpredictable. In addition to your normal meals, pack a good supply of snacks. A bite to eat can be of great assistance in keeping you warm and sharp at critical times. Have a snack handy to munch while waiting to get on rappel.
- **Water**. Drinkable water is not usually found in Zion's canyons, so most people carry enough for the day from the start. Zion is in the desert, so carry more than you might in a moister climate.

Clothing and Footwear

Clothing requirements vary with the canyon, the season and the conditions of the moment. Ask at the backcountry desk about current conditions in canyons that vary widely, like Pine Creek.

Many of Zion's canyons have cold water hidden in their depths, and the clothing discussed here provides protection from the cold water. Even when the air temperature in Zion Canyon is 100° F (38° C), a dry suit or thick wetsuit can be required to prevent hypothermia just a few-hundred feet away.

Recommendations are recommendations—you may go with less or with more. I like to wear a wetsuit for The Subway and Orderville when it is stinking hot out, so the charms of the canyons are not shivered away.

- **Shorts and Tee Shirts.** Many canyons can be enjoyed in summer with no special clothing. Spry, Behunin and Mystery come to mind as canyons with little or only brief swims. It helps to have quick-drying synthetic shorts, and shoes and socks suitable for wading and hiking with wet feet. A zip-front synthetic shirt with quick drying nylon shorts means not having to shiver in a cold, soaked cotton T-shirt between pot holes. Even if hot out, carry a fleece sweater or synthetic "puffball" in your drybag, for warming up after getting wet.
- **Wetsuits and Dry Suits.** Many canyons in Zion are most luxuriously descended clad in neoprene. While a variety of wetsuits are available, the basic "summer wetsuit" for Zion is a 3/2 (3 mm body, 2 mm sleeves and legs), full/full (full length legs, full length arms). Canyoneering

is really hard on gear, and most folks shop for economy.

The wettest and coldest canyons in Zion (Kolob, Heaps, Imlay) are usually descended using a dry suit or a "full wetsuit," even in summer. A "full wetsuit" is from 5 mm to 7 mm thick and provides considerably more warmth than a summer wetsuit. A dry suit is completely waterproof, with latex seals at the ankles, wrists and neck. It permits the layering of thermal underwear underneath, allowing adjustment of warmth to the conditions. Dry suits can be rented in Springdale.

In general, wetsuits and dry suits are carried to the first swim or wade, and removed after the last obstacle. Bring a large enough pack to carry your wetsuit in addition to the rest of your gear.

- **Socks.** Neoprene socks (Neos) are the canyoneer's best friend, keeping your feet warm, and protecting your feet from sand and the rough places in your shoes. Neos should be snug-fitting, but loose enough in the front to allow your toes to spread while hiking. Popular models are 2–6 mm thick.
- **Shoes.** Specialized canyoneering shoes work best, but most any sturdy trail-running shoe will do. Climbing approach shoes with sticky rubber can work well. Make sure they fit comfortably over your neoprene socks–this may require a half-size larger than your usual fit. Leather boots tend to be a big problem when hiking through water.

  Sandals? Are you crazy? Sandals offer zero protection while canyoneering, but are great around camp after a long day in the canyons.

  Five Ten Canyoneers and Sportiva Exum Rivers are the best performing footwear, and can be rented in Springdale.

Carrying Stuff

Most likely, you will be carrying a pack. Canyoneering-specific packs work best, especially when doing wet canyons that involve climbing in and out of potholes all day. Canyon specific packs from Imlay Canyon Gear, Metolius and Petzl are simple and durable, and allow water to drain out quickly.

Other packs work fine too, and since canyoneering beats gear up, the frugal canyoneer will choose a pack that is simple, sturdy, inexpensive and maybe already pretty used up. Place grommets in the pack for drainage—10 to 15 sturdy large-size (number 2, 3 or 4) grommets to drain all compartments, including the lid. Since canyoneering gear is bulky, a fairly large daypack (40 liters or 2300 cubic inches) is most useful.

Keeping Stuff Dry

The days of carefully sealed garbage bags are over! Rafting-style

A relaxing float at the end of a long rappel. Chris Avery in Kolob Creek.

drybags are inexpensive and fairly secure. Buy one that fits the main compartment of your pack and can hold all your stuff in one bag. The Pneumo Drybags from Pacific Outdoor Equipment are lightweight and work very well.

Canyon Dry Kegs from Imlay Canyon Gear offer more secure protection from water, and also protect your stuff from crushing. They are easier and faster to get in and out of than drybags–perfect for your camera. Available at several stores in Springdale.

Accessories

- **Trekking Poles.** When hiking in the murky, boulder-strewn waters of The Narrows, poles are almost a necessity, but in technical canyons they are a major liability—difficult to deal with for all but the most skilled. Poles get in the way on rappels, put scratches on canyon walls and poke holes in packs and friends. Not recommended in technical canyons. If you must, bring the rubber tip covers to lessen your impact, or pull them apart and stow inside your pack.

- **Water Tanks, Bottles.** On dayhikes, canyoneers usually carry all their water for the day with them. Watertanks (bladders, CamelBacks) can be a liability, as the rough handling your pack experiences in the canyons can be hard on tanks. Plastic bottles tend to be more reliable and provide floatation when empty.
- **Treating Water.** Backcountry water, when available, needs to be treated to be safe for drinking. For overnights, and for long day trips, lightweight backpacking filters or ultra-light systems like the ULA H2O Amigo are useful for filtering water. Some people use chemical treatments effectively, and clear water can often be found with a little looking around.

Group Gear

- **Ropes.** For easy canyons in Zion, pretty much any climbing or caving rope will do. Dynamic climbing ropes used for canyons in Zion should not be used for leading again–wet sand worked into the core by swimming and rappelling could compromise the dynamic properties of the rope. If buying ropes specifically for canyoneering, tightly woven canyoneering-specific static ropes are preferred to dynamic.

  Extensive discussion revolves around rope diameter, which is a matter of personal taste. Most people are using ropes of 8 mm, 9 mm, or 10 mm diameter. While experienced canyoneers chose 8 mm ropes so they do not have to lug around quite so much weight, less experienced canyoneers should carry larger diameter ropes as they are more durable, provide a higher safety margin and provide more friction when rappelling.

  A key point of rope selection is to make sure that ALL of your canyon companions are equipped and prepared to rappel on the chosen rope.

  The length of the longest rappel is given for each adventure. You will need at least TWICE that length to both rappel and recover your ropes. A standard rope length for Zion is 200 feet (60 meters), which in tandem with a similar rope or a 200-foot pull-cord, will get you down all but a few canyons.
- **Extra Ropes.** If your group is large, carry an extra set of ropes. This greatly increases efficiency and flexibility. More ropes allows greater speed through multiple-rappel sections, can save the day if ropes get stuck, and allows the team to split in the case of an accident.

Group Leader Gear

- **Slings, Rapides, Knife.** As a rule of thumb, the group (or leader) should carry enough webbing and rapides (Rapid-Link, quick-links) to re-rig all the anchors in the canyon.

  Anchor slings in canyons are maintained by the general public—that includes you. If slings look suspect to you, cut away the old slings and re-rig with new. Carry a knife for removing old slings, and for cutting new slings to the ideal length. A steel ring (rapide or round ring) should be used on every rappel point. Aluminum rappel rings used by climbers wear out quickly in the canyon environment and should be inspected carefully or replaced when encountered.

  If you do not have the skills to re-rig anchors, then you should obtain proper training. Zion's canyons attract a large variety of canyoneers, some of whom have poor rigging skills, and anchors are often in bad shape. The wise canyon leader will understand rigging and evaluate each anchor carefully.
- **Rope Climbing Gear.** Though climbing the rope is seldom required, it is a good skill to know. Some folks carry small ascending tools (Tibloc, Ropeman, or Prusiks) for when the need arises. It is also good to know how to climb a rope using slings and biners (using Prusik, Kleimheist or Bachman knots).

  Getting the rope stuck is a bad thing, and the savvy canyon leader will set and pull the ropes carefully to avoid sticking them. Climbing a stuck rope (without the other side secured) is very dangerous, and should be avoided at all costs. Often, it is better to cut the rope and complete the canyon with the rope available, rather than risk a dangerous fall trying to retrieve a stuck rope.
- **Bolt Kit.** A bolt kit is not required for any of the canyons in this book. Zion's canyons are well traveled, and tend to have more bolts than really needed. Placing good, reliable bolts in the soft Navajo sandstone is difficult, and should only be undertaken by experienced canyoneers. Then again, most experienced canyoneers will have good natural anchor skills that make placing bolts unnecessary.
- **Hooking Kit.** A hooking kit consists of a drill, drill holder, two hooks and a hammer. A hooking kit should ALWAYS be carried in Heaps and Imlay, even when conditions are reported as easy; since escaping from a keeper pothole that resists other techniques might be required.

CHAPTER FIVE

Classic Moderate Technical Canyons

The canyons presented in this section are THE classic technical canyons, and make a good introduction to the canyons of Zion.

18 The Subway from the Top

The "Subway," (the Left Fork of North Creek) is Zion's second most popular backcountry hike for good reason. In a park of exemplary beauty, The Subway is one of the most diverse and beautiful canyons. Not to be missed. A few short rappels and a couple of short, mandatory swims add spice to the adventure.

"The Subway" is a short, spectacular section of the Left Fork of North Creek. The canyon system is called the Great West Canyon, including both the Left and Right Forks. The Subway section is not marked on maps, but is where the Left Fork tightens up and twists sharply, between North Guardian Angel and Guardian Angel Pass. The hike is also known as "The Left Fork."

The route starts at the Wildcat Canyon Trailhead and descends to the Left Fork via a cross-country route that crosses Russell Gulch, walks out a ridge and descends a steep gully. The Left Fork is followed through The Subway, then downcanyon a few miles. A steep trail is then climbed to the road.

Due to its popularity, The Subway is managed under a quota system. Reservations are distributed by lottery several months in advance and are recommended. Call the Backcountry Desk (435-772-0170) for the latest information. If you do not have reservations, don't fret—there are permits available one day in advance of, or the day of, your hike at the Main and Kolob Canyons Visitor Centers. Be flexible and plan ahead to avoid being denied.

Opposite: Jason Robertson on the last rappel in Mystery Canyon

Classic Moderate Canyons Locator Map

Classic Moderate Canyons:
- **18** The Subway from the Top
- **19** Pine Creek
- **20** Keyhole Canyon
- **21** Middle Echo Canyon
- **22** Mystery Canyon
- **23** Behunin Canyon

Virgin
Springdale
Rockville

North

Scale of Miles 0.0 2.0 4.0 6.0 8.0 10.0 Miles

Skills Required

The Subway is a strenuous and demanding backcountry hike with several short rappels and a couple of pools to swim. Good navigational skills and a map are required. Straying into the more difficult terrain on either side of the approach trail, or missing the exit trail, is hazardous. There are three short drops that most people will want a rope for. Folks should know how to rappel, and how to set up and use obvious anchors. The Subway also throws a few cold swims at you, so you'll need drybags for your gear, and if it is not stinking hot out, you might want a wetsuit.

For the less ambitious hiker, the best part of The Subway is accessible by hiking up from the bottom (see Subway from the Bottom under Off-Trail Hikes).

Rating:	3B III
Time required:	6 to 12 hours
Preferred season:	Summer or fall.
Cold water protection:	Wetsuits recommended in all but the hottest weather.
Longest rappel:	30 feet (10 m)
Special difficulties:	None

GETTING THERE: The Subway starts at the Wildcat Canyon Trailhead on the Kolob Terrace Road, and ends at the Left Fork Trailhead. In the summer, it is easy to hitch a ride from the Left Fork Trailhead the further 8 miles to the Wildcat Canyon trailhead. If you have one car, leave the car at the bottom (Left Fork Trailhead) with water, food and clothing. Hitching a ride is easier at the beginning of the day, when you are clean and smell nice. In summer, get an early start to avoid the hot sun.

From Springdale, drive south and west 14 miles to the town of Virgin. Turn right (north) on the Kolob Reservoir Road (KR road, sometimes called the Kolob Terrace (KT) road). The paved KR road winds through town, then climbs a dramatic ridge in making its way to Kolob Terrace. Six and a half miles from Virgin, the road enters the park and three trailheads are soon encountered–the Right Fork, Grapevine Springs, then the Left Fork. Park at the Left Fork Trailhead. The trailhead is not shown on many maps, but is close to the Bench Mark labeled BM 5248. Mileage from the town of Virgin is 8.6 miles. Driving time from Springdale is 45 minutes.

By car or thumb, continue up the road another 7.0 miles to the Wildcat Canyon Trailhead. Start your hike here. Toilets are available at both trailheads.

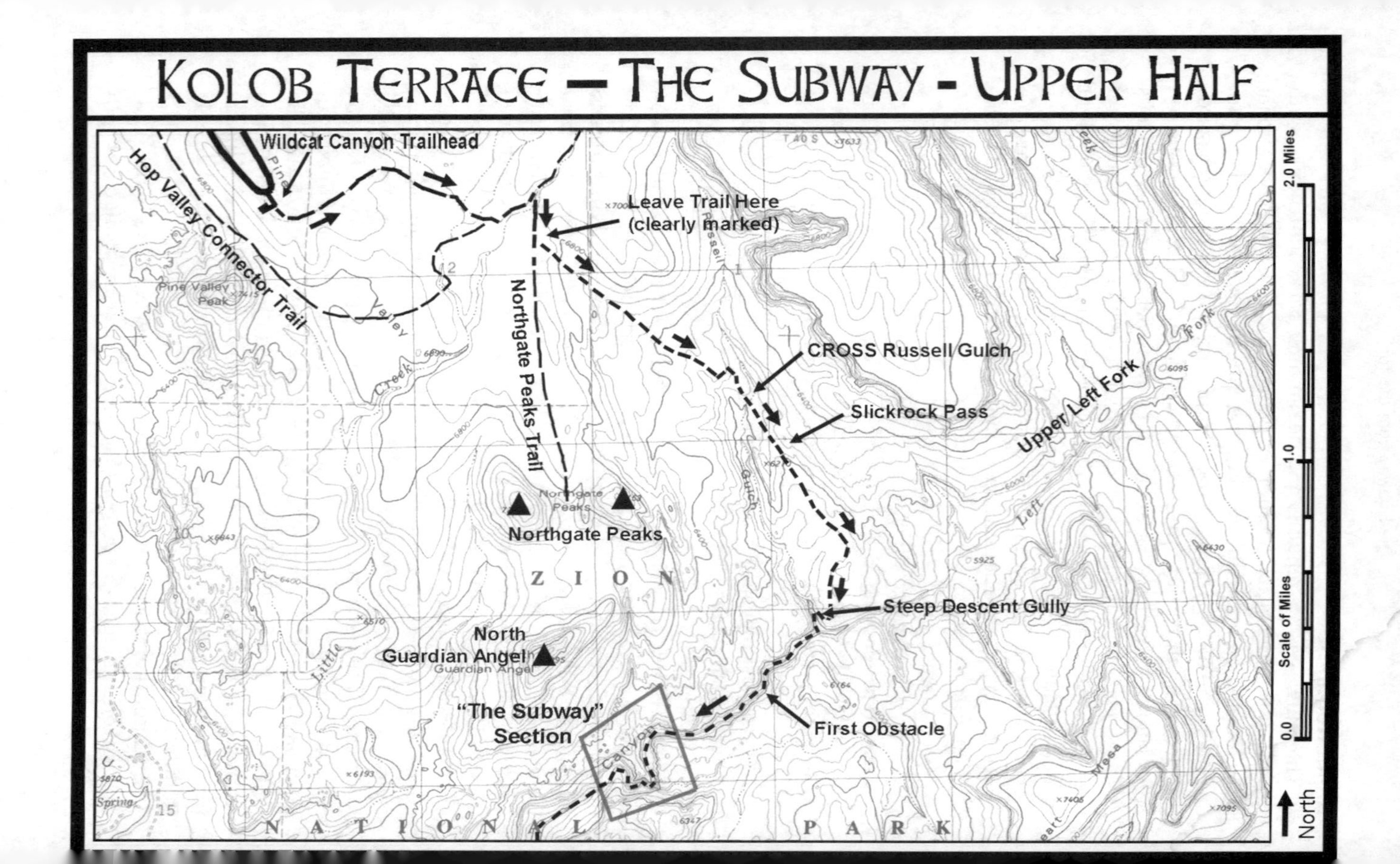

Kolob Terrace – The Subway - Upper Half
Wildcat Canyon Trailhead
Hop Valley Connector Trail
Pine Valley Peak
Leave Trail Here
(clearly marked)
Northgate Peaks Trail
CROSS Russell Gulch
Slickrock Pass
Upper Left Fork
Northgate Peaks
Z I O N
Steep Descent Gully
North
Guardian Angel
"The Subway"
Section
First Obstacle
N A T I O N A L
P A R K
Scale of Miles
0.0
1.0
2.0 Miles
North

APPROACH: The hike starts as a pleasant stroll across the open meadows of Kolob Terrace, headed in an easterly direction. Open areas are interspersed with stands of ponderosa pine. After 25 minutes, the signed Hop Valley Connector Trail comes in from the right. This trail is not shown on some maps. Continue straight. Five minutes later, the signed Northgate Peaks Trail comes in on the right—take this to the south. A few minutes down the Northgate Peaks Trail, take a trail left (east) to the top of a slickrock area. There is a sign: "Subway Hikers." The maintained trail ends here.

It is important to find and follow the unofficial trail that leads to the gully down to the Left Fork. For the most part, the path is clear, but there are a few places where it is easily lost. Make SURE you follow the trail. In 2002, two different parties strayed from the trail. One fell over a 30-foot cliff and broke both legs and some vertebrae. The other party spent a cold night on a small ledge.

Work your way down the slickrock into the drainage before you, trending right and following numerous small cairns. At the base of the slickrock, pick up a small trail leading through a delightful forest. (Take the right-most of 2 trails).

After a few minutes, the trail enters a rocky area with scattered bushes, and heads down and left into a shallow drainage. Follow the drainage, then walk a ridge to its end, and a good view of Russell Gulch below.

Take a good look at the terrain across the way. The trail can be seen below CROSSING the watercourse of Russell Gulch above a 30-foot drop, then making its way into the woods and toward a slickrock pass with a pinnacle in the middle. Descend a steep step and follow the trail across the slickrock streambed, through the woods and along a slickrock bench leading up to the pass. Descend the slabs on the other side and pick up a small trail that continues at the same elevation out to a wooded point overlooking the confluence of Russell Gulch and the Left Fork. Descend a steep, sandy gully to the bottom of Russell Gulch.

If, at any point on the approach, the trail is lost, backtrack to where you are definitely on the trail. Though unofficial, the trail is marked with cairns and heavily used, but it takes a few sharp turns that can be missed. Wandering off the trail is dangerous.

The hour-plus hike to this point is mostly in the full sun. At the bottom of Russell Gulch, a pool and shade offer respite from the heat–a good place to grab a bite to eat and a drink.

THE CANYON: Fifty feet from the bottom of the gully, Russell Gulch intersects the Left Fork. Turn right and follow the dry canyon ten minutes to the FIRST OBSTACLE—a jumble of giant boulders. Scramble right to a 20-foot (6 m) drop where a giant boulder sits against the right canyon wall.

FIRST OBSTACLE: There are several ways to manage getting your group past this obstacle.

To the right, against the canyon wall, is a V-slot with a small chunk of log at the top. This is not the way. Six feet (2 m) back along the canyon wall from the V-slot is a pinch, where a boulder leans securely against the wall, forming a place that can be slung for an anchor. It might have a sling on it. This is the anchor. To the left of the V-slot is a giant boulder. The boulder has a large, flat face downcanyon—this is the face to descend.

Passing the First Obstacle:

1. The recommended and most conservative method is to rappel the face of the boulder using the pinch as an anchor. This requires about 60 feet of rope, plus a sling and rappel ring. Run the rope over the crest of the boulder, making sure the rope does not slide to the side. Given the friction across the top of the boulder, it is imperative to use a rappel ring or retrieving the rope will prove difficult.
2. The left side of the boulder's face (left looking downcanyon) provides a downclimb (5.5) for the experienced climber. The holds are fairly big and the landing flat. However, it is still 20 feet to the ground, and extreme caution should be used. More than one leg has been broken in this spot—and the evacuation is difficult.
3. In many cases, all members of the party but one can rappel the face of the boulder, and the most agile member can downclimb the face, with spotting and encouragement from below. Leave the best climber for last.

Continue downcanyon. A few nice potholes are avoided by clambering around the sides, but about 15 minutes below the First Obstacle, the Triple Pool presents the canyoneer with the first required swim. Make sure your gear is properly drybagged, and swim the three pools. Bonus style points are awarded for swimming an underwater arch on the left, just past the exit of the second pool. A few minutes downcanyon, small springs start to provide a fresh flow of water in the canyon. Fifteen minutes downcanyon, the canyon forms a slot filled with water. Downclimb a couple of short drops and swim under a chockstone, then out a long, cold corridor. (Variation: The slot can be avoided by a high, awkward traverse on the left, followed by a short rappel).

TO THE SUBWAY: The canyon in this section is exceptionally beautiful. Five or ten minutes downstream, the final section begins at Keyhole Falls. The stream drops through a slot with a small arch on the left. Rappel 10 feet from bolts on the right, into water that is usually waist deep. Downclimbing this waterfall is difficult because the landing is very uneven.

You are in an amazing corridor. Swim through an arch on the left for bonus style points. At the end of the corridor, the canyon turns sharply right and forms nice pools. The famous "North Pole" log is in this section. Downclimb a small drop and wind downcanyon. At a logjam, the stream plunges through the logs to make a waterfall. Carefully cross the top of the waterfall to the ledge on canyon left. Walk out this ledge 50 feet (15 m). A bolt anchor allows a rappel 30 feet (10 m) to the canyon floor, or a series of ledges before the bolts allows the more agile to downclimb and traverse ledges to drop to the canyon floor 20 feet (6 m) close to the base of the waterfall. Duck under the waterfall to enjoy the Waterfall Room.

Continue downcanyon past some lovely pools. The footing can be slippery here, so be careful. This is the famous "Subway" section, the curving canyon walls and parallel cracks in the floor calling to mind underground trolleys. The canyon opens up and flattens out. Groups often remove their wetsuits and harnesses here, and warm up in the sun. If it is really hot out, take a siesta until the sun is lower in the sky.

THE WALK OUT: The walk out is long and rugged. The first part descends marvelous and photogenic red ledges with waterfalls. A few minutes below the red ledges, a spring drops water into the stream on the right. Following paths on both banks and crossing the stream many times, make your way downcanyon. Most parties take a little more than two hours for the hike out. About one hour downcanyon, look for two large tumble-down boulders close to the water on the right. Their flat, gray faces hold many dinosaur tracks. Admire, but do not touch these fragile remnants of the past.

Another hour downcanyon and it's time to exit up to the road. Missing the exit is easy, so make sure you pay attention. Two streams come into the Left Fork from the north (right). One third of a mile (0.5 km) past the second stream, the exit gully will be in front of you. The north (right) wall of the canyon is a 400-foot (120 m), steep, tree-covered talus slope with 400-foot (120 m) vertical sandstone walls above. Downstream, the sandstone at the top ends and a black lava flow replaces the steep talus. The trail out climbs the crease below the left edge of the vertical sandstone to where it meets the lava flow.

The climb out can be extremely hot—the black rock traps afternoon heat. Take a final dip in the stream before starting the steep, 400-foot climb. Find a well-established trail on the right side of the creek that starts up a gully. Do not begin the climb up without finding the trail. At the top of the slope, the trail traverses left to the top of the lava flow and works its way left through ledges to the mesa top above. Follow the trail through the piñon-juniper forest 0.5 mile (800 m) to the parking area. Enjoy the ice-cold beverages you left in your cooler.

In the (geologically) recent past, lava flowed over the edge and into the Left Fork, forming a dam. The creek gradually built a lake until it over-topped the dam and cut its way through. Soft sandstone from the lake deposits can be seen lying on top of the lava in a few places just after reaching the top of the steep climb out. Look for these thin-layered, soft sand- and siltstones. For a map of the Lower Subway, see page 109.

The Subway from the Top—Minimum Times

Landmark	hours	hrs total	miles	miles total	km	km total
Wildcat Canyon Trailhead	0:00	0.0	0.0			
Northgate Peaks Trail	0:30	0:30	1.3	1.3	2.1	2.1
Turnoff to Subway Route	0:05	0:35	0.2	1.5	0.3	2.4
Cross Russell Gulch	0:25	1:00	1.0	2.5	1.6	4.0
Bottom of Russell Gulch	0:30	1:30	1.0	3.5	1.6	5.6
First Obstacle	0:10	1:40	0.3	3.8	0.5	6.1
Triple Pool	0:20	2:00	0.3	4.1	0.5	6.6
Slot Swim	0:30	2:30	0.4	4.5	0.6	7.2
Keyhole Falls	0:30	3:00	0.4	4.9	0.6	7.8
End of Subway/Red Ledges	0:30	3:30	0.3	5.2	0.5	8.3
Dinosaur Tracks	1:00	4:30	1.5	6.7	2.4	10.7
Start of Lava Slope Exit	0:50	5:20	1.2	7.9	1.9	12.6
Climb Steep Slope	0:20	5:40	0.1	8.0	0.2	12.9
Stroll to Carpark	0:20	6:00	0.6	8.6	1.0	13.8

19 Pine Creek

The Narrows of Pine Creek are THE classic introduction to technical canyoneering in Zion. Rapid-fire rappels, beautiful soaring walls, and constantly changing conditions of light and water make Pine Creek a wonderful learning experience for the intermediate canyoneer, or a delightful jaunt on a summer evening for the grizzled veteran.

Pine Creek demonstrates the ever-changing nature of Zion canyons. Full of water from spring runoff or recent thundershowers, it is a freeze-fest requiring thick wet suits or dry suits to prevent hypothermia. After a period of extended drought, it can be completely dry. Be sure to check at the Backcountry Desk for current conditions and, more importantly, believe them when they say you NEED wetsuits.

Pine Creek is also Zion's most popular technical canyon for misadventure. Rappelling off the end of the rope, losing control of a rappel, or getting stalled out by too large a group and too little experience are common ways of demonstrating stupidity in Pine Creek. Don't do this. Pine Creek is a serious canyon with serious obstacles, and should not be taken lightly.

Here are some suggestions for avoiding misadventure:

- Know what you are doing. It may seem obvious, but Pine Creek requires canyoneering skills to descend. Everyone in your party should know how to rappel BEFORE entering the canyon. Many rappels feature awkward starts, or require disconnecting while swimming.
- Keep your group small, to six or fewer people. If your group is larger, break it into two smaller groups. If you do not have enough experienced people to do this, break the group in two, and have the experienced people run through the canyon twice.
- Bring the right equipment. Everyone must have his or her own harness, gloves and rappel device, plus a helmet and proper clothing. Do not underestimate the need for wet suits.

Pine Creek is divine, though the thunder of traffic in the tunnel kind of cuts into the wilderness experience. The technical section is done by competent small parties in an hour or less, and struggled through by large groups of incompetents in 12 hours or more. Expect to encounter other parties when descending Pine Creek.

Rating:	3B II
Time required:	2 to 6 hours
Preferred season:	Spring, summer or fall.
Cold water protection:	Highly variable. Wetsuits generally required.
Longest rappel:	100 feet (30 m)
Special difficulties:	None

DRIVING: From Springdale drive north a few miles to Canyon Junction. Follow Rte 9 up Pine Creek Canyon to the second switchback and park. This is where you will exit. Continue up the road and through the tunnel. Park at the east end of the tunnel in a small parking lot on the right. If you have only one car, park at the top and have one person hitch back to the car after completing the canyon.

APPROACH: From the east end of the tunnel: Descend a small, rough trail from near the outhouse to the canyon floor and turn right. You should be in a dry wash. If there is ANY flow, the canyon is a very different beast.

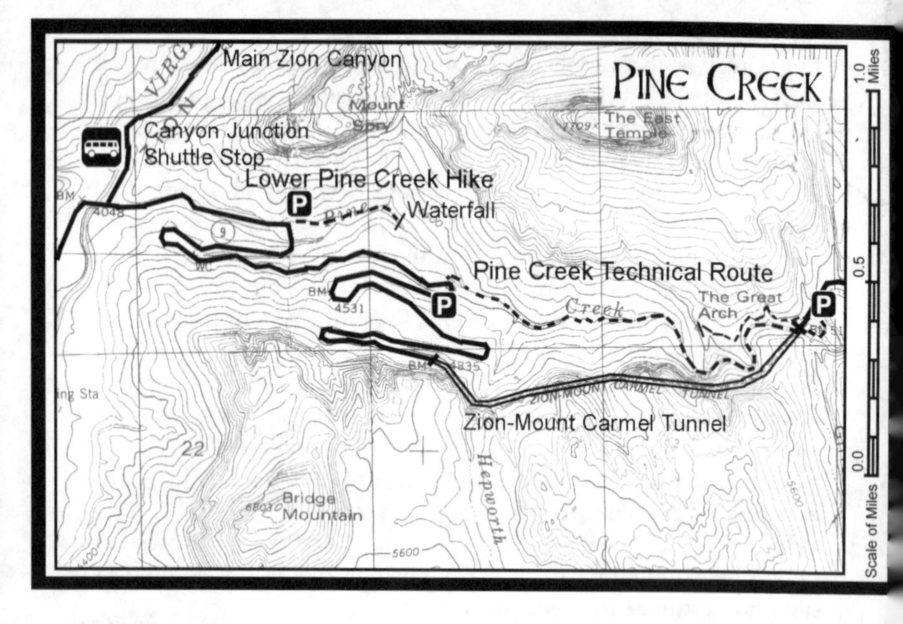

THE CANYON: Follow the canyon downhill under the bridge. Five minutes of walking and downclimbing leads to the first rappel. Wetsuits and harnesses are commonly put on in the shade of the canyon a few meters short of the first rappel.

FIRST OBSTACLE: A short drop and pool must be dealt with before getting to the first rappel. There are several options depending on water level and skills. Straight down the watercourse often is the best choice. An exposed climb up left, then down on a ramp can work better when the pool is full.

Historical Note: In ancient times, the first few rappels were avoided by walking the rim of the canyon and rappelling from a tree. **Don't do this.** The possibility of knocking rocks onto canyoneers below is too high, and you miss some nice canyon.

R1 (Rappel 1): 70 feet (20 m) Rap from a bolt anchor to a pothole. Walk to the exit of the pothole and continue the rappel another 20 feet (6 m) to the ground (sometimes pool). The last person should flip the ropes left around a horn, to avoid sticking the rope in the crack on the last part of the rappel. Pull the rope carefully, slow and steady.

Walk 20 meters, then downclimb a log under a rock. Walk 20 meters past a small arch.

R2: 10 feet (3 m) off a log into a pothole.

R3: Great Cathedral Rappel. Walk carefully out a slippery ramp to the anchor. (May require a belay in some conditions). Rap 65 feet (20 m) off a bolt anchor past 2 arches.

Walk or swim out the end of the pothole (through arch). Walk down a beautiful fluted corridor 100 m to the next obstacle. Downclimb a log into a slot (and often a swim), or follow the rim on the right up and over to a bolt anchor and short rappel (20 feet, 6 m), avoiding the deepest part of the swim. Walk or swim a long corridor. The canyon turns sharply right. Walk and downclimb 100 meters or so to a short drop.

Carefully downclimb some logs into a pool. Walk 200 yards (200 m) to one last swim where the canyon turns sharply right. Downclimb a log and make your way to where the canyon opens up. This is a good place to have lunch and warm up.

Work through large blocks 200 meters, trending right near the end to a flat ledge and a bolt anchor near a small tree.

R4: Rap 65 feet (20 m) down a corner. Pull the rope carefully to avoid getting it stuck in the corner crack. Walk through a neat keyhole to an open area. Climb slabs left to a bench, then walk down to an arch and a bolt anchor for the final rappel.

> Safety Note: The canyon "floor" in the open area is debris wedged in-between giant boulders, and is unstable. It forms the roof of a cavern below. Use caution when moving across this possible collapse area.

R5: Rap 100 feet (30 m). A spectacular free rappel leads to a delightful Fairy Glen with a small spring.

Relax, swim, drink some water, remove harnesses and pack the rope. Sometimes it is best to wait until the canyon goes into the shade for the walk out.

EXIT: Descend the canyon. The floor of the canyon is littered with large blocks and the walk out is strenuous. Very difficult in the dark. Take it slow and have fun. It usually takes at least an hour, not including time for playing in pools. The masonry wall of the 2nd switchback is clearly visible from the canyon bottom just before the largest and best swimming hole. Find a small trail in the woods from just above the pool, or from the level of the pool, leading to the road.

ALTERNATIVE EXIT: It is possible to follow a traversing trail across to the end of the top switchback of the Pine Creek road. As of 2005, the trail is closed except for emergencies, REAL emergencies. The Zion Canyoneering Coalition is working with the park to stabilize the eroding parts of the trail so it can be used as egress from Pine Creek. Please do NOT use the trail until it is re-opened.

20 Keyhole Canyon (Starfish Canyon)

A brief, wonderful and definitely chilly canyon involving a few rappels and a long swim, Keyhole is a good introduction to technical canyoneering and a delightful way to spend an hour or two on a hot summer day. It is often combined with Pine Creek—no need to strip off the wetsuit and harness in-between.

An arch can be seen far above the canyon from the parking spot. Is this the Keyhole?

Bring as little gear as possible. It's not unusual to put on wetsuits and harnesses at the car and dash up the approach as fast as possible, before being overcome by heatstroke.

Rating: 3B I
Time required: 1 to 2 hours
Preferred season: Spring, summer or fall.
Cold water protection: Wetsuits recommended even in summer.
Longest rappel: 60 feet (20 m)
Special difficulties: Awkward 1st rappel, cold water.

DRIVING: Keyhole is a small canyon north of Highway 9, just west of Point 5538 on the Springdale East quadrangle. It is 2.1 miles west of the East Entrance, or 1.9 miles east of the small tunnel. Park where the drainage crosses the road.

APPROACH: The narrow nature of the canyon makes carrying a pack difficult, so bring a minimum of gear. Walk east on the road 0.25 mile and around the corner, then cut left and climb slabs in a beautiful slickrock bowl to a pass at the top. The pass is distinctive, as it has a nice Hoodoo right in the center. Cut left of the Hoodoo and descend a steep gully on the other side to the canyon bottom. Total approach about 15 minutes.

Please be certain you are on the correct approach trail. The park has been concerned about erosion in this area. The Zion Canyoneering Coalition and Park have identified the best approach, hardened the preferred route and restored the eroded areas next to the route. Please do your part and STAY ON THE TRAIL.

THE CANYON: Descend the canyon. The first section requires a little downclimbing and some wading up to waist deep, before coming out into the open. This section is called "Middle Keyhole."

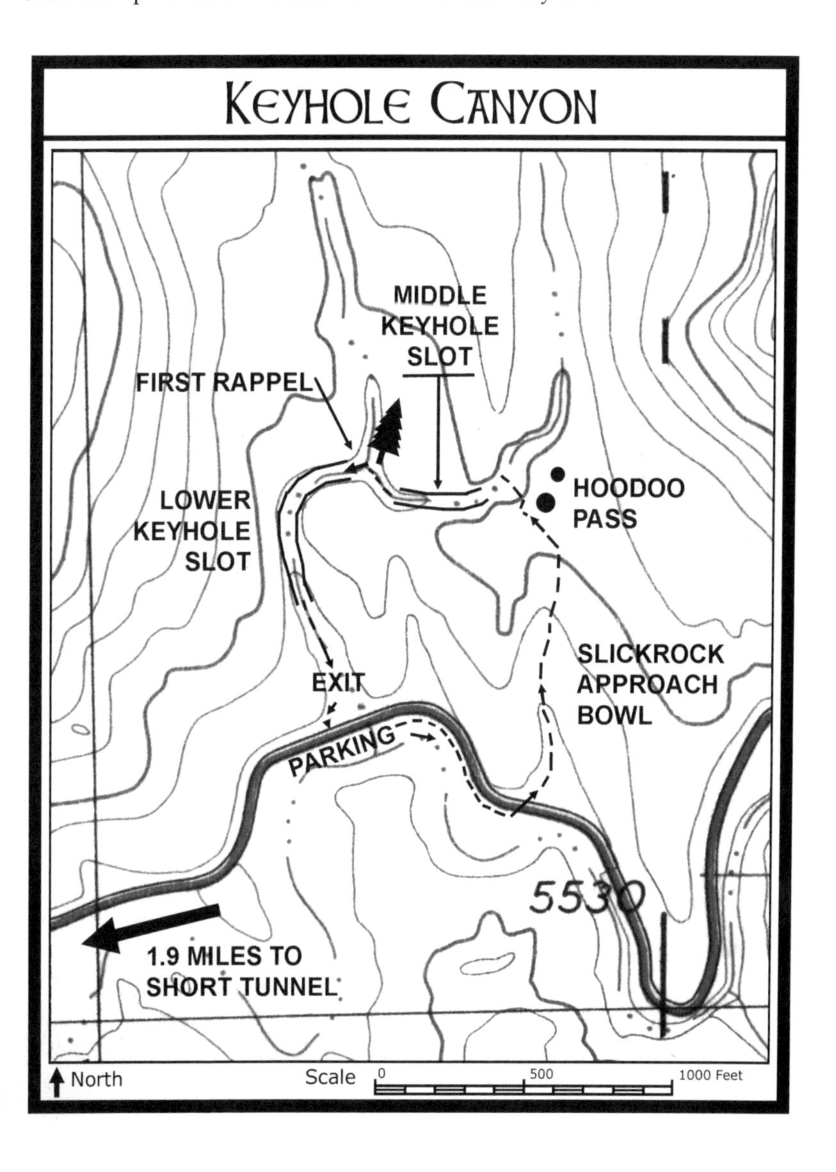

A little further, the fun resumes. The broad, sandy watercourse feeds into a narrow slot on the left, and drops 15 feet to the edge of a pool. This is "Lower Keyhole." Rappel the slot using a bolt anchor on the wall above, swinging into the alcove to the side to avoid water at the bottom. A short distance down canyon, the second drop can be rappelled by throwing a rope over an overhead log. The third drop is rappelled from a bolt. The fourth drop can be rappelled from single, suspect bolt on the right, or downclimbed to a ledge, then down a crack in a slab to the edge of a pool. Put away the ropes and get ready to swim.

The canyon continues with deep, dark, twisty and very cool narrows. Downclimbs are interspersed with walking sections until the dreaded "slanted corridor" is reached. A slot is downclimbed (very dark, headlamp helpful) to the start of the long, slanted corridor. Swim the corridor, then wade and swim the following pools to attain the delightful heat of the full sun at the end. Traipse downcanyon to the road.

21 Middle Echo Canyon

Echo is a large canyon complex that drops into the main canyon at Weeping Rock. The middle part of Echo offers a delightful canyoneering adventure. A couple of short rappels and some very chilly swims access a long section of narrows deep underground. Due to its large watershed, the pools are often full of water, and they maintain their coldness long into the summer. The pools can be filled with decaying vegetable matter and smell like poo. Canyoneers sometimes wonder if they will pass out from the smell before making it through the pool section.

Echo collects a lot of snow and ice over the winter, and should be avoided in the spring. Check with the Backcountry Desk for current conditions.

The Echo Canyon Trail is the oldest trail out of Zion Canyon. In the late 1890's, Utah pioneer John Winder reworked the existing Paiute foot trail to drive cattle up to the rim. The trail was improved and the Observation Point Trail cut into the side of the mountain in 1925.

The Observation Point Trail leaves from the Weeping Rock shuttle stop and switchbacks up the slope below the vertical face of Cable Mountain. 900 feet (300 m) above the canyon floor, the trail traverses left below the smooth face and crosses into the gravelly wash of Echo Canyon. The trail follows the wash about a hundred feet (30 m) then ascends the left side of the canyon (left looking up). The section of Echo Canyon above this crossing is called Middle Echo. The section below is Lower Echo (Variation 1).

Rating: 3B II
Time required: 3 to 6 hours
Preferred season: Summer or fall.
Cold water protection: Wetsuits required even in summer.
Longest rappel: 30 feet (10 m)
Special difficulties: None

CAUTION: In certain conditions, one pothole exit can be difficult to do without a partner assist. Soloing Echo is not recommended. During the winter, Echo collects an unusually large quantity of snow and ice. The canyon should be avoided in the spring, until the snow melts out. In big snow years, this can be as late as June.

DRIVING: Route starts and ends at the Weeping Rock shuttle stop.

APPROACH: Ascend the Observation Point Trail to the crossing of Echo Canyon. This is where the route ends. From the crossing, continue up the trail 0.5 mile (800m) to where the Echo Canyon Trail branches off right. The main trail continues up to Observation Point. The smaller Echo Canyon Trail descends diagonally toward the bottom of the canyon. Follow the Echo Canyon Trail 0.25 mile (400m) to where it crosses a shallow drainage. Follow the trail about 50 feet (15m) further, then step into the woods and follow small trails along the rim, then down steep dirt into the canyon.

THE CANYON: The canyon narrows up right away. Enjoy the cool shade of the canyon after the sun-scorched slickrock of the approach. Suit up before the first wading pool. The first rappel shows up after 20 minutes. Chose an anchor carefully, test and evaluate, then rap down a V-slot into a pool. The second rappel follows soon after, into a pool. And then the third, also into a pool. This pool can be difficult to exit and might require a partner assist. Downcanyon a few minutes, one more rappel into a pool completes the rappelling.

Fabulous canyoneering follows, down one of the best slot canyons in Zion. Downclimb and walk down the soaring corridor. Enjoy the excellent acoustics of the Echo Chamber. After half an hour, a few wades or short swims lead to familiar ground where the trail crosses Echo Canyon. Warm up in the sun and pack your gear.

Variation 1: Lower Echo Canyon

Lower Echo Canyon can be descended, although the last rappel is dangerous and closed to the public. The canyon is deep, with numerous short drops and nice pools. Lower Echo is done "caving style"—ropes are fixed and re-ascended to get out. There are pools that require swimming. The final drop is longer than 300 feet and is illegal due to the danger to the many tourists on the Weeping Rock trail below. Please respect this closure.

START: From where the trail crosses the canyon, walk downcanyon. Where it slots up, follow the left rim to a bolt anchor. There are about 15 drops to about 100 feet. Wetsuits will be required. Longer ropes can be re-belayed on some of the drops. See map on page 115.

22 Mystery Canyon

Mystery is my favorite Zion canyon. Oh my heck, it has everything–a rough-tough smackdown approach; a verdant, wooded canyon with spectacular soaring walls; multiple rappels through intimate, sculpted narrows; some walking in the hot sun; a monstrous rockfall that creates a seasonal lake; a big rappel into a pool; wading pools in a jungle paradise; and finally a slippery slab rappel to the whirring camcorders of numerous tourists. Not too long, not too short—Mystery is a great outing.

Though information is sketchy, Mystery was first descended in the 1960s. Numerous "interesting" anchors attest to the improvisatory skills of early descensionists, including chunks of rebar pounded into drilled holes. Anchors in Mystery are generally fixed, though judgment is required to figure out which of the antique anchors to use. An interesting feature of the canyon is a giant sand pile created by a landslide in the early 70's–a 400-foot pile of rock and sand that dams the canyon and creates a "Devil's Hole." On occasion, the lake before the slide is up to 10 feet deep and provides a long and stimulating swim. Most of the time it is dry or a boggy gumbo. This small "lake" is similar to larger lakes that had a profound effect on Zion's topography in the geologically recent past.

Mystery can be approached from either the Weeping Rock shuttle stop in the main canyon or from the East Mesa trailhead on the Zion Ponderosa Ranch. The second option saves you 2100 feet (640 m) of climbing on a steep trail, but requires a car shuttle. Mystery is a popular canyon, and permits can be hard to get. Expect to share the canyon with other parties, especially on weekends.

Rating: 3B III
Time required: 5 to 8 hours
Preferred season: Summer or fall.

Cold water protection: Wetsuits recommended in spring and fall.
Longest rappel: 120 feet (38 m)
Special difficulties: None

GEAR AND DIFFICULTIES: Mystery has about 12 rappels up to 120 feet (40 m) in length. Bring a half-dozen slings and rapid links in case slings are missing or damaged. Bring drybags or dry kegs for your gear–there can be two mandatory swims near the end. The swims are short, so wetsuits are not required if the weather is hot and the lake is dry. In the fall, wetsuits are recommended. Mystery does have an exposed traverse that most parties will want to protect using a safety/zip line or a belay. Each member of the party will need a tether and locking carabiner to clip the zip line. There is no drinking water in the canyon until the very end—bring your own.

Finding the top of Mystery can be a problem, so bring a map and use it. I'd like to think these directions alone are sufficient, but they are not. One or two parties a year start down the next drainage to the west (Miss-me), thinking they are in Mystery, and end up requiring a rescue. Make certain you are in the right place before heading down. If the approach does not look well traveled, you are in the wrong place–go back!

GETTING THERE: Zion Canyon/Weeping Rock Approach. Get an early start to avoid the heat. From Weeping Rock, ascend the Observation Point Trail. The trail switchbacks up the mountain below the face of Cable Mountain, then cuts left into Echo Canyon, briefly following the streambed before climbing up the side on a cutout and getting back into the sun. More climbing across mixed slickrock and brush leads to the base of a buttress. Climb steeply up the buttress, switchbacking to the rim of the mesa. The trail follows the rim west toward Observation Point. One-third mile from Observation Point, the East Mesa Trail comes in on the right–this takes you to Mystery Canyon. Allow 2 hours to climb to the trail junction–(2.7 miles (4.3 km), ascent of 2100 feet (640 m))–most of which is in the full sun after mid-morning.

The stroll out to Observation Point (0.33 mile, 0.5 km) provides a dramatic view of Zion Canyon, and is well worth a 45-minute diversion, if not pressed for time.

From the trail junction, follow the East Mesa Trail north then east through brush and ponderosa pines. After 20 minutes, and just after passing the trail's highpoint, a gorge can be seen through the brush to the left, starting about 30 feet (10 m) from the East Mesa Trail. Numerous small trails lead to the rim–follow them to the apex of Mystery Canyon.

GETTING THERE: Ponderosa Ranch approach. The East Mesa Trail begins on the park Boundary and is accessed through the Zion Ponderosa Ranch Resort. Allow an hour driving time from Springdale.

From Springdale, take Route 9 up Pine Creek Canyon toward Mt Carmel Junction. From the East Entrance, continue 2.4 miles east, then turn Left (N) on the paved North Fork Road. Follow the winding road 5.1 miles to the Zion Ponderosa Ranch Resort—turn left into the Ranch. The following mileage points are given from the entrance.

The dirt roads from here are rough and not well signed. Please be respectful of Ponderosa residents you encounter—afoot, on ATV, on horse or in cars. You are a guest on the Ranch. A few, but not all, of the turns are marked for "Observation Point."

0.0 miles: At the entrance, go straight (avoid going down to the main resort building to the left) past a residence. Pavement ends.
0.4 miles: Y—go Right.
0.7 miles: T—go Right for Observation Point (Twin Knolls Road).
1.5 miles: T—go Right.
2.3 miles: Fir Road crosses—go straight. Road gets worse. Stop here if the road is wet.
2.6 miles: Deeply rutted hill—this is the worst spot. Some 2WDs will want to park at the top of the hill.
2.65 miles: Pine in center of road, rough. Go Right down the hill.
2.9 miles: Y—go Left.
3.0 miles: End of Road at Park Boundary: Parking lot.
For those of you with GPS: UTM Nad83: 331502 mE 412942 mN

THE TRAIL: Stroll west on the wide, smooth trail winding between huge ponderosa pines with many signs of recent fires. Reach the top of Mystery Canyon at 2.1 miles (3.4 km). Mystery can be seen on the right for some time–continue on the trail until it starts uphill to go around the left side of a small knoll. At this point, follow small trails through the brush right 30 feet (10 m) to the edge of the canyon.

THE CANYON: Make certain you are in the correct place–at the very apex of Mystery Canyon. The canyon should plunge spectacularly below you, and extend straight north, with a series of mountains on the left all in a row. On the right, a steep, straight wall stretches north below a tree-topped mesa. A small but distinct trail leads down and right across a steep shale slope. (The trail is about 50 feet (15 m) east (right) of the very apex of the canyon).

Carefully follow trails and gullies steeply down through the woods

MYSTERY CANYON

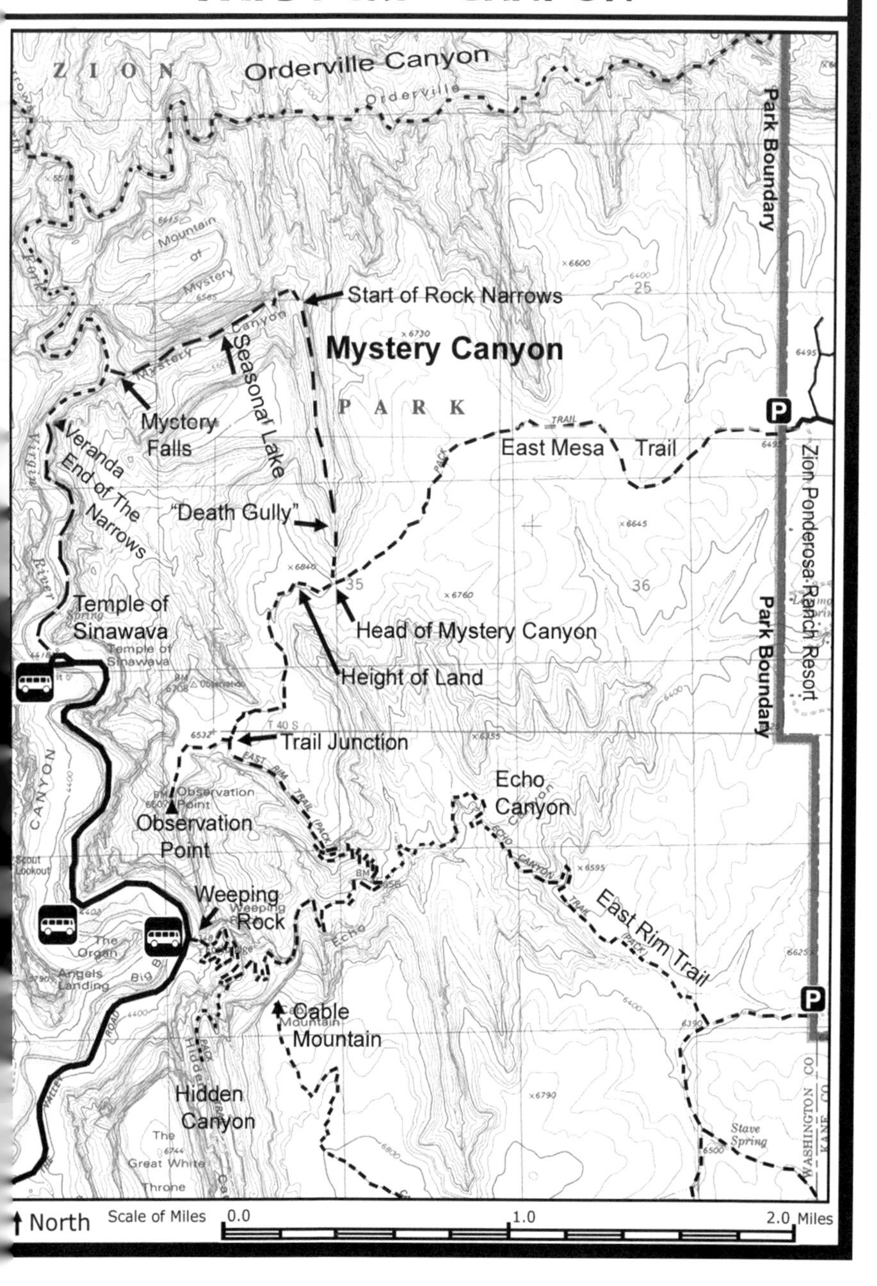

for about half an hour. Take it slowly and carefully. This section is known as "The Death Gully."

Mystery Canyon is popular, and is showing wear and tear from all our boots and sneakers. The Death Gully descends a natural erosion gully, and our passage does little to make it worse. In the next section of the canyon, several small drops are encountered. With a few exceptions, please descend these drops directly, rather than taking the eroding paths to the sides. By doing so, you minimize your impact on this wonderful canyon.

The Death Gully ends at a short, steep downclimb. Descend carefully–the boulders may be unstable. This used to be a short rappel, but a debris-slide in spring 2005 altered the bottom 2/3rds of the Death Gully. Six minutes downcanyon, a short, clean drop is encountered. This one is bypassed using a good trail to the right.

A few minutes further downcanyon, a short drop blocks the canyon. A shallow groove in the slab provides a surprisingly easy butt-slide descent. A rope can be used to sequence down all but the last member of the party, who can be spotted from below.

Sequencing is a technique for moving a group down short drops, especially low-angle drops. One person (usually the best climber) anchors the rope off their harness and braces themselves as needed to provide an anchor. The others rappel off the anchorperson, then spot as she downclimbs the drop. It is wise to consider the "sequence" of rappellers—usually heavy persons are sent first, while the rest of the team clips in and backs up the anchorperson.

Another 10 minutes downcanyon leads to another short drop, with a bolt anchor.

Two minutes further, a small drop is bypassed by a trail on the right, through the woods and down some steep slabs.

About five minutes further on, the canyon drops and is clogged with big logs. Downclimb the logs, then rappel from a bolt anchor at the end of the slot.

About 10 minutes further downcanyon, the slot jogs left and enters a section of cool, sculpted narrows with numerous rappels from fixed anchors. This is the Rock Narrows, and the count of "real rappels" begins here.

R1: 45 feet (15 m) down a chute. Walk 40 feet.

R2: 30 feet (10 m) down a chute. Slide down a short step. Walk about 50 feet (15 m) downcanyon. A single, ancient bolt is positioned

Mystery Springs rappel

above a short, easy downclimb (8 feet (2.5 m), 5.2). Twenty feet downcanyon, downclimb a log to a two-bolt anchor.

R3: 12 feet (4 m) to the canyon floor. Walk 20 feet.

R4: Rap to a pothole, then down a lower slab (50 feet (15 m)).

The canyon turns left and opens to the sun. Follow the slot 100 feet, including two short downclimbs, to a big log sticking vertically in the canyon.

R5: Rap 30 feet (10 m) off a 2-bolt anchor next to a big log (!). Walk 50 feet, then downclimb a V-slot to a 2-bolt anchor at a chockstone.

R6: Rap 40 feet (14 m) down a slab to a pothole ledge. Walk 10 feet. Rappel off a single bolt (30 feet (10 m)) or downclimb (5.6) to a round pothole.

This is a good place for lunch—the next section of the canyon is in the full sun. Apply sunscreen.

The canyon opens up, with the impressive face of the Mountain of Mystery to the right. This section of canyon is often very hot. Follow the canyon past a few short scrambling sections to a flat area and a giant ponderosa log.

> The flat area is the bed of a lake formed behind a giant landslide that crashed into the canyon sometime in the early 70's (definitely before 1976). When the upper canyon flashes, sediment is brought down to the point where the canyon is blocked, then deposited to build a flat plain. This is what happened in Zion Canyon a couple thousand years ago, building a flat area from below Zion Lodge to the Temple of Sinawava.

Ascend the sandpile that blocks the canyon. A trail can be found, starting at the left margin and climbing diagonally across to the rock on the right. Drop down the far side of the sand pile, then carefully traverse a sandy ledge on the right side of the canyon, and downclimb back into the bottom. Follow the canyon for a few minutes to the top of a steep slab blocking the canyon.

R7: Rap 50 feet (15 m) from bolts down a slab.

Follow the watercourse as the canyon tightens up. A short drop is bypassed by hopping over a rock on the right and downclimbing a chimney. Another short drop is passed by climbing under a log (the log itself is very slippery). By now, the canyon is delightfully shaded and cool. A few shallow pools are tiptoed around, then a groove followed to some larger pools. Stemming around these pools leads to a slot and the slabs at the top of Mystery Springs. Carefully climb left a few feet, then down to the comfortable pothole ledge. This is a good place to gear up for the last section of the canyon, and secure all your gear in drybags or kegs.

This is the exciting rappel into Mystery Spring. The anchor is at the far end of the slab. A single bolt at the near end can be used to set up a safety line, or for belaying folks out to the rappel anchor. Getting to the anchor is only 3rd class, but rather exposed.

R8: Rappel 110 feet (33 m) into the pool at the base of the wall. This is a bit tricky, because the rappeller must rap to the top of a boulder in the slot below, which is to the side of the fall line; then continue the rappel off the boulder, down a slippery slot and into the pool. There is a small chimney stance inches above the water where one can disconnect from the rope before swimming.

(The winter of 2004/2005 washed a lot of sand into this pool, and it was only waist deep in 2005. Hopefully, it will be restored to a full swim within a few years).

Also of note, there is an old bolt anchor in the pool behind the boulder in the slot. If someone does go down the back side of the boulder, there is an anchor available over there.

When pulling the rope, be sure it does not fall onto the boulder in the slot and get stuck. As it comes free, give it a gentle tug so the end falls towards you.

Note: If concerned about speed or ability, set up a guided rappel. By not having to make the top of the boulder or rappel the slippery slot below, those of lesser skill will move faster and easier through the rappel. A guided rappel can also be used to keep people out of the pool, but that's no fun. The guided rappel plus safety line requires three sections of rope.

Downclimb a small cascade into a waist-deep pool. Further on, a boulder blocks the width of the canyon, creating a short drop with a turquoise pool below it.

There are several ways to deal with the pool. A small tree 10 feet back from the edge allows for a rappel. The chimney to the right can be downclimbed (5.6), though it is a little tricky. This pool used to be a good jump, but floods in 2005 washed a lot of sand into the pool, and it is now too shallow to jump.

Continue downcanyon, downclimbing a short waterfall. After a short walk through the jungle, you arrive at the final rappel down Mystery Falls into The Narrows.

R9: Rappel 120 feet (36 m) from bolts down the slippery cascade to the river. Many an expert canyoneer has been embarrassed on this rappel–try not to be among them. This is a good place to provide a bottom-belay for all rappellers.

The Narrows is followed downcanyon about a half-mile (800 m) to a stone structure (The Veranda) at the end of the paved trail. Follow the Gateway to The Narrows Trail one mile (1.6 km) to the Temple of Sinawava shuttle stop.

23 Behunin Canyon

In 1863, Utah pioneer Isaac Behunin built a small cabin near the current location of Zion Lodge, across from the Emerald Pools cirque. He grew melons and tobacco during the summer, and wintered in Springdale. A narrow canyon that drops into that cirque was named for him, and it is a fine canyoneering adventure. Two hours of hiking up the West Rim trail takes the intrepid canyoneer to the head of the canyon. Nine rappels and a bunch of fun hiking lead to a final precipitous drop 165 feet (50 meters) into the Emerald Pool cirque. Behunin is a great backcountry canyon, with mostly fixed anchors and only one short swim.

Behunin is one of the more straightforward of Zion's backcountry canyons, and is popular. Those with good anchor and rappelling skills will find it pleasant and easy; for those without, this is not a good choice. Many rappels provide numerous opportunities to get the rope stuck, and the backcountry nature of Behunin means you are on your own. This is not a good canyon for groups larger than six.

Behunin has become popular in winter and spring, because people think it is dry. Sometimes it is, but in winter and spring, melting snow water vastly complicates the descent. At least one canyoneer recently spent a few hours stuck on a rope under a waterfall, contemplating his fate. Luck was in his favor, as the Zion SAR team responded in time to save him.

The popularity of Behunin is also its curse, and makes it a showcase of the impacts canyoneers have in the fragile desert environment. As you descend, notice the eroded social trails in several places, cutting around drops and pools. Where possible, avoid further erosion by traveling in the watercourse, rappelling and downclimbing rather than scrambling around. Many of these eroded areas are returning to a natural state since canyoneers have stopped using them.

Rating: 3B III
Time required: 5 to 9 hours
Preferred season: Spring or fall.
Cold water protection: Wetsuits advisable in cold weather.
Longest rappel: 165 feet (50 m)
Special difficulties: None

APPROACH: From The Grotto shuttle stop, head up the West Rim/Angels Landing Trail to the top of the Scout Lookout ridge. Turn left (north) toward the West Rim. The trail follows the crest of the ridge with spectacular views, then cuts left and down to cross a branch of Telephone

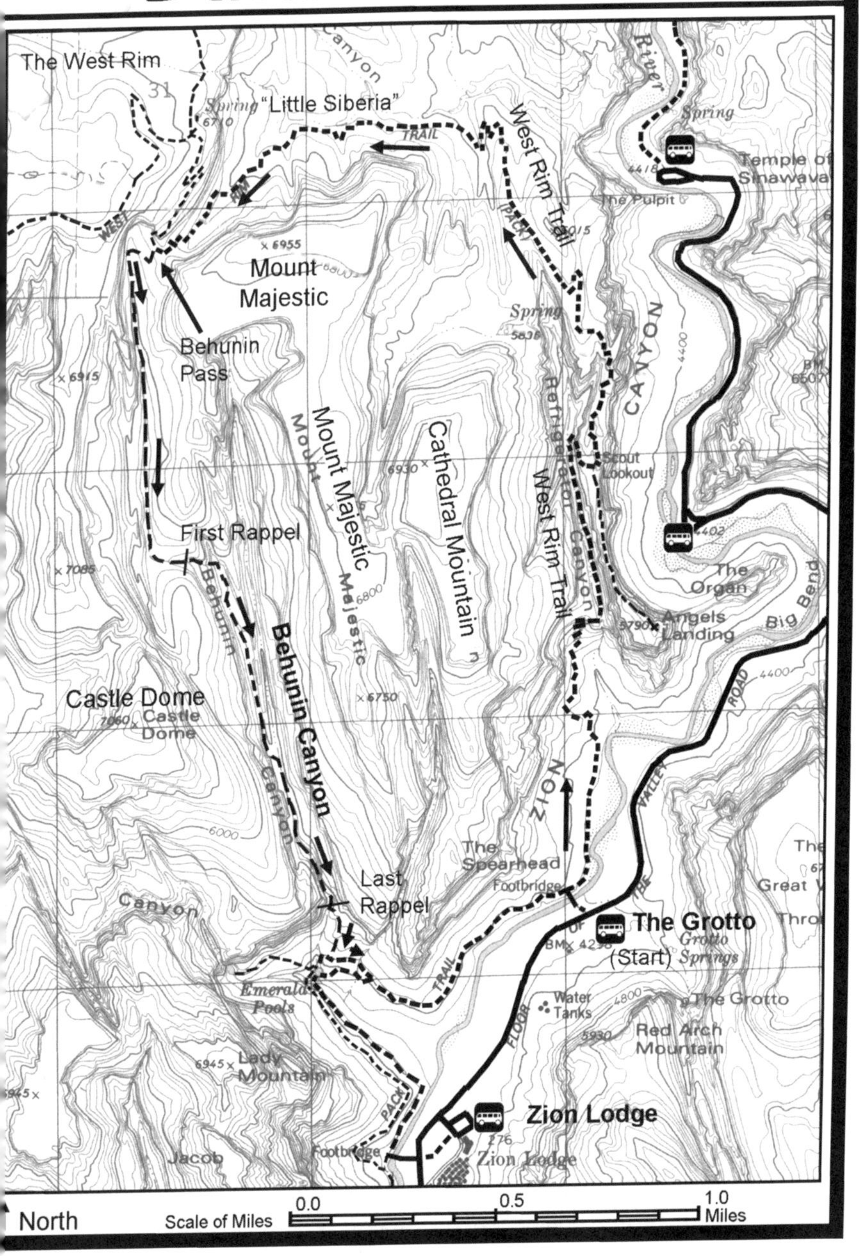

Behunin Canyon
The West Rim
"Little Siberia"
Mount Majestic
Behunin Pass
West Rim Trail
Refrigerator Canyon
Scout Lookout
Angels Landing
Cathedral Mountain
Mount Majestic
First Rappel
Behunin Canyon
Castle Dome
Last Rappel
The Spearhead
Footbridge
The Grotto
(Start)
Emerald Pools
Lady Mountain
Zion Lodge
Red Arch Mountain
Temple of Sinawava
The Pulpit
The Organ
Big Bend
North
Scale of Miles
0.0
0.5
1.0
Miles

Canyon. Following slabs around the north end of Mount Majestic, the trail crosses slickrock and works its way into a steep-walled north-facing canyon, then up to a pass. The West Rim Trail continues to the right, switchbacking up the steep sandstone on cut steps. The canyon over the west side of the pass is Behunin.

The approach is 3.8 miles (6.0 km) with 2000 feet (600 m) of altitude gain. Allow 2 to 3 hours.

THE CANYON: Drop over the pass and follow trails down and right about 120 feet (40 m), then cut right and carefully traverse across the top of steep slabs, then down to the base of a striped wall and the crease of the watercourse. Follow the bottom of the drainage, occasionally scrambling left to avoid the worst of the brush. After about 45 minutes, the canyon turns left and starts to descend. A short section of slickrock leads to pools and the first drop.

R1: From the lip of the drop, follow a narrow ledge right 30 feet (10 m) past a tree to a larger ledge and a two-bolt anchor. Rappel two short steps for a total of 90 feet (30 m) to a flat area.

R1 variation a: From the lip, look up and left—find a large ponderosa pine with slings around it. Climb up and traverse over (4th class, exposed) to the pine, possibly belaying off an intermediate tree. Rappel 165 feet (50 m) off the large tree to a flat area.

R1 variation b: From the lip, traverse left 60 feet (20 m) to a one-bolt anchor, and an 80-foot (25 m) rappel down a slab.

R2: From a large ponderosa, rappel slabs and a few short, steep walls 150 feet (45 m) to a small tree and ledge at a rollover. The course of the water can be slippery, so stay on-rope all the way to the tree.

R3: From a small tree, rappel 150 feet (45 m) down a slab, then steeper down a banded sandstone wall to a bowl/ledge. When wet, this rap can be difficult to retrieve.

R4: Rappel 120 feet (40 m) from a bolted anchor to the canyon floor. Hike downcanyon 0.25 mile (400 m).

R5: From a bolted anchor right of the watercourse about 50 feet (15 m), rappel 90 feet (30 m) to the edge of a pool.

Hike downcanyon 0.25 mile (400 m). The watercourse comes to a complex small drop.

R6: From a large rotten log, rappel 60 feet (20 m) into a pool. Swim across the pool (10 feet, 3 m). Packs can be lowered on a zip line to avoid immersion. A guided rappel can be set up to avoid the swim, for all but the first and last people.

R6 variation: Pass the drop and climb a small trail into the woods. After 40 feet, a trail leads left and down to a tree with slings. Rappel 50 feet back into the canyon at the edge of the pool.

Hike downcanyon. A small drop is downclimbed directly—much easier than it looks. Continue downcanyon through some nice narrows.

R7: The canyon turns left in a complex series of short drops and pools. Rappel 80 feet (30 m) from a bolted anchor following the watercourse. The first part rappels to the edge of a pool. The second part rappels into a knee-to-waist-deep pool—take a few giant-steps right (rappeller's right) to avoid the deeper part of the pool, and to place the rope over a gentler edge. A guided rappel can be used to avoid the deep wade (or swim, in winter and spring). (Do NOT take the trail up and left to a dirty and thoroughly annoying 2-stage rappel).

Avoid a pool by traversing a narrow ledge on the right. Continue downcanyon. The end of the canyon appears shortly. Scramble through large blocks to avoid pools, climbing to the top of a large boulder that blocks the end of the canyon. Climb carefully down the right side of the boulder on large holds to a sloping, insecure stance under the boulder.

R8: Rappel 130 feet (40 m) from slings around a pinch, down a steep wall, over some steps and down to a ledge above a slot on the left. (The final person may want to pull the rope from the ledge above the slot, then downclimb into the slot). This is a common place to get ropes stuck–be careful.

R8 variation a: (150 feet (45 m)) with a large group, or when the pool at the end of the canyon is full, a rappel anchor up and left, 20 feet above the big boulder (a small tree and a single bolt can be used).

R9: Climb down into the slot, then under a chockstone to the front. Clip into the bolt garden under the chockstone, then set your rope off a bolt anchor around the corner a few feet on the face. Rappel 165 feet (50 m) mostly free to a wet nook in the talus below.

If you have trouble pulling the rope, walk away from the cliff as far as possible, down to "The Beach."

EXIT: Pack up the gear and shoulder the packs. From the shallow pool or sand flat below the large rock, boulder-hop directly down the streambed to the Middle Emerald Pool and the trail. Turn left to return to The Grotto.

The fastest way back to Zion Lodge is to take the trail left. After a few minutes, a trail junction is found among giant boulders. Turn RIGHT and follow the trail steeply DOWN to the lower Emerald Pool and behind the waterfall. Follow to Zion Lodge.

CHAPTER SIX

Technical Canyons

The following canyoneering descriptions are presented in somewhat less detail than the previously described Classic Canyons.

24 Fat Man's Misery

Fat Man's Misery (West Fork of Misery Canyon) is a classic canyoneering adventure just outside the east boundary of the park on BLM land. Getting to the canyon and escaping back to your car requires good navigation skills–have a map and use it. Unfortunately, the Trails Illustrated Zion National Park Map does not cover this area, so the USGS "The Barracks" and "Springdale East" quadrangles are required.

A cross-country route is followed to Misery Canyon, then the canyon followed through a series of short, interesting narrows with a few rappels and swims. Misery then drops into the East Fork of the Virgin River through a beautiful grotto–the highlight of the trip. The East Fork is followed briefly, then a steep climb up a ridge leads back to civilization. The climb out can be scorching in summer, so Fat Man's is best reserved for spring and fall. Water can be filtered from the East Fork.

Legend has it, one of the rappels could be avoided by worming down a narrow passage between boulders—thus the name "Fat Man's Misery." This feature has eroded away, but the hike out still provides a dose of misery for those not in top condition.

In several places, single old bolts COULD be used for rappels. These things are dangerous–please admire their antiquity, but rig your rappel off more reliable (typically natural) anchors.

The technical sections of Fat Man's are entirely outside the park, so a permit is not required.

Exiting from Misery Canyon requires a short walk down the East Fork. If the Canyon is in flood stage, this short walk could be difficult or impossible. Check the level of the river before starting on this adventure, especially in the spring.

Opposite: *Brian Cabe entering the grotto, Fat Man's Missery*

Rating: 3B III
Time required: 6 to 10 hours
Preferred season: Spring, summer or fall.
Cold water protection: Wetsuit advisable in cold weather.
Longest rappel: 40 feet (15 m)
Special difficulties: Challenging navigation, possible flood in East Fork.

DRIVING: Fat Man's starts by ascending the canyon west of Checkerboard Mesa. From the East Entrance, drive into the park ¾ mile and find a safe place to park on the edge of the highway.

APPROACH: Your objective is the west fork of Misery Canyon, the north-south running canyon just east of the park boundary. The canyon runs south from just west of Point 6445.

Ascend the canyon west of Checkerboard Mesa to a sandy pass, then descend the other side about ½ mile to where the canyon flattens out. Traverse left (east) around the nose of a round sandstone buttress. Cross a shallow drainage, then cross a second, larger drainage. Ascend the ridge on the far side, then descend into the Misery Canyon drainage. A 200-foot cliff blocks access to the canyon floor–traverse the rim downcanyon, then descend a steep slickrock bowl to reach the watercourse.

THE CANYON: Open, sandy wash alternates with lovely, sculpted narrows. A few rappels are required–avoid using the single, ancient bolts and find safer, natural anchors instead. One section of narrows is a good place to practice your partner-assisted downclimbing skills. There are four natural bridges, and often swimming or deep wading. Please do NOT use the natural bridges as rappel anchors, to avoid scarring them with rope-pull grooves.

After several narrows, the canyon intersects the East Fork of Misery Canyon. Avoid small potholes by traversing slabs left, then re-enter the canyon near the big drop, downclimb or rappel a short chimney (tricky!) to a large flat ledge overlooking the East Fork. Rappel 20 feet (7 m) from a tree to the slabs below.

Below the confluence, the canyon soon narrows up. A dirty section of canyon usually requires a rappel–this is where the "Fat Man's" down-crawl used to be. Choose your anchor carefully–the canyon is eroding rapidly and the rocks might be unstable.

Shortly past this obstacle, the canyon enters an amazing grotto, its deepest and neatest section. The grotto leads to the East Fork of the Virgin River. A warm, sulphurous spring creates an interesting and fragile

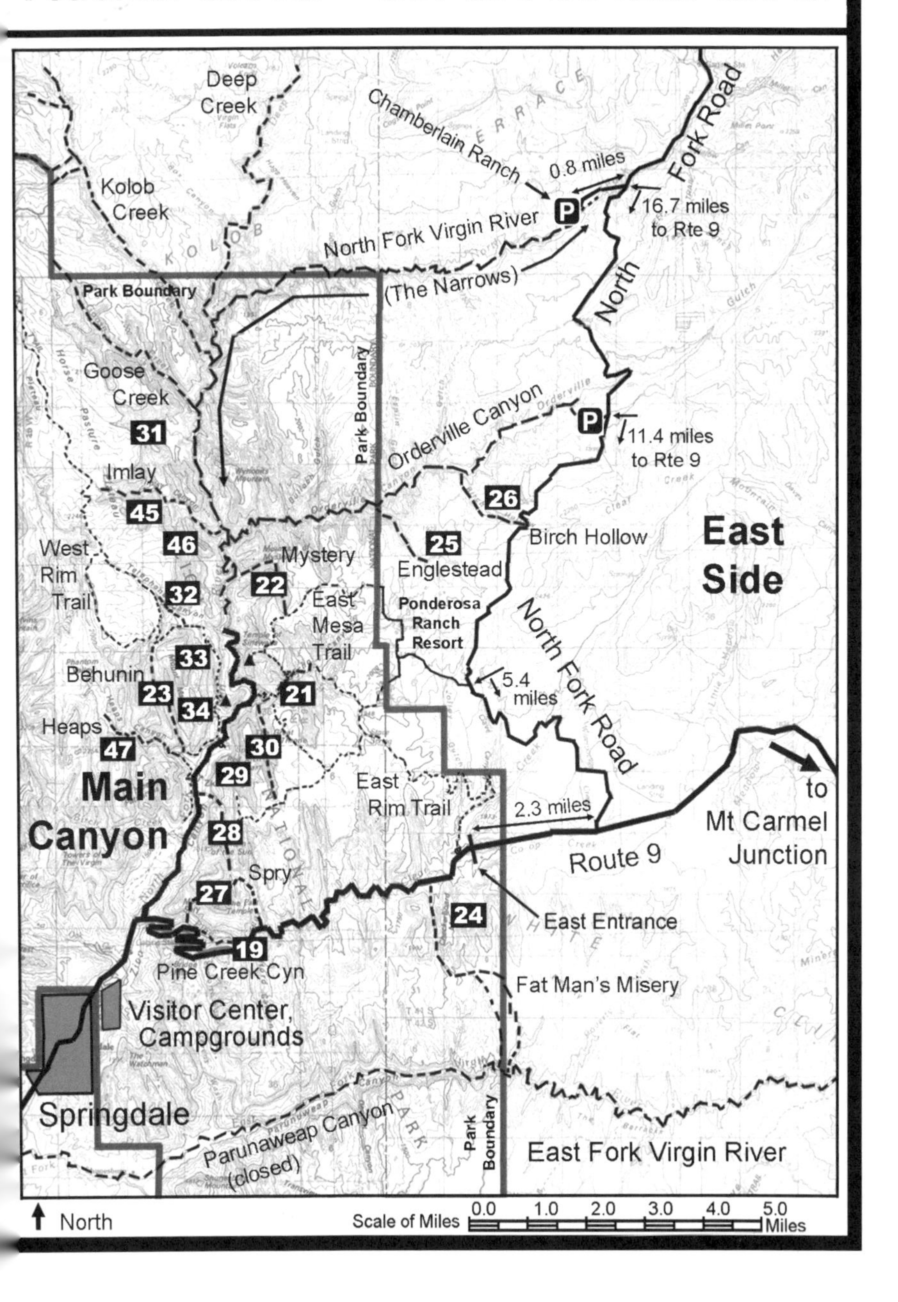
Technical Canyons—East Side and Main Canyon
Deep Creek
Chamberlain Ranch
0.8 miles
Kolob Creek
North Fork Virgin River
(The Narrows)
16.7 miles to Rte 9
North Fork Road
Park Boundary
Goose Creek
31
Imlay
45
46
Orderville Canyon
11.4 miles to Rte 9
26
Birch Hollow
East Side
West Rim Trail
32
22
Mystery
25
Englestead
East Mesa Trail
Ponderosa Ranch Resort
33
Behunin
23
34
21
5.4 miles
Heaps
47
30
29
Main Canyon
East Rim Trail
2.3 miles
to Mt Carmel Junction
28
Route 9
Spry
27
24
East Entrance
19
Pine Creek Cyn
Fat Man's Misery
Visitor Center, Campgrounds
Springdale
Parunaweap Canyon (closed)
East Fork Virgin River
North
Scale of Miles
0.0 1.0 2.0 3.0 4.0 5.0 Miles

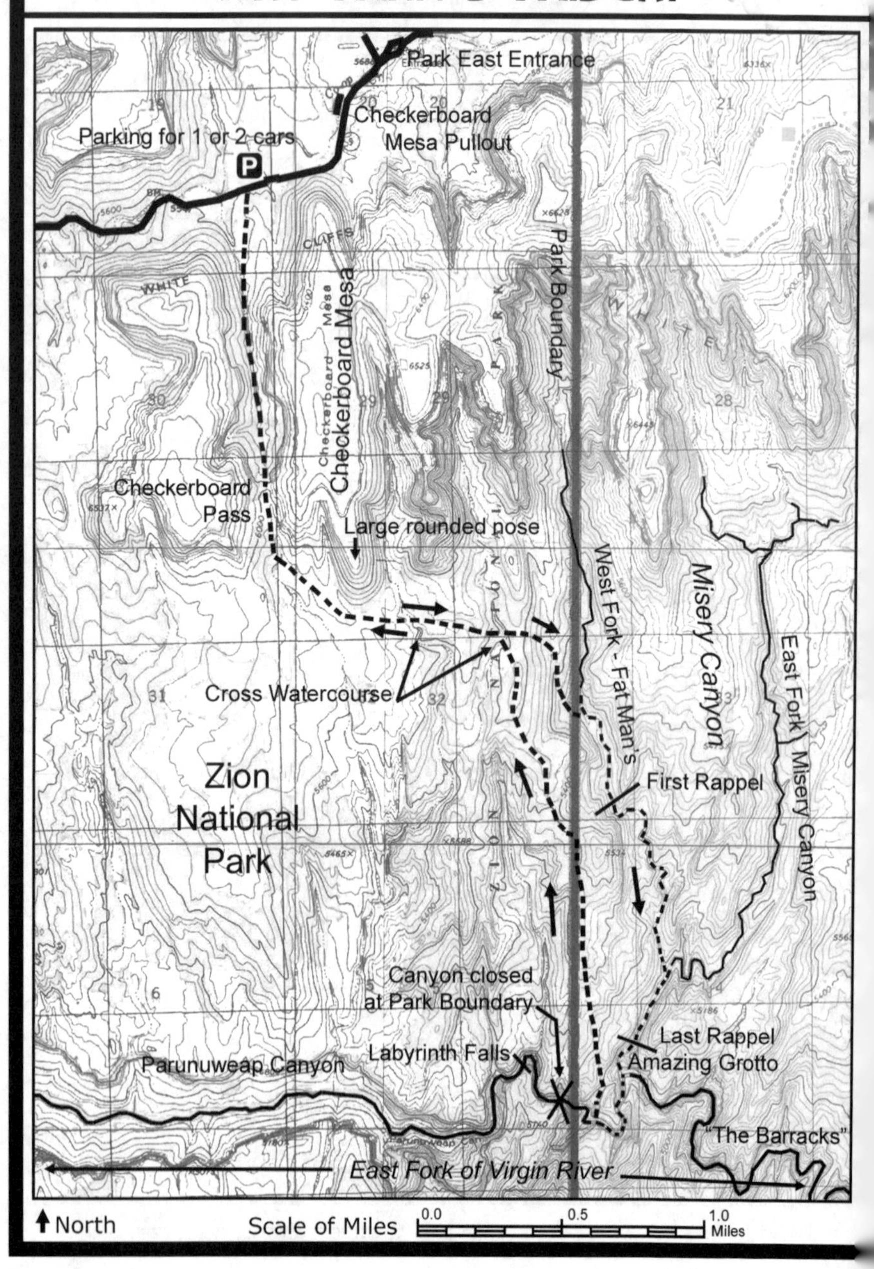
FAT MAN'S MISERY
Park East Entrance
Checkerboard Mesa Pullout
Parking for 1 or 2 cars
P
CLIFFS
WHITE
Checkerboard Mesa
Park Boundary
Checkerboard Pass
Large rounded nose
West Fork - Fat Man's
Misery Canyon
East Fork Misery Canyon
Cross Watercourse
Zion National Park
First Rappel
Canyon closed at Park Boundary
Labyrinth Falls
Last Rappel Amazing Grotto
Parunuweap Canyon
"The Barracks"
East Fork of Virgin River
North
Scale of Miles
0.0
0.5
1.0 Miles

riparian area—minimize your impact here. Enjoy the coolness and soaring walls of the East Fork.

EXIT: From the Misery/East Fork confluence, wade downcanyon about 0.33 of a mile (500 m), 10 to 15 minutes. On the inside of a sweeping bend to the right is a grassy/reedy/brushy area. This is the exit. Take a trail into the grass, then climb a steep gully toward the rim. (A plaque commemorating the Powell expedition of 1872 can be found on the downstream side of the grassy area, behind some brush).

The East Fork is closed to public access at the park boundary, 1/10 mile west of the Powell Plaque, near Labyrinth Falls.

Above the gully, follow a ridge north toward Checkerboard Mesa. Approaching the mesa, trend left to the round sandstone buttress, then cut left into the approach canyon. Follow this back to the road.

25 Englestead Hollow

Englestead is a deep canyon with a dramatic start. After an initial 700 feet of rappelling, the canyon continues through marvelous narrows with some downclimbing and a few short rappels to intersect with Orderville Canyon just inside the park boundary. One can turn left and enjoy the best parts of Orderville, exiting out The Narrows, or turn right and climb up Orderville Canyon.

Other than a few bolts at the beginning, Englestead is bolt-free. Please keep it that way. The drops lower in the canyon can be easily rigged using natural anchors.

Rating: 4B III or IV
Time required: 6 to 10 hours
Preferred season: Summer or fall.
Cold water protection: If going down Orderville, wetsuits are recommended in cold weather.
Longest rappel: 300 feet (91 m)
Special difficulties: The long initial rappel gets special respect, and has been the scene of several incidents.

DRIVING: Englestead is approached using an old logging road off the North Fork Road. Drive north on the North Fork Road 5.4 miles to the entrance of the Zion Ponderosa Resort. Continue on the North Fork Road 2.8 miles to a small dirt road on the left (west), between two fenced ranches. Park here (2WD) or drive the small dirt road ¼ mile to a small parking area at the top of a hill. The road from this point is an ATV trail, not suitable for even 4X4 vehicles.

APPROACH: Follow the old road down through the scrub. After 15 minutes, an ATV trail branches right toward Birch Hollow. A couple minutes further down, a campsite is seen to the right. Twenty-five minutes from the car, a log staging area is reached, with an interesting log-loader rusting back into the environment. Continue following the road off the end of the ridge and down into the wash below. Follow the wash 15 minutes further to the BIG DROP at the head of Englestead. Approach time is about 45 minutes.

Alternatively, Englestead can be approached from a trailhead near the East Rim Trailhead.

ALTERNATIVE DRIVING: From the East Mesa (Mystery Canyon) Trailhead, drive back 0.1 mile to the last intersection–turn left. At 0.2 mile, turn right on an ATV trail. At 0.4 miles, another trail comes in from the right–go straight. At 0.7 miles, park at the end of the road.

ALTERNATIVE APPROACH: From the carpark, find a small trail heading down and right. Follow the trail right a couple hundred yards (200 m) to a fork left, and follow this down to a piney wood. Head left through the wood and find an old road. Follow this about 200 yards (200 m), then head right and down to a second overgrown old road. Follow this past several gullies and ribs to the head of the canyon, then descend easily a dirt rib 100 meters to the canyon floor. Follow the canyon 10 minutes to the big drop. Approach time is about 45 minutes.

THE CANYON: Walk about 50 feet (15 m) along the left edge to a tree overlooking a steep wall. Rappel from this tree to a 1st pothole ledge, then further to a 2nd, larger pothole. Total length is 300 feet (91 m).

R1 variation: Rappel 90 feet (28 m) from tree to a small stance with 2 bolts under a block to the rappeller's right. Rappel from bolts 200 feet (60 m) to the upper pothole ledge. Rappel from a bolt anchor 50 feet (15 m) to the larger pothole ledge.

Several rappels follow, one after the other. The last is the longest (120 feet, 40 m), off a long sling tied to a tree wedged above the canyon floor. Though difficult, inspect the entire length of the sling. The rappel drops 10 feet into a pothole, then across the pothole and 100 feet down beautiful flutes to the ground. Carefully rig this rappel, because the pull is often difficult.

Mark Mallory over the edge in Engelstead

Follow the canyon to Orderville. Several short rappels off logs and other natural anchors present the only obstacles. There's a really nice natural bridge that some people miss. At the last drop (intersection with Orderville), climb up left and downclimb a crack (5.2, exposed) to the ground.

Hiking down Orderville gets the best parts of Orderville, but involves splashing through quite a bit of water, and usually at least one swim. Exiting UP Orderville makes for a shorter and dryer day, and requires climbing one short chimney (5.2) that can be muddy (5.5 M1?). See map on page 103.

26 Birch Hollow

A technical start to Orderville Canyon, save Birch for a nice day in the spring or fall when its charms will not be lost in the hot sun. Birch was a showcase of natural anchor technique, at least it was before some ass bolted it up. Contemplate how YOU would get anchors at each of the many drops, if the bolts were not there. Descending Birch and exiting UP Orderville is entirely outside the park and does not require a permit. This has become popular as a straightforward, reasonably short technical day for beginners.

Birch enters Orderville near the top of the Orderville hike, therefore descending Birch and going DOWN Orderville makes for a long day. Plan on 3 to 5 hours for Birch, then either 1.5 hours to ascend Orderville, or 6 hours to descend.

Rating:	3A III
Time required:	3 to 5 hours to Orderville
Preferred season:	Spring, summer or fall.
Cold water protection:	None required unless descending Orderville
Longest rappel:	100 feet (30 m)
Special difficulties:	None

CAR SPOT: If walking out the top of Orderville, spot a car at the well-signed Orderville Trailhead, 11.4 miles up the North Fork Road. A real 4WD road descends from the Orderville Trailhead 2.5 miles and, when dry, is drivable by high clearance 4WD vehicles only.

DRIVING: Birch Hollow is approached using an old logging road off the North Fork Road. Drive north on the North Fork Road 5.4 miles to the entrance of the Zion Ponderosa Resort. Continue on the North Fork Road 2.8 miles to a small dirt road on the left (west), between two fenced ranches, the Gifford and the EZ Acres. Park here (2WD) or drive the small dirt road ¼ mile to a small parking area at the top of a hill. The road from this point is an ATV trail, not suitable for even 4X4 vehicles.

APPROACH: Follow the old road down through the scrub. After 15 minutes, an ATV trail branches right (somewhat hidden) toward Birch Hollow. Follow this around the head of a wash, through a meadow and up a hill. At a fork in the road, go right and follow the road out to the edge of a canyon. Follow the best of several social trails steeply down the hillside into the canyon. Allow 90 minutes to get to the first rappel.

ALTERNATIVE APPROACH: From the road between the two ranches, continue 0.4 miles on the North Fork Road to where Birch Hollow crosses the road and park. Drop down into the wash and follow the watershed. After an hour of thrashing through the brush, a 100-foot drop is encountered. Rappel this using a block or tree. (Do not add to the erosion of the nasty trail around the side).

THE CANYON:

R1: Rappel 100 feet (30 m) off a block. Continue hiking downcanyon. The main narrows section is soon reached. The canyon narrows up and a few small drops are encountered. These can be rappelled or carefully downclimbed. Soon, the first of a series of rappels is encountered.

R2: Rappel 80 feet (25 m) from one of the trees to the side into the slot.

R3: Walk down-slot 50 feet (15 m) and rappel 80 feet (25 m) off bolts to the canyon floor.

Several more rappels from bolt anchors lead down beautiful fluted chambers to Orderville Canyon. Turn right to exit up Orderville Gulch and back to the North Fork Road. Turn left to descend Orderville to the Zion Narrows. See map on page 103.

27 Spry Canyon

A splendid canyon in the heart of Zion, the rugged approach and a bit of spicy downclimbing give Spry a more serious air than many canyons at the same rating. Best done in spring or fall, or with an early start in summer.

Spry Canyon is not named on the map, but is the canyon between Twin Brothers and The East Temple, dropping into Pine Creek below Mount Spry. Mt. Spry is named for William Spry, third governor of Utah (1909-1917), and an early supporter of Zion National Park. He is most famous for signing the death warrant of labor organizer Joe Hill—the case generated international attention, with critics charging the trial and conviction were unfair.

Rating:	3B III
Time required:	5 to 7 hours
Preferred season:	Spring, summer or fall.
Cold water protection:	None required.
Longest rappel:	165 feet (50 m)
Special difficulties:	None

DRIVING: Spry starts where Pine Creek crosses Highway 9 one third of a mile (500 meters) east of the main tunnel. There is poor parking at this spot—park closer to the tunnel at a real parking spot and walk the side of the road to the crossing of Pine Creek.

Spry ends in lower Pine Creek, where the highway crosses the creek on a beautiful masonry bridge and starts climbing toward the tunnel. This is 0.5 mile (800 meters) east of Canyon Junction. Spot a car here.

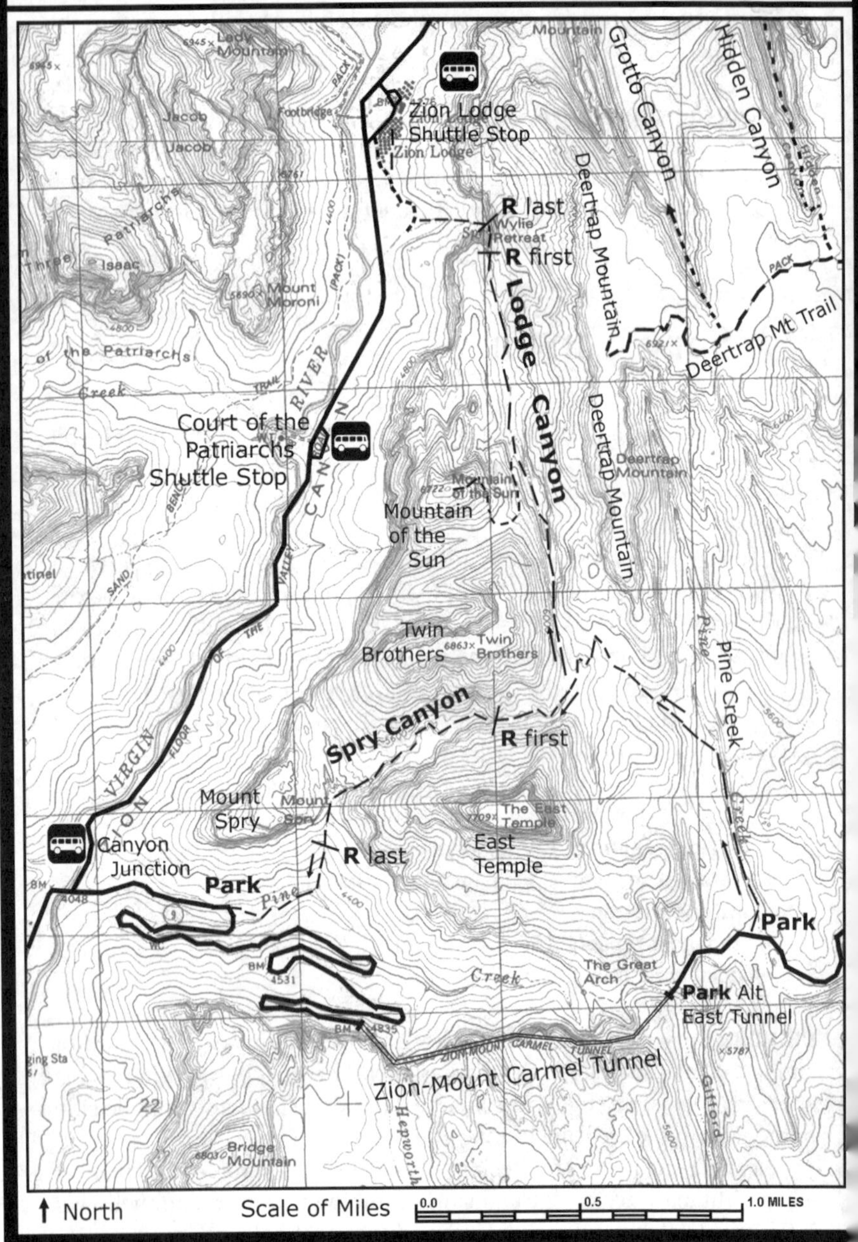

Spry Canyon and Lodge Canyon
Zion Lodge
Shuttle Stop
Grotto Canyon
Hidden Canyon
Deertrap Mountain
R last
R first
Lodge Canyon
Deertrap Mt Trail
Court of the Patriarchs Shuttle Stop
Mountain of the Sun
Deertrap Mountain
Twin Brothers
Pine Creek
Spry Canyon
R first
Mount Spry
The East Temple
East Temple
Canyon Junction
R last
Park
Park
Park Alt East Tunnel
Zion-Mount Carmel Tunnel
North
Scale of Miles
0.0
0.5
1.0 MILES

APPROACH: The approach to the bowl of upper Spry is shared with Lodge Canyon. From Highway 9, follow social trails north into the bed of Pine Creek. Walk this wide and sandy wash about 15 minutes (0.5 mile, 800 meters) to where the canyon starts to narrow. Exit the bed of the canyon left up a 4th class slickrock watercourse and climb up and a little right several hundred feet to a bench. Follow the bench north then west into a slickrock bowl below the impressive south buttress of Deertrap Mountain. Climb the center of the bowl (4th class), then up and right to the top of the pass. Keep your eyes peeled for faint petroglyphs on vertical orange wall a couple hundred feet below the pass.

From the top of the pass, looking west, left to right you see: The big peak of the East Temple; then the upper bowl of Spry Canyon; the Twin Brothers; a notch pass next to Twin Brothers; then a ridge leading up to Deertrap Mountain. From the top of the pass, traverse right and slightly down toward the slot pass and to the head of a narrow slot that cuts across the slope below. Climb into the head of the slot and, pushing through some brush, follow the slot most of the way down to the canyon floor. When convenient, exit to the right and descend steep broken slabs to easier terrain. You are now in the upper bowl.

THE CANYON: Descend the watercourse between huge, colorful walls. The canyon winds its way through trees and brush, soon arriving at a lovely slickrock bowl. Downclimb to a bolt anchor, then rappel (R1) 165 feet (50 m) past a swampy pothole to the ground.

The canyon again winds its way through a delightful forest. A couple of small potholes lead to a mossy area of short drops in the canyon bottom, usually downclimbed. Stay in the watercourse. The second drop is tall, but yields easily to the "elevator" technique–staying back in the corner and using outward pressure to control one's slide. Or rappel off a tree. The last drop into a dark slot requires a rappel off the most solid of the abundant debris. The dark slot may require a little wading.

After another mellow section, the canyon gets going. Moderate downclimbing is interspersed with about 10 rappels. In one spot, a narrow slot is down-slid elevator-style, then a pool delicately stemmed over. After an interesting rappel, the canyon opens out, then a slabby slope is downclimbed by cutting right. This leads down to a bolt anchor for a 90-foot (27 m) rappel into a black slot. The edge here has been cut up badly by canyoneer's ropes–don't get your rope stuck in one.

Soon after, a block allows rappelling into a mysterious pool in a slot. This is not to be missed. Swim the pool, then continue the rappel (total 30 m or 100 feet) down a second drop. (Variation: Those wishing to avoid swimming can rappel off a large tree directly to the large sandy area below.

A trail leads past the large tree to a really ugly rappel down a dirty slot.)

Toward the end, a diagonal rappel is made to gain the top of a flute, thus avoiding dropping into a skanky pool. Most of the anchors are bolted—certainly no more bolts are required.

Finally, the canyoneer downclimbs (4th class) a scary-looking, narrow slot (easier with pack off) into a pool (ankle to nose deep, depending) to a 100 foot (30 m) rappel to a ledge. The final rap is made by climbing up and left onto a shelf, and rapping off a tree to the top of the talus.

EXIT: Work your way directly down the watercourse (large blocks) to a big ledge with a 90-foot (27 m) drop, the Lambs Point Tongue layer of Navajo Sandstone. Rappel or follow the ledge right to a landslide, then back to the watercourse under the drop. Descend to Pine Creek. Turn right and walk out Pine Creek to the bridge.

28 Lodge Canyon and Mountain of the Sun

Lodge Canyon (Employee Canyon or Mountain of the Sun Canyon) offers but modest charms and several opportunities for misadventure. Mountain of the Sun is one of the more-accessible technical wilderness summits in the park, and the ascent of the one, and descent of the other, makes for a quality day. The big-wall exit out Lodge is a common place to get ropes stuck, so this adventure can only be recommended to experienced canyoneers.

Lodge Canyon runs north between Mountain of the Sun and Deertrap Mountain, dropping into the main canyon south of Zion Lodge, through the alcove known as Wylie Retreat, and coming out to the road through the employee housing area of Zion Lodge.

Mountain of the Sun catches the first and last rays of the sun, as seen from Zion Lodge. It used to be called one of the Three Brothers, but "left the family" when the lodge became popular. The other two became the Twin Brothers. Before the lodge, the Wylie brothers operated a motorcar tour with tent-camp at the present Lodge location (1917-1925). The waterfall and glen behind the lodge is known as Wylie Retreat. The lodge was built by the Union Pacific Railroad in 1925.

Rating: 4A III R
Time required: 5 to 7 hours

Preferred season: Spring, summer or fall.
Cold water protection: None required.
Longest rappel: 200 feet (60 m)
Special difficulties: Famous for getting ropes stuck. Bring lots of webbing for extending anchors.
Overall rating (Lodge Canyon and MOS): 4A IV 5.4 R

DRIVING: Lodge starts where Pine Creek crosses Highway 9 one third of a mile (500 meters) east of the main tunnel. There is poor parking at this spot—park closer to the tunnel at a real parking spot and walk the side of the road to the crossing of Pine Creek.

Lodge Canyon ends at Wylie Retreat, behind Zion Lodge.

APPROACH: Follow the same approach as Spry Canyon into the upper bowl of Spry. Turn north and climb to the notch pass between Twin Brothers and Deertrap Mountain, and drop over the other side. Descend small trails steeply through trees and around a few minor drops to an open slickrock area below Mountain of the Sun (see Variation 1).

THE CANYON: The canyon soon slots up. Avoid the first slot section by following the left edge about 50 feet to a weakness that is descended into the canyon. Downclimb as far as possible, then cross the canyon to a narrow, sandy ledge and traverse to a small tree.

R1: From small tree 165 feet (50 m) to the edge of a small pool. SCAAAARY!–as of 2005, the small tree is not long for this world. Evaluate carefully, then find another anchor in the area.

R2: From bolt anchor on left 165 feet (50 m) to the edge of a large pool. This rappel tends to get stuck—extend the anchor as far as you can.

R3: From bolt anchor on right 30 feet (10 m) to ledge.

R4: From bolt anchor, rap 40 feet (12 m) to the top of a buttress on the right—**NOT down the chute**. Walk right (east) to the other side of the buttress.

R5: From bolt anchor at right side of buttress, rap off right side of buttress 200 feet (60 m) to a ledge. Watch out for loose rock. Ropes get stuck on this one—extend the anchor as required.

R6: From bolt anchor 165 feet (50 m) beside waterfall to the ground.

Special Warnings: You MUST exit the watercourse part way down rappel 4. The final drop down the watercourse is longer than 300 feet (100 m). The descent route is on the other side of the buttress—be SURE to go that way.

This canyon is famous for sticking ropes. There are long slings on a couple of the anchors, and they may not be long enough to place the rappel point over the edge. Rig your rappels carefully and test-pull. Carrying an extra rope or two is a good idea in this canyon, and might prevent an unplanned bivy.

Loose rock falling on the last rappel station has been responsible for one fatality. Wear a helmet, clip into the belay, and pay attention to what you are doing.

EXIT: Follow game trails down and left, past a small waterfall to the main canyon. Find a discrete way to the road, then follow the road to the back of Zion Lodge. You are walking through people's backyards, so be polite.

Ascent of Mountain of the Sun (4th class/5.4 R)

From the open slickrock area in Lodge Canyon, follow a huge, tree-spotted ramp up and left, then right to the MOS—Twin Brothers pass (3rd class). Climb dirty slabs with brush on the right-hand corner of the south face to the base of an orange vertical wall facing Deertrap Mountain. Follow the ledge/gully at the base of the orange wall north (right) several hundred yards (200 m) to near its end, where a steep gully allows easy escape up and left. Follow a faint trail up and around to the summit. Pay attention—the trail can be difficult to find on the way down. Enjoy the expansive views, then return the way you came. Allow 2 hours for the round trip from the canyon floor.

29 Grotto Canyon

Grotto Canyon descends between the Great White Throne and Red Arch Mountain ending at, you guessed it, The Grotto. It is not a very appealing canyon. Since it gets very little water flow, it is more like a fault-following gully than a canyon. I did it, so you don't have to.

The Grotto used to be the end of the road, and is the site of the first ranger cabin and the first park campground. If you are camping in the South Campground and wonder where the North Campground might be, think The Grotto.

Rating: 3A III
Time required: 4 to 6 hours
Preferred season: Spring, summer or fall.
Cold water protection: None.
Longest rappel: 260 feet (80 m)
Special difficulties: None

APPROACH: Follow the Deertrap Mountain Trail to near the head of the canyon.

THE CANYON: Cross the mesa top, then downclimb into the canyon near its head. Downclimb until forced to rappel. A handful of rappels lead to a big drop. Follow ledges out right, then rappel 260 feet (80 m) to the canyon bottom. Eventually, rappel about 100 feet (30 m) over the dripping overhang of The Grotto. Walk out the little stream to the bus stop.

30 Hidden Canyon from the Top

A fine adventure in a wilderness setting, descending Hidden from the top makes for a great day of downclimbing and rappelling. Hidden has been ascended, and has been the scene of numerous broken legs and difficult extrications, from people who tried to ascend it. There are some difficult and dangerous climbing sections near the top.

In big snow years, Hidden could hold snow and ice until well into the spring. Caution is advised.

The Hidden Canyon Trail was blasted out of the rock in 1928, a year after rangers "discovered" the canyon when looking for W. H. Evans, the first ascensionist of the Great White Throne.

Rating: 3A III
Time required: 5 to 7 hours
Preferred season: Spring, summer or fall.
Cold water protection: None.
Longest rappel: 100 feet (30 m)
Special difficulties: None

APPROACH: The top of Hidden can be approached from either the East Rim Trailhead or from Weeping Rock via Echo Canyon. The latter is quite long, but requires only one car. From the crossing of the wash near the top of Hidden, make your way to the north end of the blocky bluff, and find the very head of the canyon. A few cairns mark a faint trail leading down to the edge, at the apex.

THE CANYON: Carefully descend steep dirt to any of several trees overlooking the head of the canyon. A huge pine right at the apex might be your best choice. Rappel. If you need to, pick another tree and rap further.

Hidden throws many obstacles at the intrepid canyoneer. Most are

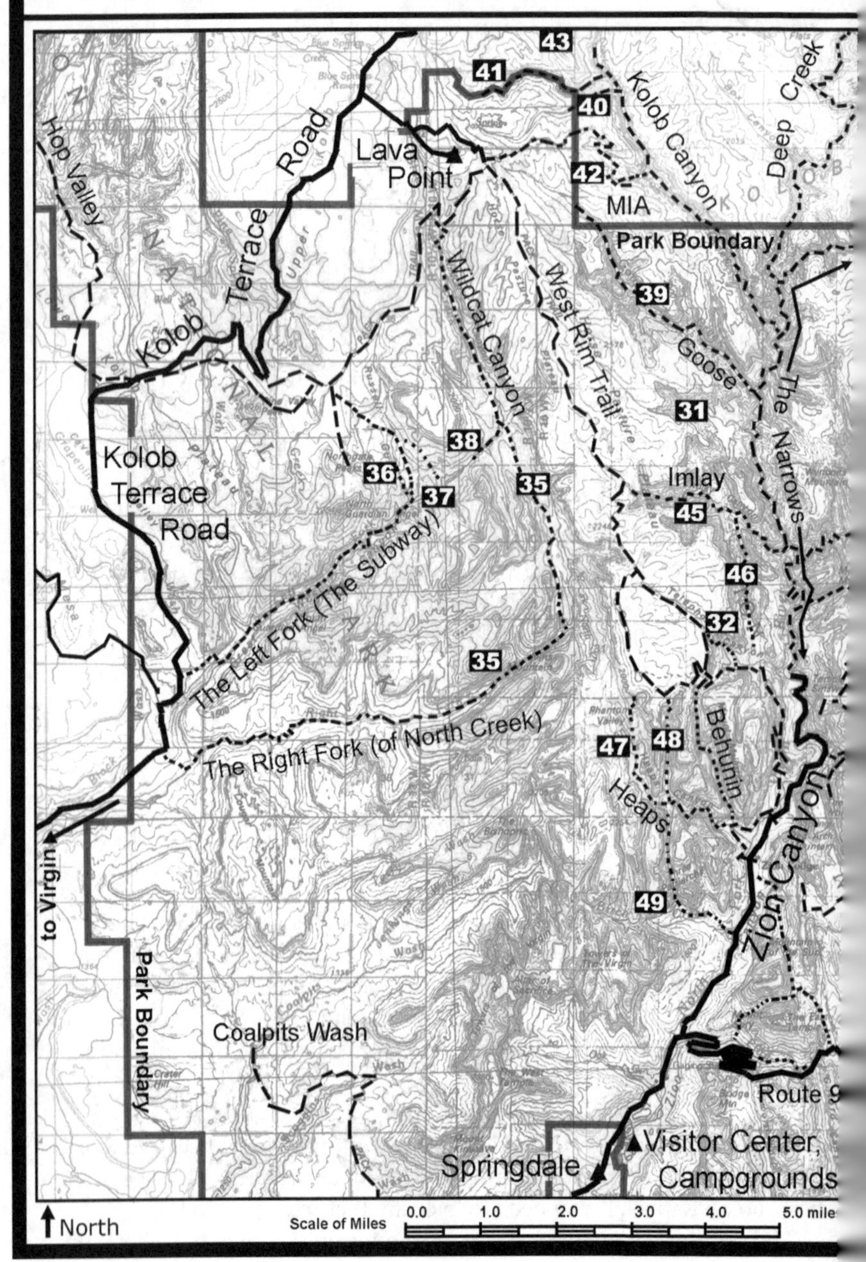
Technical Canyons – Kolob Terrace
43
41
40
42
MIA
Park Boundary
Kolob Canyon
Deep Creek
Lava Point
Kolob Terrace Road
Hop Valley
Wildcat Canyon
West Rim Trail
39
Goose
31
The Narrows
38
36
37
35
Imlay
45
46
32
Kolob Terrace Road
The Left Fork (The Subway)
35
The Right Fork (of North Creek)
47
48
Behunin
Heaps
Zion Canyon
49
to Virgin
Park Boundary
Coalpits Wash
Route 9
Visitor Center, Campgrounds
Springdale
North
Scale of Miles
0.0
1.0
2.0
3.0
4.0
5.0 mile

downclimbable, but a few require a rappel. Abundant trees, logs and rocks provide many opportunities for natural anchors. A few bolts pop up in surprising places, as do a couple of nice arches.

EXIT: At the end of the canyon, the well-constructed Hidden Canyon Trail heads right, connecting with the Observation Point Trail and leading down to Weeping Rock.

31 Corral Hollow

A nice canyon in a remote setting, Corral is beautiful in the fall and seldom visited. If you are looking for a place to not encounter other parties, this is a good one. Unlike most Zion canyons, the middle section of Corral is a shallow canyon on a slickrock bench, rather than deeply entrenched, and is open to the sun. Hot in summer.

Rating:	3A IV
Time required:	8 to 12 hours
Preferred season:	Fall.
Cold water protection:	None.
Longest rappel:	200 feet (60 m)
Special difficulties:	Getting to the head requires good navigation skills.

DRIVING: Begin at Lava Point, end at the Temple of Sinawava.

APPROACH: Hike down the West Rim Trail 3.4 miles to a point just past the dramatic viewpoint straight down The Left Fork. Head east into the woods, and follow the stream course to the head of the south fork of Corral Hollow. It is somewhat brushy, long pants are recommended.

THE CANYON: Follow the drainage. The upper section features downclimbs and four raps up to 120 feet, from bolts and natural anchors.

The middle section is a shallow canyon set in the slickrock bench. Following the watercourse is a pain in the butt–instead, walk out left (north) and walk down the bench to the big drop at the end.

The big drop section starts with a dramatic view 800 feet to The Narrows below.

R5: From tree, 150 feet (45 m) to another tree on canyon left. Ignore intermediate bolt.

R6: From tree, 200 feet (60 m) to ledge.

R7: Two-stage, low angle, 100-foot (30 m) rappel down slabs and across ledges.

Scramble down ledges and step across (exposed) to a ledge with bolt anchor.

R8: Rap 170 feet (55 m) to the canyon floor.

The final section scrambles down a small, wooded canyon to The Narrows. Several short rappels will be required.

Corral Hollow hits The Narrows just above Big Springs. Walk down The Narrows.

32 Upper Telephone Canyon

A nice little slot high on the West Rim, the technical part of Telephone makes a great canyon by itself, or can be combined with Behunin for a longer day. The long approach hike, many rappels and substantial downclimbing make it a good outing for experienced canyoneers in small groups.

Telephone Canyon starts out as a drainage atop the West Rim, then drops steeply to the bench level 1000 feet lower, wanders across the bench with some slotting, then drops suddenly into The Narrows in a dramatic, 900 foot drop. This technical route is the 1000 feet from the West Rim to the bench.

Telephone is named for the telephone line that used to run from the West Rim to the Temple of Sinawava through this canyon.

Rating: 3A III
Time required: 6 to 8 hours
Preferred season: Spring, summer or fall.
Cold water protection: None.
Longest rappel: 200 feet (60 m)
Special difficulties: None

DRIVING: Begin and end at The Grotto Picnic Area.

APPROACH: Chug up the Angels Landing Trail to the top of Scout Lookout. Continue chugging all the way to West Rim Spring. A small spring provides filterable water. Take the "Telephone Canyon" branch of the West Rim Trail and hike about 0.5 mile north. Cut down through a burned-over ghost forest to the bottom of the drainage. Follow the rim left to the canyon, or the stream right to the head of the drop.

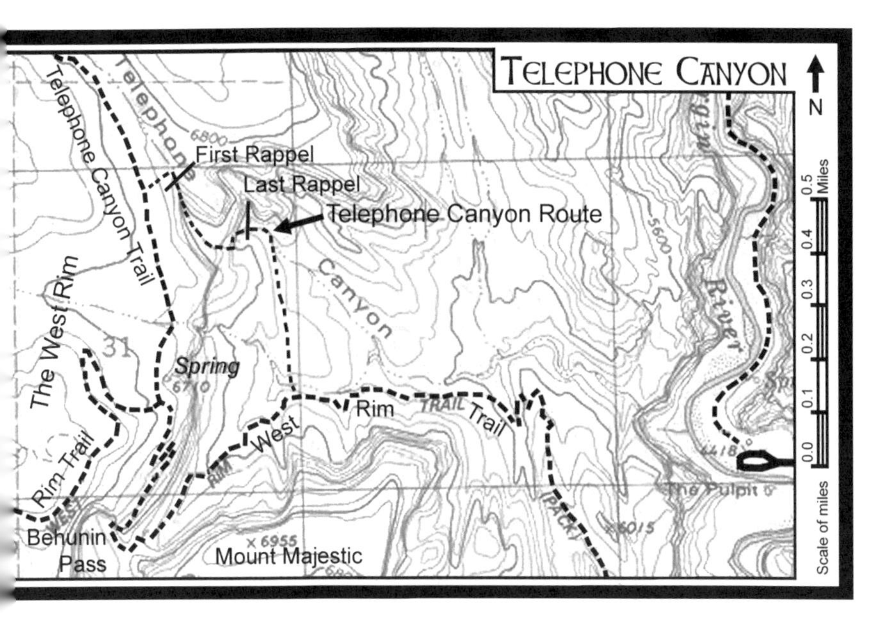

THE CANYON: On the right side of the drainage, rappel 30 feet (10 m) to a shelf with a few trees on it. Rappel from the lowest tree 100 feet (30 m) free-hanging, then continue the rappel down past a few potholes to a ledge with a bolt anchor, then down another short drop to another bolt anchor. The rope pull from here is surprisingly good. Rap a short steep drop, then down an awkward low-angle V-slot about 200 feet (60 m) to a ledge.

The canyon continues with about 10 rappels from a mix of natural and bolted anchors. Some downclimbing is required, made spicier by the fine coating of limey dust coating much of the canyon.

Toward the bottom, after a steep rappel in an area of recent rockfall, follow a game trail right across a wooded slope to exit onto the slickrock to the side of the canyon. Traverse slickrock to regain the West Rim Trail. Climb up to Behunin Pass, or descend back to the main canyon.

33 Refrigerator Canyon

The Angels Landing Trail climbs through Refrigerator Canyon on its way to Walts Wiggles. The upper section of Refrigerator can be descended from the bench to the Angels Landing Trail, but the way is steep, brushy and unpleasant. There are about 5 rappels up to 200 feet (60 m), mostly from natural anchors. Towards the end, poo papers from the hordes on the trail add to the unpleasantness. Not recommended.

34 Spearhead Canyon

Spearhead is a nice, rarely visited canyon in a difficult to get to location. The main part of the canyon is easily descended on all natural anchors. The final, bolted chimney section is a rarely used climbing descent route.

Spearhead is the canyon running south from the pass between Cathedral Mountain and Mount Majestic. It descends behind The Spearhead into the Emerald Pools cirque.

Rating:	4B V
Time required:	The canyon itself takes a full day.
Preferred season:	Summer or fall.
Cold water protection:	None required.
Longest rappel:	200 feet (60 m)
Special difficulties:	None
Note:	Recent reports indicate that the tree for the second rappel anchor may be gone, so rappels longer than 200 feet (60 m) may be required to get into the canyon.

THE CANYON: From the very head of the canyon, note on the left wall a clump of trees about 30 feet (10 m) down from the rim, with a single tree just beyond it. This clump of trees is roughly 500 feet (150 m) along the edge of the canyon from the apex. Sharp eyes can see a large pine 200 feet below the single tree.

Hike around to the rim above the single tree.

R1: 40 feet (12 m) from a tree to the single tree in a pocket.

R2: From the single tree 200 feet (60 m) to the base of a large pine.

R3: 130 feet (40 m) to a rocky gully at the base of the wall.

Enter the brush and work your way down and right (upcanyon). Downclimb ledges and brush as far as possible and choose a tree to rappel a cliffband. Three rappels up to 160 feet (50 m) from trees lead to the canyon floor.

The main canyon quickly heads south, providing a beautiful though easy walk in a deep canyon. A couple of short rappels are intermixed with a few pools that may require swimming. This part of the canyon only drops a couple hundred feet before arriving at the final chimney. Carefully rappel the final chimney from natural anchors and bolts to the main canyon floor. Descend game trails through the woods to the Emerald Pools Trail.

35 The Right Fork of Great West Canyon

The Right Fork is a remarkable journey across the Zion landscape, offers outstanding beauty, and extracts a worthy price of admission. Rather long and hot, it is done as either a one-day, two-day or a three-day hike. Lack of palatable water for the first two-thirds of the hike will deter some. There are rappels and swims–enough to put-off the non-technical hiker but not enough for it to be a technical test piece.

For many people, finding the correct route is the crux. First descended June 29–July 2, 1966 by Victor A Schmidt and company, they pioneered the intricate route still used today to avoid a long string of linked potholes in the Upper Right Fork. Many an adventurer, paying insufficient attention to the map and the route, has found themselves unexpectedly in technical terrain beyond their skills. Follow the route carefully. If you do not read and understand topographic maps, pick another adventure.

The middle section of the canyon is where the "goodies" are. The Grand Alcove and several lovely waterfalls are the highlight of the trip, though many will also enjoy The Black Pool. Before and after the goodies section, long, hot hikes are required. Plenty of poison ivy grows in the lower Right Fork.

Rating: 3B V
Time required: 1 to 3 days
Preferred season: Summer or fall.
Cold water protection: Wetsuits generally required.
Longest rappel: 60 feet (20 m)
Special difficulties: Navigation is difficult.
USGS Quadrangle: The Guardian Angels

GETTING THERE: From Springdale, drive south and west 14 miles to the town of Virgin. Turn right on the Kolob Reservoir (KR) road. The paved KR road winds through town, then climbs a dramatic ridge in making its way to Kolob Terrace. Six and a half miles from Virgin, the road enters the park and three trailheads are soon encountered—Right Fork being the first. Park at the Right Fork Trailhead, 7.0 miles from the town of Virgin. The trailhead is not shown on many maps, but is close to the Bench Mark labeled BM 4501. Driving time from Springdale is 45 minutes. This is your exit point, leave a car here.

The top of the route can be accessed from either the West Rim Trailhead or from the Wildcat Canyon Trailhead. The first is a shorter hike, but a longer drive, and will be described here. Wildcat Canyon Trailhead will work better if you have only one car, or if the Lava Point road is closed. If you have one car, leave it at the Right Fork Trailhead.

West Rim Trailhead: From the Right Fork Trailhead, continue up the KT road 13.3 miles. Turn right between two fenced fields onto the Lava Point Road. (The Wildcat Canyon Trailhead is 8.8 miles up the KT road from the Right Fork Trailhead). Follow the Lava Point road 0.9 miles southeast to a Y. Take the left fork signed for the West Rim Trailhead. Follow this a further 1.4 miles to a small parking lot before a gate at the West Rim Trailhead. Do not park blocking the gate, and do not drive beyond the gate.

TRAIL HIKE APPROACH: Hike down the West Rim Trail 500 feet (150 m), then turn right onto the Wildcat Canyon Trail. Follow this 15 minutes (0.7 mile), then drop south off the trail through brush to the bottom of Little Blue Canyon (not labeled on the map). Follow the bottom of Little Blue Canyon southwest to where it drops steeply into Wildcat Canyon. Two 75-foot (20 m) rappels pass this section into a lush glen.

Alternatively, stay on the trail another half mile and drop into Wildcat Canyon where the trail crosses the obvious drainage, avoiding two rappels.

OFF-TRAIL APPROACH: Wildcat Canyon is an open, rugged and dry canyon with large cliffs on both sides. Follow easily the bottom of the canyon, for a mile and a half, until it becomes more rugged and brushy. Avoid difficulties by staying right of the canyon bottom on the benchland where the walking is easier.

Follow the bench for 3.2 miles, crossing a wash. Just short of where Wildcat Canyon turns right and joins the Left Fork, follow social trails that find a ramp that leads easily down into the canyon. Follow the canyon bottom for 0.1 mile (160 m) to an easy exit up slabs on the left (east) where The Seeps come in. Many people will want to filter water here, either from potholes in the canyon or from The Seeps.

Up to the pass: Hike south-southeast, climbing up a wide, open and

Kolob Terrace – Right Fork – Upper

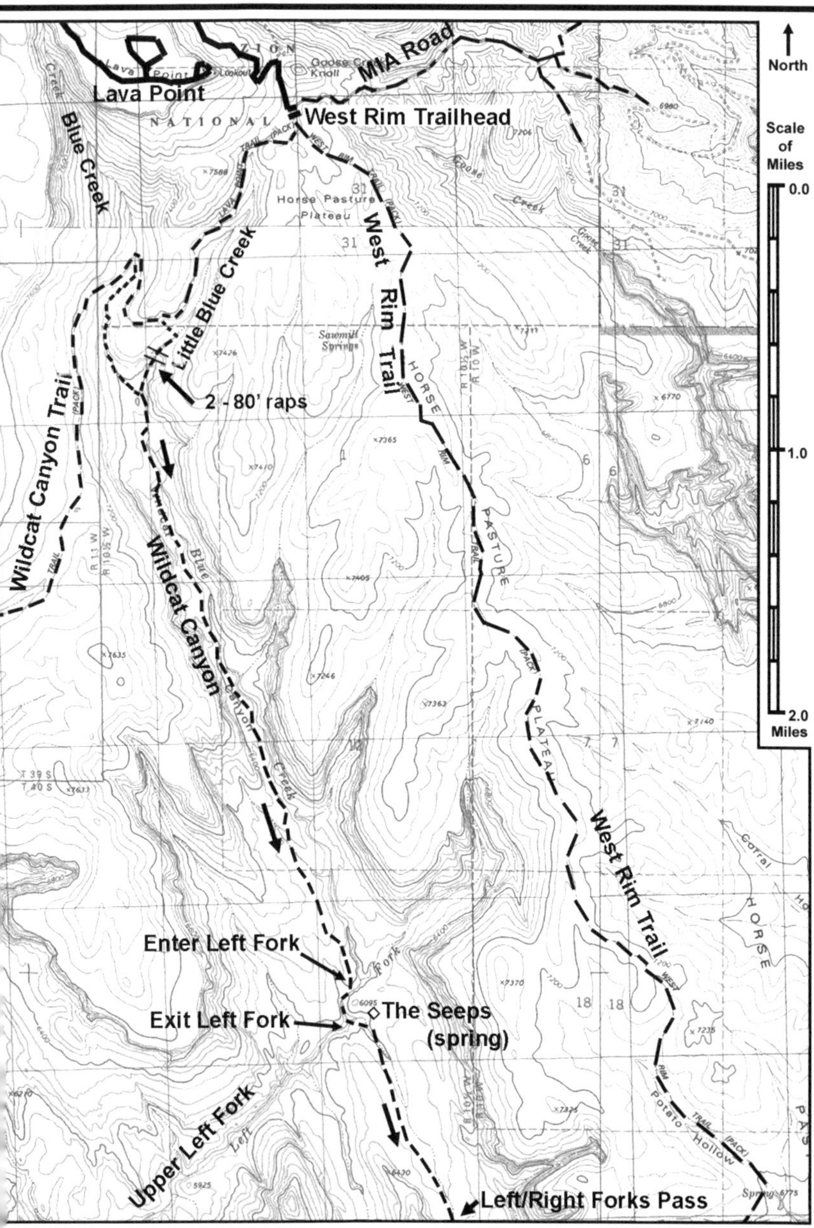

Lava Point
West Rim Trailhead
MIA Road
Blue Creek
Little Blue Creek
West Rim Trail
Horse Pasture Plateau
Wildcat Canyon Trail
Wildcat Canyon
2 - 80' raps
Enter Left Fork
Exit Left Fork
The Seeps (spring)
Upper Left Fork
Left/Right Forks Pass
North
Scale of Miles
0.0
1.0
2.0 Miles

dry valley. There are some incredible ponderosa pines in this canyon, protected by the very large sandstone walls on each side. Cresting the pass, the canyon to the south is a neat slickrock canyon of great ruggedness. A bivy site near the pass offers excellent views.

Descend The Valley and Climb to The Shelf. Stay to the right to avoid the rugged canyon on the left. Follow game trails down and into a small drainage, that in thirty minutes joins with the main canyon on the left. Follow the main drainage for only a few minutes, to where it becomes slickrock and starts to slot up and form potholes. This is the start of the more-technical, Direct Upper Right Fork section that most parties will wish to avoid.

Backtrack a few minutes and find a social trail or game track ascending the steep, wooded slope to the west. Climb several hundred feet to the crest. Once atop of the ridge, a good trail-of-use makes travel easy. Follow the crest of the rib, then drop into a shallow, beautiful slickrock canyon on the right, and follow this remarkable "Giant Staircase" to its end. (This is the last place to bivy before dropping into the narrow canyon). Where the canyon drops precipitously, downclimb steeply to the left, using the trees and carefully searching out the easiest route. Rappels should not be necessary. Near the bottom, cross the watercourse and follow a shelf 40 feet above the watercourse, until it is easy to drop into the canyon. You may need to use a handline or lower packs to get to the canyon floor. Some people bivy in this vicinity. Water may be available in potholes.

THE RIGHT FORK: Finally! we're in the cool confines of the Right Fork. The canyon is deep and shaded with a rocky bottom. The canyon is rugged and downstream travel is slow. The wise canyoneer will hunt around for options at each obstacle, then choose the fastest and safest route down. This stretch to the Grand Alcove is only 1.3 miles (2 km) long, but takes 2 to 3 hours to traverse. Several short rappels and cold swims make it more interesting.

Hike downcanyon under a giant boulder. A few minutes later, the canyon turns sharply right. In about 20 minutes, the Black Pool is encountered.

The Infamous Black Pool is a nice way to cool off. Drop into the pool, and swim 50 feet to 100 yards through a sinuous sandstone slot. Brrrrrrr. Rumor has it the pool can be avoided by a traverse on the left, then rapping off a tree into the end of the pool. But what's the point?

Walk briskly to warm back up. Other obstacles are overcome, rappels are made, pools are swum. Close to the Alcove, a little flow starts up in the canyon bottom. After several hours of rugged canyon, you arrive at:

The Grand Alcove, a magnificent overhang with multiple colorful

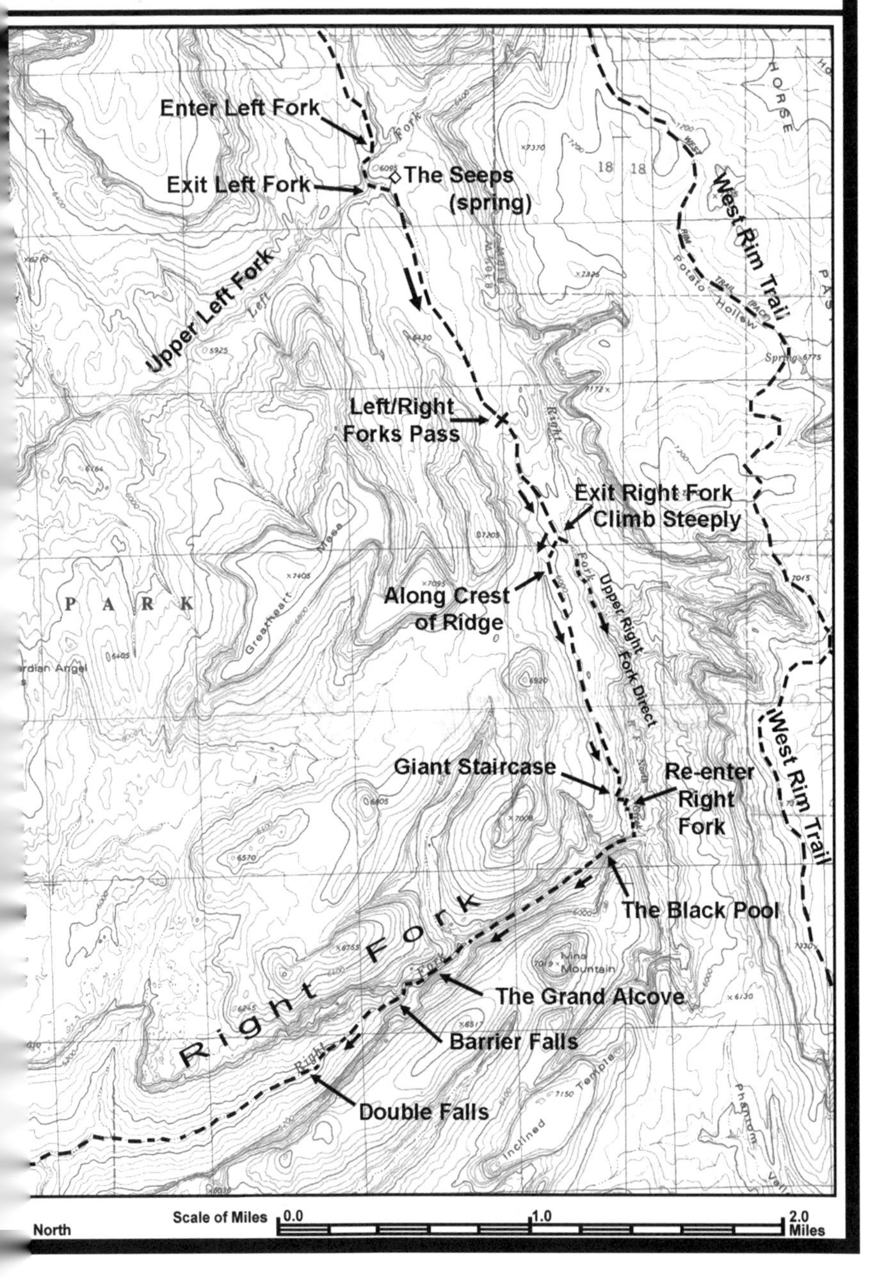

Kolob Terr.-Right Fork-Middle
Enter Left Fork
Exit Left Fork
The Seeps (spring)
West Rim Trail
Upper Left Fork
Left/Right Forks Pass
Exit Right Fork Climb Steeply
Along Crest of Ridge
Upper Right Fork Direct
P A R K
Giant Staircase
Re-enter Right Fork
The Black Pool
Right Fork
The Grand Alcove
Barrier Falls
Double Falls
West Rim Trail
North
Scale of Miles 0.0 1.0 2.0 Miles

tiers. The canyon cuts through the aquifer layer and copious quantities of clear, clean water burst out of the walls. This makes a splendid camping place—requiring your best minimum impact camping technique.

The Grand Alcove was named the "Stevenson Alcove" by the first ascent party of Ron Shofner and Bill Fisher in July 1965. Adlai Stevenson died a few days before they started their trip. Unfortunately, later authors did not propagate this name.

The Grand Alcove comes with a cliff obstacle that can be rappelled on the left at the far end of the ledges off a fixed anchor. A second, short rappel is made off a tree to the canyon floor. The streambed flume can be slid and downclimbed directly to the pool at the bottom—makes for a refreshing morning swim.

Barrier Falls. One hundred yards below the Grand Alcove, a 60-foot (20 m) waterfall is rappelled from bolt anchors. Barrier Falls represents the furthest the canyon can be hiked from the bottom. Watch out for Poison Ivy from Barrier Falls out to the trailhead. Heading downcanyon soon leads to...

More Waterfalls. A splendid waterfall appears difficult, but is easily passed by a trail to the side. The next fall is Double Falls—passed on the left. A ledge passes behind the twin waterfalls, allowing the adventurous canyoneer to dive through the waterfall into the pool beyond. Big boulders and rugged terrain make this section slow going. A short ways further downcanyon is...

THE SLOG. Unfortunately, Double Falls represents the end of the 'goodies', and the beginning of the slog out. The streambed is much like the end of The Subway, but twice as long. Follow the streambed and side trails west for 4 miles to the junction with the Left Fork. Watch out for poison ivy.

From the junction, cross the stream and head south (left) on the opposite bank. A quarter mile below the junction, a path heads up and right to the lava cliffband. Keep your eyes peeled–while the path is marked, it is still an unofficial trail, and can be easily missed. Follow the trail up through the steep talus, then up through the cliff band of black lava to the Right Fork Trailhead. Near the base of the trail up, a great swimming hole is available and recommended.

Right Fork Variations

Approach Variation 1, The Hammerhead: The hammerhead shaped canyon 0.2 miles SE of Point 7325 on the West Rim makes a reasonable, though more technical entrance to the Right Fork. Bushwhack to the northern end of the hammer. The brush is terrible and the terrain hard to read, so a GPS is highly recommended. About 6 rappels up to 165 feet (50 m) from natural anchors, and several downclimbs, are required to reach the Right Fork. At the intersection with the main canyon, descend the steep nose on canyon left to reach the floor of the canyon.

Canyon Variation 2, Upper Right Fork Direct: The series of linked potholes in the Upper Right Fork can be descended directly. Climbing skills will be required to exit some of the potholes, and rappels up to 80 feet will be found, all off natural anchors. The series of linked potholes calls for greater protection from cold water than the regular Right Fork route. This variation adds 1 to 2 hours to the normal descent.

36 Russell Gulch

While the normal route into The Subway is often called the "Russell Gulch Approach," it actually crosses Russell rather than descending it. This variation descends the canyon with three rappels of 100 feet (30 m), adding a little technical interest and another nice section of canyon to the normal Subway Route. It adds about an hour to the route, for small groups.

While this route is fairly straightforward, the rappels themselves have awkward starts and are not suitable for beginners. Don't take them, they won't have a good time.

Rating: 3B III
Time required: 7 to 10 hours
Preferred season: Summer or fall.
Cold water protection: Wetsuits advisable in all but the hottest weather.
Longest rappel: 100 feet (30 m)
Special difficulties: None

APPROACH: Follow the normal approach to The Subway to where it crosses Russell Gulch. Don't cross. Instead, traverse right (west) across the top of slabs then down steep slickrock and dirt to the canyon bottom. Find the path of minimum impact–stay on the slickrock as much as possible. The further you traverse right, the easier it is.

THE CANYON: Traipse down Russell Gulch, occasionally wading knee deep pools or scrambling over logs and rocks. The first rappel is soon found—100 feet (30 m) over a pothole and to the edge of a pool. Expect

Alicia Scotter on the last rappel, Russell Gulch

wading up to waist deep on all these pools. All rappels are bolted.

Continue downcanyon. A second rappel of the same length is made down a steep wall and into a shallow pool.

Continue downcanyon. A third rappel may require some effort to get to. Steep slabs can be downclimbed on canyon left, or a short, dirty rap made from a large tree. Rappel the overhang to the slab below, about 100 feet (30 m).

Continue downcanyon. The last drop ends in a large pool near the confluence of Russell Gulch and the Left Fork. From the top of the drop, find a small trail up and left through the woods, that leads to the bottom of the steep, sandy gully that is the normal Subway approach route. Descend to the canyon floor. Continue down The Subway.

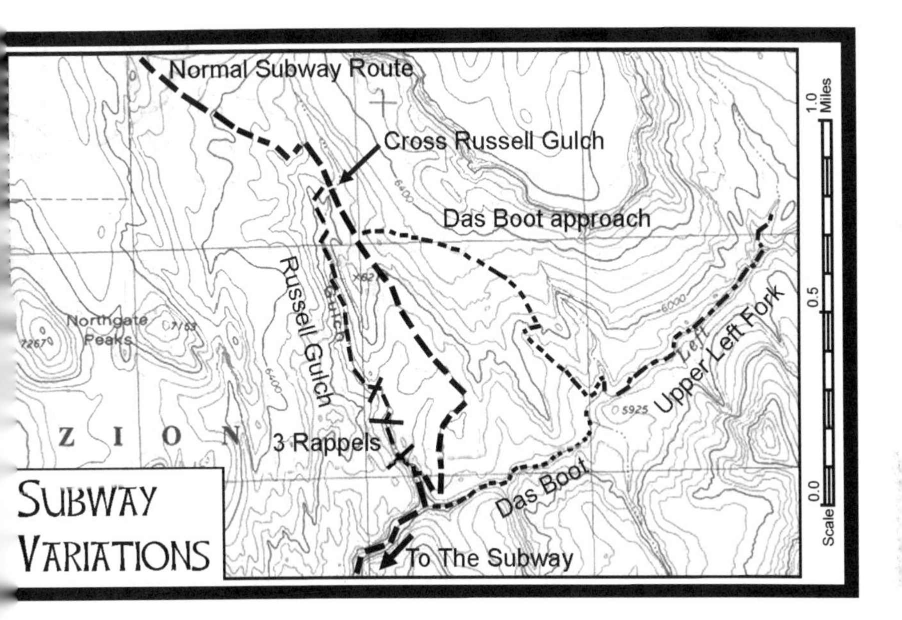

37 Das Boot

The famous "Subway" is an easy and incredibly scenic canyoneering adventure. Hidden upstream from the usual start is a wonderful, tight, dark, cold and wet canyoneering narrows that makes a much more adventurous start to the classic (and not very difficult) Subway. The Das Boot Variation offers easy access to the kind of tight, twisty and wet narrows found in more "extreme" canyons like Heaps or Imlay. Due to its unrelenting nature, this is a journey only for prepared and experienced canyoneers. Careful navigation is required to enter the canyon at the right spot.

Rating: 3B III
Time required: 7 to 10 hours
Preferred season: Summer or fall.
Cold water protection: Wetsuits even in hot weather.
Longest rappel: 60 feet (20 m)
Special difficulties: Long exposure to cold water.

What's it like? A long, underground narrows with only an occasional view of the sun. Wading and swimming for 2 hours straight. Numerous logjams to climb over or rappel from. A few short drops requiring skilled downclimbing or short rappels. A fun, underground adventure.

GETTING THERE: Follow the normal Subway approach trail through the forest and out onto a ridge. The trail then heads left, dropping into Russell Gulch.

DAS BOOT—THE STORY

By Dave Pitney

My friend Ram and I are descending Mystery one October day and we come upon two ropes still set up at Mystery Spring. After dropping them, we proceed to the drop into the Virgin and find a 3-ply 18 mm rope leading to the drop. So now we carry out 600 feet of wet rope and inquire at the ranger station if any one reported stuck ropes. Nope. Later that week we get a call from L, a podiatrist, who says "hey I heard you found my ropes, can you send one back to Vegas?" Certainly, but how did they get there? Well, L and the boys decided to do Mystery at night, rapping with hand-held flashlights, held in their teeth. OK. Our kind of people. Since I was going there in a few weeks for a trade show, I said I'd leave them at the hotel desk. One thing led to another and L and I made plans to descend the upper middle of Left Fork and then finish with The Subway. Now, this is mid-November at 6000+ feet and L does not want to rent a wet suit. Very bad idea. Most are convinced that he will die if he does not suit and eventually he is convinced to get a suit and all appears well. Appears, that is.

So we meet and head up after getting the requisite permit and we start hiking to the start in a foot of snow. Now, I was happy to just find the start as I had only been there once with Ram and was not paying particular attention. So I'm suiting up, including the taco wrap and eating all I can find and L. is waiting for me in his hiking clothes. Let's get ready I say and he tells me he is hot and won't be putting on his wet suit. A little bit of arguing and I point out that the shiny stuff in the water is ICE and get your suit on! Finally he relents (partly) and puts the top of his Farmer John on and this whole trip is going downhill, fast. So I'm tired of this and get ready to go and realize he has no neo socks on. L states that he has done many canyons before and knows what he is doing. Timing? Well June and July, mostly. You are in for a treat, I say.

So in we plunge and twenty minutes later I hear, "Duh, duh, DDDave,

Looking down from the ridge, note a slickrock pass above the usual slickrock pass. Descend and cross Russell Gulch, then climb to the higher slickrock pass. From there, climb straight up and slightly right to gain a bench. Cross the corner of the bench and descend shallow gullies heading southeast toward a complex of gullies and ridges toward the Left

I'm cold." No shit, and this is ice swirling around you. How cold? I can't feel my legs. About what one should expect, your body is working fine, let's go. No, he has to put on his bottoms. So this takes 20 minutes and despite my aerobic exercises I go from cool to cold. Now my panties are in a wad. L is slow and stumbling a little (we know what this means) and to keep him moving I keep slipping around corners ahead of him just letting him catch a glance of me. Finally we come to a place with that white winter sun and L comes up and falls face first into the stream and does not get up. I notice that he has one boot on and a sock on the other foot. I pick his head out of the water and ask him where his other boot is. "I duh, duh, don't know" he says slowly. So we still have more of this canyon segment and then 8 miles of The Subway including the hike out and L has one boot. Unacceptable I state. If you hike with me, you hike with two boots. Go get it. I don't know where it is he stutters. So how long have you not had a boot? I dunno. I can't feel my feet. Neo socks rule, I guess. So I go back and poke around in the last pool and find no boot. Probably not tied on well when he changed. Damn. What am I going to do with a hypothermic bimbo and miles to go? Does death become him? Nah.

Hike. And shortly we come to the final rap of the narrows and I try to puzzle out the best way with hypo L. Me first? Him first? Just toss his sorry ass into the pool? So I put him on rappel and then I go down and get ready to fireman him in case of mistake. But of course he has to rap down the snow covered slope in his sock. So it's pretty obvious that this canyon is over if we can get out. I go through his pack and make a boot out a stuff sack and my two socks and figure that if we can exit the Russell Gulch entrance then maybe this will end, mercifully. So up we go and L begins to warm and come out of his stupor. Sun is shining, snow is melting and all is well. We get back to the car and I give L my card and he begins to weep as the import of the day becomes clear—and the card is titled "Let's Adventure."

So how the name Das Boot? A podiatrist losing his boot in the narrows. Lessons are obvious.

Fork visible ahead. Make sure there is a substantial ridge on your right. Work your way down trying to avoid difficulties (3rd class) to a canyon bottom. Follow the canyon past some brushy sections, some sandy sections and some slickrock sections to where it drops into the Left Fork. Avoid rappelling in by traversing upcanyon (4th class) and finding an easy, secret ledge to reach a steep brushy slope that descends to the bottom of the canyon.

THE CANYON: Let the Games Begin! The narrows start immediately, so wade on in. Das Boot is much, much better when it has clean, fresh water in it. Wade, swim, climb, rappel, etc. for about 2 hours. It is beautiful and challenging down there, and even in hot weather, wonderfully cool.

The end of this section is marked by a 30-foot waterfall, with a large ledge on the right. Rappel the waterfall directly off chockstones. Downcanyon 100 yards (100 m) is the intersection with The Subway regular route. (If short on time, one can ascend the regular Subway approach, rather than completing The Subway). Enjoy The Subway, or exit.

38 Full Left Fork of North Creek

The Full Left Fork is a great adventure when the pothole water is full and fresh, but it dries out faster than Das Boot and becomes unpleasant. Most parties start by hiking down Wildcat Canyon (see the Right Fork) to The Seeps, then continuing down the Left Fork. It is also possible to traverse close to The Seeps from the Das Boot approach, though tricky route finding through cliff bands is required.

The section above Das Boot alternates sections of potholed, entrenched canyon with open canyon. Expect cold water (when in condition) and a few rappels up to 60 feet. Many will have had enough when they get to Russell Gulch, and will chose to escape at that point.

39 Goose Creek Direct Route (closed)

Goose Creek is closed as a Natural Research Area, preserving one of Zion's deep, narrow slots as a relict area. The following information is presented for historical purposes.

Goose is one of the earlier of the big canyons descended in Zion. It is possible to get into the upper canyon via a steep, loose, sandy side canyon near the head with little rappelling, but, the direct route right down the watercourse is much more aesthetic.

R1: Right down the watercourse, rap off a small tree 60 feet to a large log. Set up a long sling off the log, and continue another 30 feet to a large ledge.

R2: Rap 240 feet off the long sling to a ledge.

R3 through R10: Continue rapping. About 4 more rappels get you to the canyon floor. A few raps downcanyon appear from time to time. There is no reliable water in the canyon.

40 Boundary Canyon

A sweet canyon tucked in between "The Big Ones" up on Kolob Terrace, Boundary makes a nice day canyon exiting out the MIA, or a great way to access Kolob Creek for a high-class, technical backpack trip. The technical part of the canyon starts right AT the park Boundary, thus the name.

In the spring the canyon runs with water, so most parties will want wetsuits. In wet years, it is known to run all year round. Be sure to check the release level of the Kolob Dam by calling the Washington County Water Conservancy District (435-673-3617) AND to check the flow where the Kolob Terrace Road crosses Kolob Creek, 1.2 miles north of the Lava Point Road. Hiking in Kolob Canyon with more than 10 cubic feet per second (cfs), even just to the MIA exit, can be quite challenging.

Rating: 3A or C III
Time required: 8 to 10 hours
Preferred season: Summer or fall
Cold water protection: Wetsuits required when running
Longest rappel: 200 feet (60 m)
Special difficulties: Dam Release flows

APPROACH: From the West Rim trailhead, follow the MIA road east and northeast for 10 minutes or approximately 1 kilometer to a slight knoll at a right-hand turn. This is seen on the map as where the grid line hits the MIA road. Enjoy the view north down a moderate slope into the Boundary Canyon drainage. Follow a logging road down the ridge, then a complicated maze of logging roads more or less straight down the fall line, avoiding bushwhacking as much as possible, to

Kolob Creek, Boundary Canyon, MIA Exit

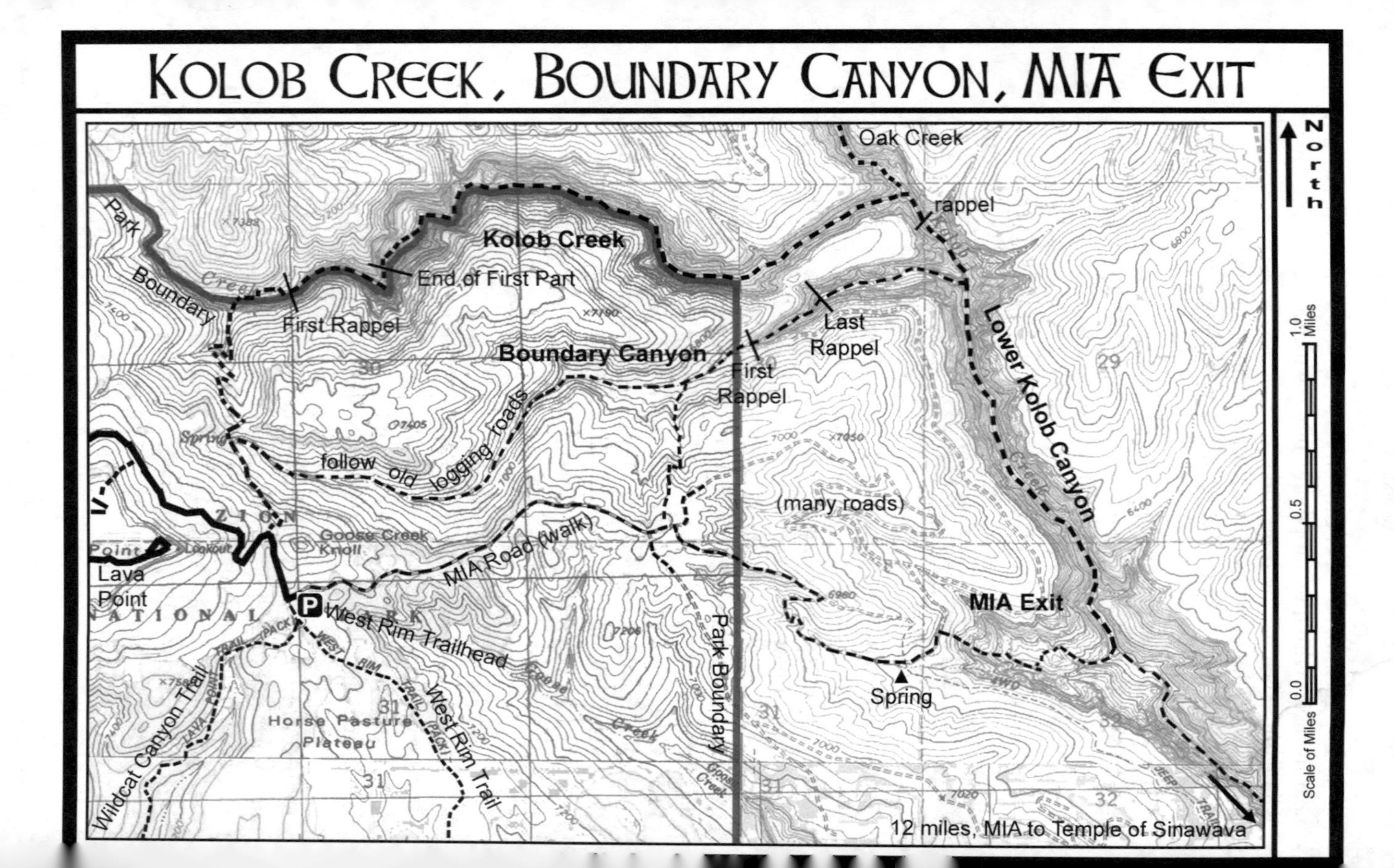

the canyon bottom. Follow the grown over logging road east along the right side of the drainage to the park Boundary (wire fence) and the head of the canyon. Allow one hour walking time to the head of the canyon.

Note: The MIA road is not always locked, but could be locked at any time. DO NOT drive the MIA road without permission.

THE CANYON: Find a small but stout pine about 70 feet from the head of the drop on the left (north) side of the canyon.

R1: 165 feet (50 m) down a steep, smooth wall to a large pothole/ledge with a logjam at its exit.
R2: 100 feet (30 m) past several ledges and down flutes to a large ledge. Very scenic! Anchor is a sling around the logjam.
R3: 80 feet (24 m) off bolts down nice flute.
R4: 100 feet (30 m) off bolts. An interesting arch!
R5: 30 feet (10 m) off natural anchors.
R6: 30 feet (10 m) off natural anchors.
R7: Off bolts, 70 feet (21 m) down a steep wall to the bottom of the canyon.

The rappel sequence leads to the floor of a beautiful canyon, lush with vegetation, with huge sweeping walls. Descent of the canyon offers few difficulties to the intersection with Kolob Creek–about 1 hour.

MIA AND KOLOB CANYON EXITS: See description under Kolob Creek.

41 Kolob Creek

And I saw the stars, that they were very great, and that one of them was nearest unto the throne of God; and there were many great ones which were near unto it.

And the Lord said unto me: These are the governing ones; and the name of the great one is Kolob, because it is near unto me, for I am the Lord thy God: I have set this one to govern all those which belong to the same order as that upon which thou standest.

—*Book of Abraham, Chapter 3, verses 2 and 3.*

In LDS Cosmology, Kolob is the place nearest God, the star nearest to the throne of God.

Kolob Creek is one of the grand adventures in Zion, invested with an unfortunate history in part because of its special situation.

On July 15, 1993, two youth-group leaders drowned while trying to descend Kolob Creek in high water conditions. Three leaders and five teen-agers were on a four-day descent that coincided with a substantial release from the dam. After a four-day wait, the six survivors were located and rescued on July 19th. The subsequent lawsuit is largely responsible for the technical canyoneering permit system in Zion today.

Is Kolob dangerous and extreme? Can be. Kolob must be respected, but the leaders made obvious blunders that led directly to their deaths. The flow in Kolob Creek is controlled by a dam at Kolob Reservoir, several miles upstream from the technical narrows. The group entered the canyon when the flow was too high for their technical skills–maybe anyone's skills.

Dam controlled flow has interesting consequences. Except in deep drought, a small flow is maintained through the canyon, so the pools stay full and cold. Water is released to supply irrigators downstream, and when the water is flowing, the technical narrows are impassable, even to those with advanced technical skills. The volume of water released is a major flood for this small canyon.

Potential Kolob-ers must first call the Washington County Water Conservancy District (435-673-3617) and determine the current release rate from the Kolob Reservoir Dam. Flows of 3 to 5 cfs will prove challenging to most canyoneers. Flows above 5 cfs are too high to safely descend the canyon. The District Office is only open during normal business hours, Monday through Friday, 9 AM to 5 PM. A Zion Park canyoneering permit is required.

So what is Kolob like? After a brief walk through the woods, the canyoneer rappels into a pocket garden. A hundred feet further, the canyon starts a drop of 700 feet through numerous pools. A total of 12 rappels are made, many into crystal clear, deep green pools followed by short swims and climb-outs to the next anchor. The canyon is incised deeply, with delightful grottos and wonderful light reflecting off the walls. From the bottom of the technical section, the canyoneer can make the long hike out to The Narrows and the Temple of Sinawava, or can ascend the steep and strenuous "MIA Trail."

Most parties will take 4 hours to complete the technical section, and will be in the water for most of this time. **Dry suits or full 7 mm wetsuits are required for descending Kolob. Do NOT underestimate the power of cold water to kill you.** While the technical difficulties in Kolob are few, the long exposure to cold water makes Kolob a step up in difficulty and danger compared to most of Zion's canyons. This makes it good preparation for the continuity of cold water found in Imlay and Heaps.

All anchors are bolted, expect a few raps off logs and trees near the start. In drought conditions, some of the pothole exits can be difficult—be prepared to do pack tosses, partner-assists and, as a last resort, drilling and hooking to exit the potholes. Most rappels require a floating disconnect—be sure everyone in your party is trained in this skill before entering the canyon, and bring a spare rap device or two.

A few of the rappels chain together two or three pools, and it is important to understand this technique. Rappel into the first pothole and either disconnect or pull through a bunch of slack. Swim across and exit the pothole, then go back on rappel and rap into the next pothole. When all canyoneers are down, the rope is pulled from the lowest pothole. Care must be taken by the last canyoneer that the rope is untwisted and will pull easily. When descending Kolob, be sure to locate the next anchor before pulling the ropes.

First Recorded Descent: 1978 Dennis Turville et al.

Rating:	3C IV or V
Time required:	9 to 12 hours
Preferred season:	Summer or fall.
Cold water protection:	Full wetsuits or dry suits
Longest rappel:	165 feet (50 m)
Special difficulties:	Long exposure to cold water.

LOGISTICS: Kolob is commonly done in two ways. For a day trip out the MIA Trail, park at the West Rim Trailhead near Lava Point. The MIA Trail returns to this point. For a two-day trip enjoying the full glory of Kolob Canyon, start from the West Rim Trailhead and exit at the Temple of Sinawava.

PREPARATION: Call the Washington County Water District at 435-673-3617 to determine the release schedule. They are only open Monday-Friday, 9am to 5pm. Obtain a permit at the Backcountry Desk. CONFIRM the water flow in Kolob by looking where Kolob Creek crosses under the Kolob Terrace road.

APPROACH: The approach to Kolob can be done entirely on old logging roads. Park at the West Rim Trailhead. Walk back along the road a few minutes to the big turn. Continue straight north across the meadow to a gap in the trees, a post and the start of a road. Follow the road down a few feet, then follow it left and traverse steeply downhill 15 minutes to the bottom of a hill. Continue straight ahead and pick up a smaller road climbing the opposite side to a pass.

Descend the road on the other side of the pass, switchbacking down the drainage. Where the road forks, stay in the drainage. About 15 minutes below the pass, after crossing a small, rocky drainage, follow an obscured switchback to the right into a small drainage with bluffs on each side. Follow this road all the way to Kolob Creek. Follow a path on the right side downstream for a ways, then cross to the left side when forced. Follow a pretty good trail on the left side to the start of the drops. Allow 45 minutes for the approach.

THE CANYON: Check the flow in the stream. The dam release schedule might have changed. Carefully consider the amount of flow you see—if it is more than 5 cfs you are out of luck—go find something else to do. The stream flow should be gentle and shallow–you will be rappelling, swimming and downclimbing in this flow–make sure it is low.

The first rappel in the canyon is 25 meters (80 feet) into a pocket garden. Put your dry suit on before this rappel. Choose a tree near the head to rappel from, and rap in. Head downcanyon and you immediately encounter your first swim. Yee haw!

Proceed downcanyon. Rappels 2 and 3 are off log jams down short drops. Rappel 4 is a chained rappel through two or three pools. Most teams will do 10 to 12 rappels. Two long rappels of about 45 meters (150 feet) are near the end of the technical section. Otherwise rappels are no longer than 30 meters (100 feet).

The final long rappel into a big pool is fabulous. This marks the end of the main technical section, though not the end of the fun. Many parties remove their dry suits here. However, there are a couple short rappels and swims a half-hour to an hour downcanyon.

TO THE MIA TRAIL: About thirty minutes downcanyon, a 400-foot waterfall comes in over the left canyon wall. The spring at its base is a good place to collect water. About one hour past the waterfall, and soon after two short rap-n-swims, Kolob joins the larger canyon of Oak Creek, and your direction changes from generally east to generally south. There is often a small flow in Oak Creek, and shortly downcanyon is a short drop into a pool. Rapping from bolts on the right might allow you to avoid another swim.

Finding the MIA Trail

(Note: Directions will be stated either as CANYON left or right (meaning when facing down-canyon) or as (blank) left or right, as seen by the ascender).

While the MIA Trail is not hard to find, many a canyoneer has walked past it due to inattention. Noting the intersection of Boundary Canyon is the key to finding the MIA Trail. The MIA Trail should not be attempted in the dark. The first time, most parties will require at least 2 hours for the MIA Trail, plus another hour to hike back to the trailhead.

The Boundary Intersection is marked by Boundary Canyon coming into Kolob Canyon on canyon right as a 50-foot wide, vegetated and not-steep canyon, and a steep, small, vegetated slot coming in across the way. There is a large flat rock right at the intersection that makes a great place to remove wetsuits and harnesses, and prepare for the ordeal ahead.

From Boundary, Kolob canyon is rocky and wide for about 20 minutes, then enters a short (5 minute), tall, narrows section. Next, the canyon opens out again and proceeds as a rocky streambed for perhaps 20 minutes, then again enters a tall narrows section, which is considerably longer (15 minutes). Approximately 10 minutes after the second narrows section, MIA canyon comes in on canyon right, as a large, obvious, lushly vegetated and steep (but climbable) sandy slope. Cairns often mark the intersection. This is the only possible-looking exit since Boundary, due to tall, unbroken canyon walls.

42 The MIA Trail

Climb the steep slope above Kolob Creek, starting in a shallow gully, then working left at the toe of a rock buttress. Traverse left, then down to the top of a short pourover. You are now in the main MIA canyon watercourse. Scramble upcanyon. A short wall is surmounted either directly, or by climbing a ramp on the right and stepping back left. At the next obstacle, climb a steep slope on the left to gain an exposed traverse ledge. The main canyon ends at a 40-foot (12 m) dryfall with a wider-than-fists crack in the back. Stop 30 feet (10 m) from the dryfall and ascend the obvious small drainage on the right.

Follow the drainage upward, to the base of a wall. Climb left along the base of the wall, then up again. Traverse left through brush to a wide pass that overlooks the upper basin of MIA Canyon (30 minutes to this point).

From this viewpoint, carefully examine the complex terrain ahead.

The upper basin is bounded on the left by cliffs and then a slinky little slot canyon (MIA Slot) dropping steeply into the basin (this is just above the "4WD" annotation on the map). To the right of this, is a complex, steep and tree-covered face that slides over into a deep slot canyon on the right. Take careful note of three snags (dead trees) at the canyon rim above the middle-left of the complex face–the three snags are where you are trying to go.

Descend to the bottom of the upper basin, and head for the bottom of the MIA slot on the left. The slot is well worth a few minutes of exploration. Follow the main watercourse past automotive debris washed down from above. Follow this canyon five minutes along the basin floor, until it turns right and heads for the right-hand wall and slot. At this point, climb steep dirt directly up the fall line, following a shallow watercourse on a fairly good social trail.

To this point, the dreaded MIA Trail is not so bad. It gets worse.

Follow the trail steeply upward. It is important to "Follow The Trail." In the brush, the trail is easy to find, but there are several sections where the trail crosses open ground and several options all look pretty much the same. At one point, stay right and scramble steeply up rocks. At other points, walking a few feet to check out the options will reveal the correct trail.

In general, when hunting for the trail, follow the watercourse. Explore, figure out which is the correct path, and follow it. Even the best trail is steep and difficult—persevere. Keep the three snags in sight.

Near the top, the trail is less well-defined and climbs a few sections of steep, loose rock. Be careful of partner-generated rockfall. Ascend to the road.

Back to the West Rim Trailhead

From the top of the MIA Trail, turn left (south) and hike about 1000 feet (300 m) to a picnic area with water coming from a pipe. Hike the road heading uphill behind the spring, then north up a roadcut, then follow the roads (generally north and west, but always up) to the West Rim Trailhead. Allow at least an hour for the MIA Trail, and at least an hour for the roadwalk back to the Trailhead.

Down Kolob Canyon to The Narrows

Kolob Canyon can be followed to The Narrows and out to the Temple of Sinawava. This makes a fine two-day trip, and includes the best part of The Narrows. Kolob Canyon itself offers a wonderful variety of narrows. The total slot length of 12.1 miles is not the longest in the area, but possibly the most spectacular long narrows.

From the MIA Trail, hike downcanyon four miles to the intersection with the North Fork. There are two short rappels with swims in icy pools within the first two miles. Plan on 3 hours.

From the end of the technical narrows, there are numerous small places to bivy in the canyon. Please use zero-impact camping techniques. Kolob has a few pools, but tends to be mostly dry. Be prepared to pump drinking water from skuzzy pools, or pump early when the water is good. If you camp after the intersection with the North Fork, you will need a Narrows camping permit. Most parties camp between the MIA trail and the North Fork.

From the intersection with the North Fork, stroll 8 miles downcanyon to the Temple of Sinawava (approx 6 hours).

43 South Fork Oak Creek

A very nice canyon, just north of the park on BLM and private land, Oak has been known by many names including "Cave," "Eye of the Needle" and "Battle Creek." Oak has several forks–the one described here is the southern-most fork, which originates near the knoll marked 7355 on the USGS Kolob Reservoir Quadrangle.

Unusual for Zion, Oak is spring-fed just above the technical narrows, and enjoys the splashing of a small stream through the technical section. Wet suits are recommended even when it is really hot out. Flow will be too high for safe descent during snow melt in the spring. No permit is required as the technical parts of this adventure are entirely outside the park.

Rating: 3C III or IV
Time required: 8 to 12 hours
Preferred season: Summer or fall.
Cold water protection: Wetsuits or dry suits
Longest rappel: 150 feet (45 m)
Special difficulties: Exposure to cold water. Private land access issues.

LOGISTICS: Oak Creek is usually done as a daytrip, exiting out the MIA Trail. You will need to spot a car at the West Rim Trailhead near Lava

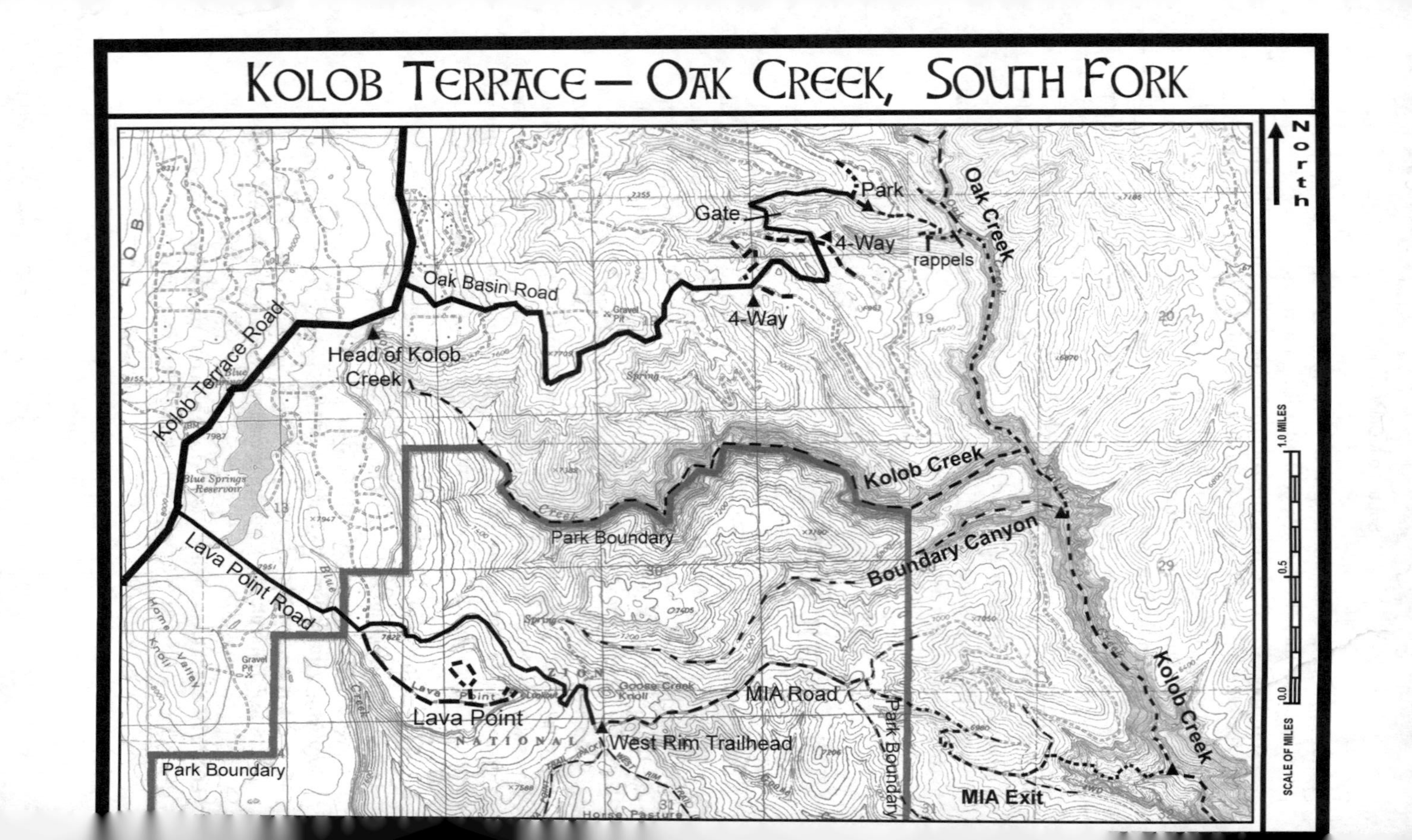
KOLOB TERRACE — OAK CREEK, SOUTH FORK
North
Park
Gate
4-Way
rappels
Oak Creek
Oak Basin Road
4-Way
Head of Kolob Creek
Kolob Terrace Road
Blue Springs Reservoir
Kolob Creek
Park Boundary
Boundary Canyon
Lava Point Road
MIA Road
Lava Point
West Rim Trailhead
Park Boundary
Park Boundary
MIA Exit
Kolob Creek
SCALE OF MILES
0.0
0.5
1.0 MILES

Point—the MIA Trail returns to this point. For a two-day trip enjoying the full glory of Kolob Canyon, start in the Oak Basin and exit at the Temple of Sinawava.

PREPARATION: Call the Washington County Water District at 435-673-3617 to determine the release schedule for Kolob Creek. They are only open Monday-Friday, 9am to 5pm. If the release from the dam is higher than 5 cfs, getting down Kolob Creek to the MIA exit will be challenging.

Confirm the water flow in Kolob by taking a look where Kolob Creek crosses under the Kolob Terrace road.

ACCESS: Access to both forks of Oak Creek (South and Main) is from a private road across private property. As we go to press, there is no access that does not involve trespassing. Please visit the Canyoneering USA website: *www.CanyoneeringUSA.com/utah/zio*n for the latest information on access to these canyons, as it develops. We hope to secure an access agreement in the next couple of months, but without that, the area should be considered closed.

THE CANYON: Walk left along the rim of the canyon about 50 feet, and find a tree to rap into the gorge. Head down canyon–a few short downclimbs are interspersed with about 7 rappels, often in the flow. The final rappel (in this section) is the longest at 150 feet (45 meters). Sly canyoneers will rappel THROUGH the natural bridge, thus threading the Eye of the Needle, but will place the pull-side of the rappel over the outside.

The canyon continues with a few short rappels and downclimbs, then opens out at the intersection with the Main Fork of Oak Creek. Sunshine can sometimes be found by heading up the Main Fork a few minutes.

Hiking down the Main Fork, one rappel and some wading are required to reach Kolob Creek. If it is not flowing, Kolob is easy to miss–it is a 5-foot wide flooded corridor coming in perpendicular to Oak Creek on the right. Another short rappel and swim (or deep wade), through a corridor, is found before reaching the intersection with Boundary Canyon.

Continue downcanyon and escape via the MIA Exit, or all the way down Kolob to the Temple of Sinawava.

MIA AND KOLOB CANYON EXITS: See description under Kolob Creek.

44 Icebox Canyon (Waterfalls Canyon)

Hidden behind Timbertop Mountain and Nagunt Mesa is an interesting canyon that makes a fine adventure on a long summer day. Two entrances are available: The Slickrock Pass start offers a big wall, technical, station to station rappel route suitable for a small party of expert canyoneers; while the North Pass start provides a dramatic 4th class slickrock couloir followed by two steep rappels–an interesting approach at a more moderate standard.

The canyon itself is narrow and lush, keeping a trickle of water even in drought conditions. A few rappels and a swim lead to the top of a huge, three-drop waterfall. From the bottom end, this canyon is known as Waterfalls Canyon. Bypassing the waterfall and descending the adjacent ridge, the delighted canyoneer passes below one of the world's largest arches (Kolob Arch) on her way to LaVerkin Creek. Then there's only the little matter of a 7 mile, 1000-foot gain (11 km, 280 m) slog back to the trailhead.

Either route can be done as a long day-canyon or as an overnight trip. However, humping bivy gear up the wooded ridge and down the rappels is a lot of work, and not recommended. The hike back to Lee Pass can be brutally hot in the summer.

DRIVING: From Springdale, drive south and west 19 miles to LaVerkin. Turn right on Highway 17 and drive north 6 miles to I-15, then 13 miles north on the Interstate to the Kolob Canyons exit and the Kolob Visitor Center. Allow an hour for the drive from Springdale.

From the Kolob Visitor Center, drive 4 miles to the Lee Pass Trailhead. Continue 0.25 to 0.5 mile (400 m to 800 m) to any of several turnouts from which a good view is available. Take a good look at the area between Beatty Point and Nagunt Mesa. Note several passes, and the wooded ridge leading up to the passes on the left. The V-notch at the top of the ridge is North Pass. The slickrock pass to the right is Slickrock Pass. Return to the Lee Pass Trailhead and park.

APPROACH: Descend the trail to the bottom of the ridge where it crosses a small wash. Turn left, down the wash, leaving the trail, and hike about 30 yards (30 m) to an intersection with the main drainage of Timber Creek. Turn left and ascend the wooded and brushy canyon 1-0.5 miles (2 km)

Kolob Canyons—Icebox Canyon Route

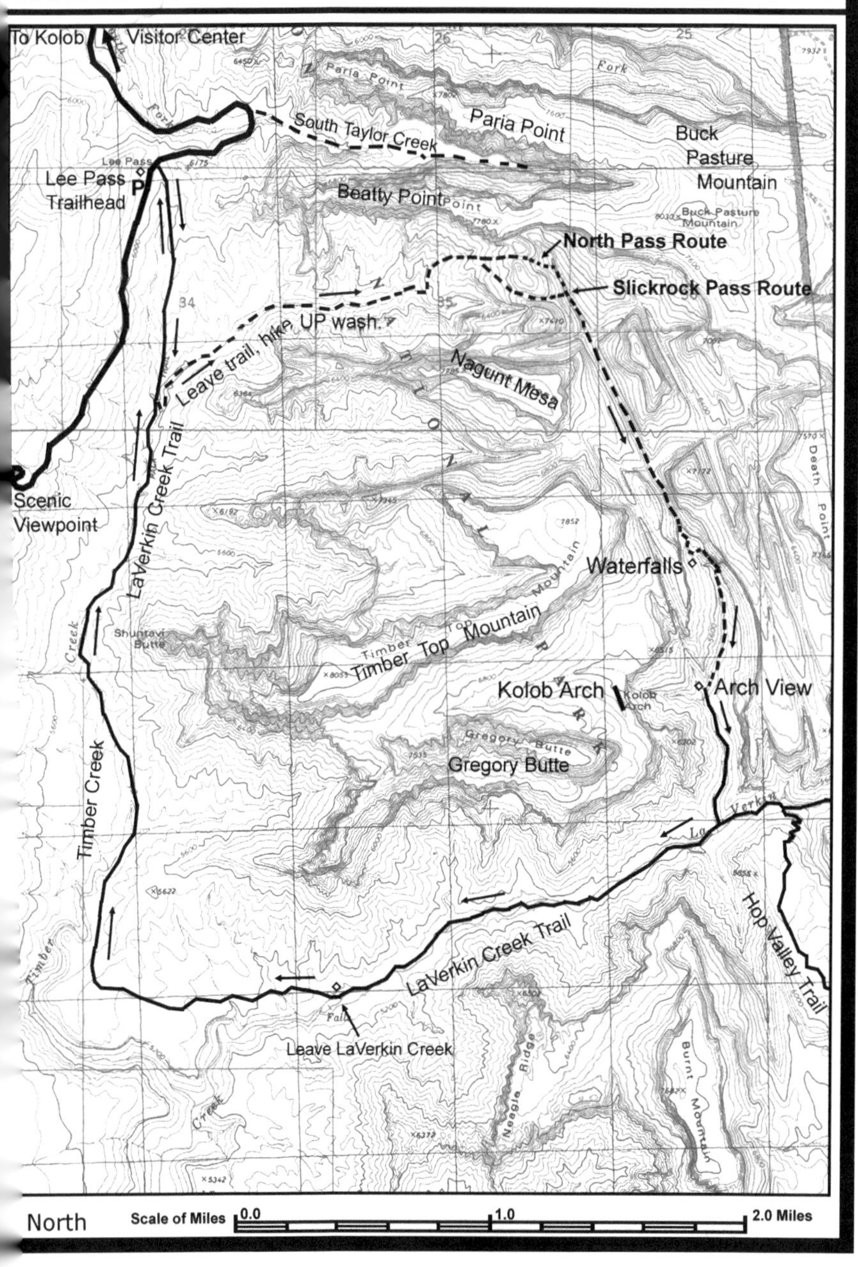

to where the canyon splits, the left hand split ending in a dry fall after a hundred feet. The fun begins here.

From the canyon junction, ascend the dirt between the arms to an alcove. At the right end of the alcove, climb a short cliffband to attain the open slopes above at the base of the wooded ridge. Head left of the crest of the ridge to find more open terrain and climb the ridge.

North Pass Entrance

Rating: 3B IV
Time required: 8 to 12 hours
Preferred season: Summer or fall.
Cold water protection: Wetsuits advisable in cold weather.
Longest rappel: 165 feet (50 m)
Special difficulties: None

THE CANYON: Follow the ridge to the top. Descend the slickrock couloir on the other side. Single bolts are available at odd intervals for setting up a rappel or handline. They can be hard to find. Descend the fall line to a ledge with several bolts. From the ledge, note a small pine tree down and right (right facing out). Rappel or downclimb to the ledge and tree.

Rappel from the pine 160 feet (50 m) to a good ledge with several bolts. Rappel from the ledge 140 feet (45 m) to the canyon floor.

(See Variation 1: Slickrock Pass Entrance)

Once in the big canyon, enjoy the lush vegetation and hike downstream. A small trickle of water will soon appear. Follow the canyon. Interesting slots come in on both sides that are worth a few minutes exploration.

Three obstacles must be overcome in this section of canyon. The first is a short drop into a slot with a pool, avoided by traversing on the right to a bolt anchor. Careful rigging and a diagonal rappel avoid a swim. The second drop goes into the pool and swims a short, cold slot. The third drop swim is again avoided on the right by a long hike out to a bolt anchor.

Enjoy a fabulous view from the top of the waterfall. From the top, traverse on a small trail left to the adjacent ridge, past the crest and down into the gully on the other side. Descend to the main canyon floor, then walk out the beautiful and dramatic canyon, mostly staying in the center of the drainage. After a half mile, Kolob Arch becomes visible on the right, and an official trail can be found. Follow the official trail out to LaVerkin Creek, then turn right and follow the main trail back to Lee Pass.

Variation 1: Slickrock Pass Entrance

Rating: 4B IV
Time required: 8 to 12 hours
Preferred season: Summer or fall.
Cold water protection: Wetsuits advisable in cold weather.
Longest rappel: 165 feet (50 m)
Special difficulties: Station to station rappels. Not suitable for parties larger than 2.

NOTE/WARNING: This entrance requires excellent rope technique and is not suitable for parties larger than 2, or 3 at the most. It is NOT a place for beginners–all members of the party must be competent. The hanging rappel stations are just that–bolts on a steep wall with no ledge. Experience in rappelling with a large pack is recommended (tip: Clip the pack to your belay loop and let it hang below your feet while rappelling).

THE CANYON: Ascend the wooded ridge about half way, then work your way over to the slickrock below Slickrock Pass. Climb to the pass, then descend the opposite side. A short section of slab climbing (5.2) leads to a cool slanted corridor. A bit of 4th class downclimbing leads to the top of a slab leading to a steep dropoff. A single bolt at the top of the slab can be used to set up a handline down to the first anchor.

R1: Rappel 160 feet (4 m) to a bolt anchor on a steep wall.
R2: Rappel 164 feet (50 m) to a bolt anchor on a steep wall.
R3: Rappel 140 feet (40 m) to the canyon floor.

Follow the main route from the canyon floor.

INTRODUCTION TO IMLAY AND HEAPS CANYONS

"Their Own Introduction?" the querulous reader asks.

Heaps and Imlay are unlike other canyons in Zion, and deserve their own introduction. Deeply incised into the stone, Heaps and Imlay have a character that is both sublime and perilous. Sublime because the dark hallways, carved stone and subterranean pools offer an experience only hinted at in other canyons; perilous because what accompanies these beauties are continual exposure to water, difficult pothole exits and a degree of strenuosity giant leap greater than other Zion canyons.

So what's the big deal?

There are several factors that make these a big deal:

- **Extreme Condition Dependency.** When the potholes are full, Imlay and Heaps are a romp; a cold, strenuous romp, but a romp nonetheless. The technical difficulty in these canyons is the long chain of continuous potholes. When full, rappel into the pothole, swim to the other side, and exit with ease. As the water level works its way down, the pothole exits become more and more difficult; and the number of difficult exits becomes large. So, if your buddy says "way over-rated, not hard at all," ask her how many potholes she had to hook out of.
- **Leadership Counts.** Do not underestimate the difference between leading and following in these canyons. If you were "taken down" one of these canyons, don't think it is easy to be in the lead.
- **Big, deep potholes with water in them.** Imagine yourself swimming in a pothole. You swim to the other side. Th`e lip is 6 feet above water level, the sandstone smooth, polished and slightly overhanging. Can you get out? There are 4 or 5 potholes in both canyons that CAN be in this condition. Be prepared to deal with them–because you might have to.
- **Hours and hours in the freezing cold water.** The "extreme" sections of both Imlay and Heaps take from two to eight hours for a party to traverse. Much of this time is spent in pools, swimming and wading, and walking between pools. This alone requires a great deal of energy, and will wear you down.

Opposite: *Rappel in Upper Imlay*

- **Excess Baggage Charges.** Getting yourself through these puppies is hard enough, schlepping your stuff through is even worse. Unfortunately, their length encourages people to do them as overnights. Of course, with camping gear, the canyons take even longer…

So how do you prepare for these canyons, and stack the odds in your favor?

Bring a strong team. By which, I would suggest:

- Someone who has done it before—an obvious candidate.
- Conditioned Athletes Only! People who are not fit enough become a big liability in these canyons.
- Everybody Climbs! There are climbing sections that are hard to belay in both canyons. Everybody needs to be able to climb.
- The Right Size: Three to five is the best group size. Less than three cuts down the options in partner climbing and pothole exits, more than five definitely slows the group down. The small ledge on the last rappel of Heaps fits no more than 4 people.
- Variety is the Spice of Life: Physical variety is of great benefit in partner climbing and pothole exits. It helps to have one small, lightweight expert climber, and one big strong guy that can boost the petite gymnast when needed.

Here's some specific skills you should know:

- ALL members of your party should be capable of rappelling quickly. With 20 or 40 rappels each, folks not real comfortable or safe rappelling are a big liability.
- For Heaps, ALL members of the party should be ready for a 300-foot (90-meter) single-line free rappel on a skinny cord. One canyoneer recently broke his back on that rappel. Why? Because he had not rappelled single strand before, had inadequate skills and equipment, and lost control of his rappel.
- Escaping Potholes: Do you know how to escape? Techniques used include Pack Tosses, Cheater Sticks (like the Happy Hooker), partner climbing techniques, and, as a last resort, hand-drilling small holes and bat-hooking out. You should have ALL of these tools and techniques available to your team, AND some practice in deploying them, so you can choose the best tool at each point.
- Experience! Unfortunately, there are few Zion canyons that have these kinds of obstacles. I recommend doing Kolob and Das Boot in preparation, as well as The Squeeze and Quandary Direct (in

the San Rafael Swell) before considering yourself ready for Imlay. Try taking your team with 30-lb packs through Pine Creek in wet conditions, in less than 45 minutes (for the technical section). Now you're getting there.

And did I say **BRING LESS STUFF**? Moving the baggage around can be half the effort–don't bring stuff you don't need.

Gear

Here are some special things you probably should bring:

- **Hooking Kit:** Hammer, 3/8" drill, drill holder, 2 Black Diamond Talons, and etriers or a bunch of slings (10) to tie into Aiders to hang on these things.
- **More on Escaping Potholes:** Drilling and Hooking should only be done as a last resort. Spend at least an hour trying pack tosses, partner assists, floating assists from rafts, etc, before reaching for the hardware. If drilling, minimize your impact by using already drilled holes as much as possible. A geologic hammer ("Geo-Pick") is not considered a valid technique, as it is crude and overly destructive.
- **Family Band Radios:** Are extremely helpful on the final rappels in Heaps.

Rope Notes

IMLAY: Imlay Sneak Route: The longest rappel is 130 feet (40 m).

Full Imlay: From Potato Hollow, longest rappel is 175 feet (54 m).

Most of the rappels are quite short. Bring along a 40-60 foot piece of rope to use on the short rappels. Ropebags are quite useful, an excellent way to manage your rope.

HEAPS: The longest rappel is the last one, almost 300 feet or 90 meters. If you carry a 300-foot (90 m) rope through the canyon, seal it carefully in a drybag. Some people use a 200-foot (60 m) rope, a 100 to 150-foot (30-45 m) rope, a 200-foot (60 m) pull cord, and a 300-foot (90 m) rope stashed in the rocks on the ground. In the bulk of the canyon, you will want to have two working ropes at least 100 feet (30 m) long. The Phantom Valley entrance includes one 200-foot rappel (60 m).

The second to last rappel often surprises people. It is steeper than it looks. You will want to hang your pack for this one, and set up your rappel with plenty of friction.

The final rappel can be handled a variety of ways. Carrying a 300-foot rope through the canyon just for this rappel is popular. With two shorter ropes, a lower-and-rappel can be rigged, and a 300-foot rope stashed in the talus below sent up. Careful rigging of the final rappel is highly recommended. It is a free rappel for all but the first 10 feet (3 m).

Comment 1: If you stash a rope below the final rappel, hide it from view. That three-leafed plant among the rocks is poison ivy–don't touch. I like to stack the rope into a pack, so it is ready to go. Attach a sign to the pack that says (something like): "Please leave this rope here. We left it on July 21. If you take it, we will DIE."

Comment 2: Bring radios. Family band radios make communication through the long rappels much easier.

Comment 3: Don't wear your pack on the last two rappels. Hang it by a sling from your harness.

IMLAY AND HEAPS: There are two ways to do Imlay, and two ways to do Heaps. The "Imlay Sneak Route" hikes up from Zion canyon and catches the best part of the canyon. It is usually done in one long day, but also makes a nice overnight, bivying in the Alcove before getting wet.

From Potato Hollow on the West Rim, the "Full Imlay" route is a little longer, and is usually done in two days, camping near the Crossroads where the Sneak route comes in.

Heaps can be done via the Gunsight entrance, or by the Phantom Valley route which includes the nice narrows at the bottom of Phantom Valley. Either version can be done in a long, long day by very fit people; or in two days, camping near The Crossroads.

45 Imlay Canyon from Potato Hollow

Rating: 4B V R
Time required: 12 to 16 hours
Preferred season: Summer or fall.
Cold water protection: Thick wetsuits or dry suits required at all times.
Longest rappel: 175 feet (54 m)
Special difficulties: Pothole Escapes (many).

Full Imlay is often done from Potato Hollow, though there are other entrances into the complex upper drainage.

APPROACH: From Lava Point, hike the West Rim Trail 5.1 miles (8 km) to Potato Hollow. A side trail leads left to a small pond and a designated camping site. Follow the outlet of the pond to the head of the canyon. There is often a trickle of water in the stream. (Can also be hiked from the Main Canyon floor—add 1.5 hours at least).

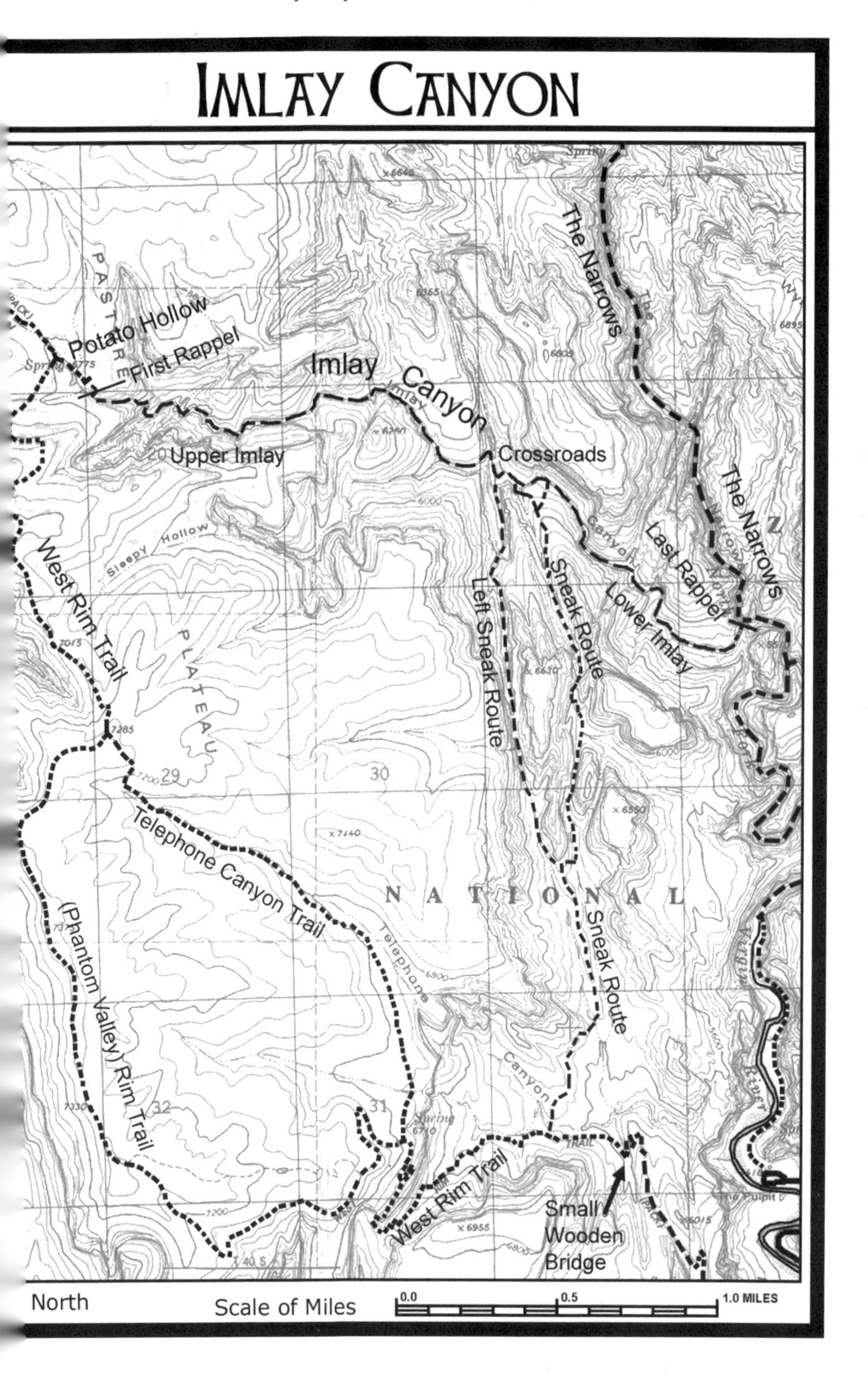
IMLAY CANYON
Potato Hollow
First Rappel
Imlay
Canyon
Upper Imlay
Crossroads
The Narrows
The Narrows
Last Rappel
Lower Imlay
Sneak Route
Left Sneak Route
Sleepy Hollow
West Rim Trail
Telephone Canyon Trail
(Phantom Valley) Rim Trail
Sneak Route
West Rim Trail
Small Wooden Bridge
NATIONAL
North
Scale of Miles
0.0
0.5
1.0 MILES

THE CANYON: Traverse the left rim 250 yards (200 m) to a small bowl with two pine trees. Downclimb through a break in the cliffband to the lowest pine.

R1: Rap 140 feet (40 m) to a large pine tree.

R2: Rap 120 feet (35 m) to the creek bottom.

R3: Rap 120 feet (35 m) off of logs in the streambed through multiple pools past an old piton. The pools are usually waist deep.

Climb down the canyon. One section may be easier to rappel. At a steep pouroff, climb left up dirt and brush, then down to a small tree.

R4: Rap 120 feet (35 m) past a large tree to a ledge with bolts at the rollover.

R5: Rap 175 feet (54 m) down a steep wall to a big ledge atop a ridge.

Downclimb to the end of the ridge, then off the right side down steep dirt into the wash. Several hours of interesting canyon with numerous short rappels lead to The Crossroads. The pools get deeper as the canyon progresses–suit up after encountering the first waist-deep pool.

The Crossroads and Lower Narrows

The Crossroads is a complex area where numerous canyons come in from both sides. The Sneak Routes comes in on the right, in several places. After The Crossroads, the canyon provides about an hour of moderate canyon with rappels and swims. Near the beginning of this section, after a couple of nice pools, is a large overhang sheltering a sandy beach with easy access to higher ground—a good place to bivy.

An hour later, the first section of extreme narrows begins. Work your way through this section, enjoying the beauty of these deep, dark and heavily sculpted narrows. Strenuous climbing, pack tosses, ingenuity and, as a last resort, drilling and hooking may be required to pass the numerous obstacles. After a few hours, the canyon relents and opens up briefly. A safe bivy can be found by climbing slabs out of the canyon bottom to the left.

Note: It is possible to exit the canyon right at the start of the first section of extreme narrows, and proceed overland to bypass them–but it is reported to be ugly.

The second extreme narrows (the Terminal Narrows) is somewhat shorter, but still takes several hours to traverse. It culminates in a long rappel (60 feet, 20 m) to a long pool. At the end of the pool, the canyon jogs left to a large ledge overlooking the North Fork Narrows. Rappel 130 feet (40 m) to the river. Hike out to the Temple of Sinawava (about 2 hours).

46 Imlay Canyon Sneak Route

Imlay is commonly done in a day using the Sneak Route. There are several variations on the Sneak Route, but the most popular starts from the main Zion Canyon and hikes up the West Rim Trail. Just past the little wooden bridge, the route leaves the trail and cuts across the Telephone Canyon basin, then between Point 6550 and Point 6630 (no elevations are marked on the Zion Park Map) and enters Imlay at any of several spots. The "extreme" narrows start an hour downcanyon. By sneaking into Imlay, the very best parts can be experienced in a long but reasonable day. The other sneak route (west of Point 6630) can also be used.

Rating: 4B IV R
Time required: 9 to 14 hours
Preferred season: Summer or fall
Cold water protection: Thick wetsuits or dry suits required at all times.
Longest rappel: 130 feet (40 m)
Special difficulties: Pothole escapes (many)

APPROACH: From The Grotto Picnic Area, ascend the West Rim Trail to Scout Lookout. Follow the trail left along the ridge, then down the end to a small wooden bridge crossing a branch of Telephone canyon. Continue along the trail 10 minutes until a clear route can be seen down into the slot of Telephone canyon and up rock on the other side. Cross the canyon and proceed north, staying on the slickrock left of the canyon bottom until forced into the canyon. Cross the canyon and climb onto the south ridge of Point 6630.

Follow the ridge until 100 yards short of where it steepens up, then find a way down into the canyon on the right (east) (see Variation 2). Climb up this canyon to a pass, then down the other side. Continue straight ahead and climb to another pass. A steep and dirty slab can be bypassed by backtracking 100 yards, climbing steep dirt to the west to the base of a steep, clean slab. Traverse upcanyon to the top of the dirty slab and continue up the watercourse to the pass. Descend the canyon on the other side, until it becomes smart to climb out right onto the slickrock buttress (see Variation 1). Follow the slickrock buttress down, then right to the edge of the inner gorge across from a deep alcove. Work carefully down very steep slabs to the alcove. This makes an excellent bivy site.

VARIATION 1: After stepping right onto the slickrock buttress, descend the buttress following the edge of the slot you just left. When overlooking Imlay canyon, find a place to cross the aforementioned slot easily and traverse onto steep, sandy, tree-covered slopes beyond. Descend until possible to traverse into a very-steep sandy bowl on the left, then down to the canyon floor. This variation accesses 4 to 5 more interesting potholes.

VARIATION 2: It is also possible to Sneak the route between Point 6630 and the West Rim, the Left Sneak Route. Follow the ridge until it steepens, then find a way down into the canyon on the left (west). Follow this canyon up over a pass and down the other side. A steep, broken up area about halfway down the approach canyon can be descended without rappels, but it may be easier to just rappel. There is a hidden natural bridge in this section. This variation accesses Imlay canyon a few raps higher than the buttress-to-alcove route.

Whatever Sneak Route used, continue downcanyon to the Lower Narrows.

47 Heaps Canyon via Phantom Valley

Rating: 4B V R
Time required: 12 to 20 hours
Preferred season: Summer or fall
Cold water protection: Thick wetsuits or dry suits required at all times.
Longest rappel: 280 feet (90 m)
Special difficulties: Pothole escapes (many)

William Heap, John Rolf and Isaac Behunin were the first European settlers in upper Zion Canyon. In 1863, Isaac Behunin built a cabin near the current location of Zion Lodge and established a farm. The cabin was used to tend fields on a seasonal basis. Heap and Rolf moved in a few years later, Heap establishing his cabin and farm west of the river, north of the Emerald Pool stream.

The three settlers agreed on the name Zion–the place of refuge. Isaac Behunin had been with the Mormon pioneers since they had left New York, had helped build the Kirtland Temple, and survived the numerous persecutions of the Saints. At last he had found a place to live his life in peace: Zion.

Heaps can be approached either from the valley floor via the West Rim Trail, or from Lava Point. Both approaches take about 4 hours, but the

Heaps Canyon and Isaac Canyon

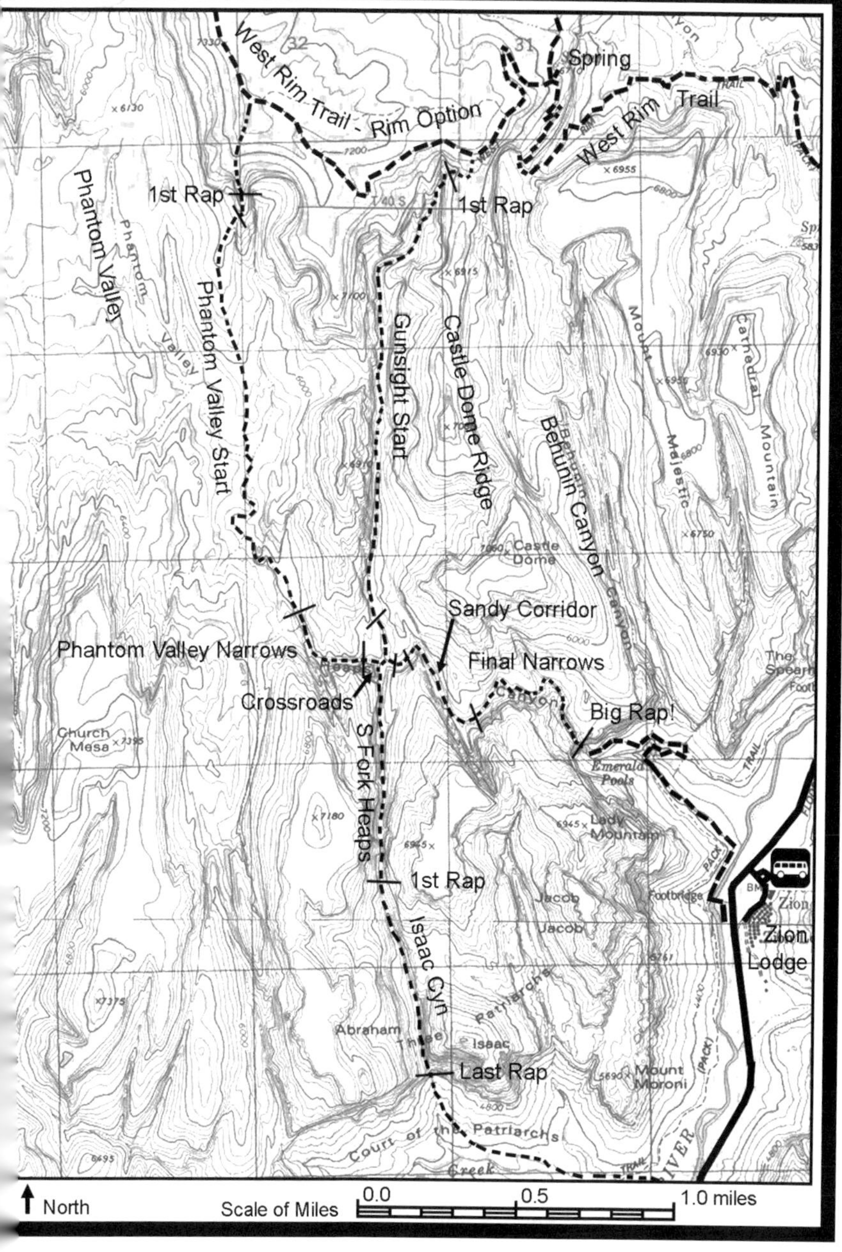

Lava Point approach uses considerably less energy than climbing 3000 feet (900 m) from the valley floor. First recorded descent: October 1982, Norman Harding and Royce D. Trapier.

APPROACH FROM LAVA POINT: This approach uses less energy, but does require a car spot. Follow the West Rim Trail south 6.5 miles (10.4 km) past Potato Hollow to a trail junction. The West Rim Trail splits here–take the right branch that continues along the West Rim. Walk 1.5 miles (2.4 km) to around campsite 4. Leave the trail and follow the edge of the escarpment another 1/8 mile to the top of a ridge between an amphitheater on the left and Phantom Valley on the right.

From the Valley Floor: From The Grotto, skip up the Angels Landing/West Rim trail 4.3 miles (7 km) with 3000 feet (900 m) of gain to West Rim Spring. This is a very small spring that provides reliable water, but requires treatment. Take the "Rim Route" (left fork) of the West Rim Trail 1.3 miles to around campsite 4. Leave the trail and follow the edge of the escarpment another 250 yards to the top of a ridge between an amphitheater on the left and Phantom Valley on the right.

The ridge is at UTM NAD83: 12S 323930 mE 4128070 mN

Work your way down the ridge, carefully following small social trails to avoid the worst of the brush. Progress on the ridge is blocked by a short cliffband. A small tree with slings above a dirt and gravel slope provides a possible rappel anchor, but a cleaner rappel can be found by stepping west 10 feet (3 m) over a rock ridge and slinging a block (may require a long sling). Rap 60 feet (20 m) to the ground. Continue down the ridge, downclimbing on the left side when needed. Delicately climb an exposed, crumbling knife-edge ridge to a large tree on the right. Rap from tree 205 feet (62 m) to the high point of the ground, 20 feet (6 m) right of a large ponderosa pine. Alternatively, rappel to a tree on the face below, and rappel from there to the ground. Bag the ropes and walk down the slope to the slickrock, then follow the ridge all the way to the bottom of the wash. Walk the wash one hour to where it drops into a dark slot, and suit up.

THE CANYON–THE PHANTOM VALLEY NARROWS: After a few walking and wading sections, the real fun begins with a rappel through a series of beautiful pools. After a few rap 'n swims, the canyon opens up briefly, before closing in for another pool drop section. When full, this section is easy and fun. When the water is a little lower, as many as eight challenging pothole escapes may be required.

The canyon then opens up and works its way through a section with canyons coming in on both sides. This is "The Crossroads." Escape to the south out Isaac Canyon is possible here, if needed. Traverse around

Chris Avery in the Iron Room, Heaps. Photo by Lin Alder/AlderPhoto.com

a pothole and rappel off a tree. A few minutes of hiking takes you to the Sandy Corridor. At the end of the Sandy Corridor, the canyon turns sharply left and plunges into darkness.

The next section of narrows is long and intense. Work your way through it. Near the end, there are potential bivy spots high enough above the stream course for most conditions. Strenuous climbing, pack tosses, ingenuity and, as a last resort, drilling and hooking may be required to pass the numerous difficulties.

Many hours later, the intense narrows relent and the huge, smooth face of Lady Mountain can be seen on the right. A flat sandy corridor leads to a flat rock and a plunging slot on the left. The flat rock is often used to remove dry suits and prepare for the final rappel sequence.

Take a look down the slot on the left. This is NOT the exit–a rappel from the lip is about 500 feet. Instead, climb a sandy chimney on the right (30 feet (10 m), 5.4) to the crest of a lump. Downclimb a slot on the other side to a small tree. Rap carefully 60 feet (18 m) down a slot to an exposed sloped ledge at a large tree. Be careful not to release any of the loose blocks perched in the slot–there are tourists below.

From the large tree, rappel 165 feet (50 m) to a small ledge in the chimney. There is some loose rock on this rap too. Do NOT underestimate this rappel–it is vertical the entire length and very exposed. Do NOT wear your pack for these last two rappels–dangle it from your harness using a sling.

From the small ledge, rappel 280 feet (90 m) free to the talus below. Carefully rig the final rappel. There is a lot of poison ivy at the base of the rappel—avoid touching it.

Stroll down the Emerald Pools trail to Zion Lodge.

48 Heaps Canyon via The Gunsight

Heaps can be accessed by descending The Gunsight, rather than through Phantom Valley. Follow the description below for the Gunsight, then head down Heaps from the Crossroads. This route bypasses some of the best, and most challenging narrows of Heaps.

49 Isaac Canyon via The Gunsight/ Escape from Heaps

Isaac Canyon runs between Abraham and Isaac into the Court of the Patriarchs. It is accessed by climbing up the South Fork of Heaps Canyon, which can be reached either by the Gunsight route, or via Phantom Valley. This description is via the Gunsight, and is included as a possible ESCAPE route from Heaps after the Phantom Valley narrows, should escape be advisable.

Rating: 4B V
Time required: 12 to 16 hours
Preferred season: Summer or fall.
Cold water protection: Wetsuits might be needed.
Longest rappel: 280 feet (90 m)
Special difficulties: A rarely traveled route.

APPROACH: From the valley floor, hike up the West Rim trail to West Rim Spring. Take the Rim Trail west (left) from the spring, and up a steep hill. Soon after passing the head of Behunin Canyon, a ridge leading out toward Castle Dome can be seen. Soon after, the steep drop into the head of Gunsight Canyon is admired. Gunsight is not marked on the map, but is the canyon between Castle Dome and Point 6910. Backtrack from the viewpoint to the start of the ridge, and bushwhack down to the ridge, then down the side into the head of the canyon. Climb down as far as possible, then rappel off any of several sturdy trees into the canyon. Downclimb and rappel into the slot.

THE CANYON: The Gunsight is formed by faulting, and is amazingly straight. The same fault forms the South Fork of Heaps and Isaac Canyon. Descend the Gunsight. Numerous rappels and downclimbs will be required. Anchors will not always be obvious, and might require some skill to set. After a long and impressive V-slot section, a more-normal canyon ramble begins, with nice walking in a lovely canyon interspersed with a few interesting rappels. In dry conditions, getting wet can be avoided, but in normal conditions, deep wades or short swims should be expected. After a couple hours, a huge slab that runs into a vertical wall is encountered, which is almost downclimbable, but easily rappelled from a large pine tree. Soon after, the Gunsight feeds into Heaps Canyon at The Crossroads. The canyon is exceptionally lush here.

To continue the Isaac adventure, head up-canyon about 50 feet to where the South Fork of Heaps comes in. The South Fork can be recognized as a 10-foot wide slot that ends in a 7-foot dryfall about 30 feet in. An interesting boulder problem can be surmounted by a strenuous mantle, or an assist from your partner.

UP THE SOUTH FORK OF HEAPS: Hike up the canyon. A few climbing obstacles up to 4th class are easily overcome. A steep sand pile leads to lush garden of pricker bushes, then a final climb up rocks and logs leads to the pass between Heaps and Isaac.

ISAAC CANYON: Since this canyon is seldom visited, you may get the chance to exercise your natural anchor skills and demonstrate judgment. Proceed downcanyon, hiking, downclimbing and rappelling. Rappels up to 200 feet may be required. A few old pins and slings are in place for some of the rappels–evaluate these carefully before use. Better anchors may be easily available.

The end is near when the massive walls of The Sentinel across the Court of the Patriarchs come into sight. Downclimb or rappel to an airy perch, then rappel 280 feet to a lovely spring. (An old climber's rappel station can be seen about half way down this final rappel, so it may be possible to do this route with a 200-foot rope. The anchors at that station should be checked carefully before being used!)

EXEUNT: Follow big boulders in the watercourse down to a cliffband, then follow water pipes and social trails left and down to the floor of The Court. Follow horse trails out to the Court of the Patriarchs shuttle stop.

Appendix

Selected Accident Reports from Zion National Park

Zion National Park has one of the best technical rescue teams in the National Park System. Still–backcountry visitors should be prepared to take care of themselves. The existence of an excellent rescue team is no excuse for reckless behavior. Rescue is always several hours to several days away, and does little for people who are already dead.

The first section excerpts and paraphrases incidents from the very entertaining book by Charles R. "Butch" Farabee, Jr.: ***Death Daring and Disaster–Search and Rescue in the National Parks,*** and is presented for historical interest.

July 27, 1927—First Big Rescue In Zion

> *... there remains no doubt that he succeeded in reaching the summit of our greatest mountain. I had hoped that no one would ever succeed in this climb, but nothing seems impossible anymore, and if he had failed, it would only be a question of time until someone did succeed.*
>
> *—Superintendent Ev Scoyen*

The towering sandstone summits of Zion were destined to call to climbers, and the first to succumb to their charms was W. H. W. Evans, a California adventurer who was "distinctly of the daredevil type, and a seasoned mountaineer."

The obvious target–The Great White Throne. Not only is it grand and impressive, but up the backside (the south face) it is downright reasonable, only 600 feet tall and slabby. (Modern rockclimbers can follow a 5.8 route up this side).

Mr. Evans climbed to the summit, but failed to return to camp that evening. The rangers were called out and searched in the staggering heat of June. Poking around the base of the south face, the team "noticed a notebook at the foot of the cliff, and at practically the same moment saw Evans stretched out in some brush and sand a few feet away." Having tumbled several hundred feet and lain in the June sun for two days, Evans was in bad shape, but still alive. The rangers constructed a litter and removed him to the Valley floor.

The search led to the discovery of Hidden Canyon, and a trail to it was built the next year.

July 8, 1930—Fatality on Lady Mountain

The Lady Mountain trail was constructed in 1925 by cutting steps in the rock and installing ladders. A 19-year-old visitor from St. Louis, Eugene, staying at Zion Lodge, ducked out of the lodge late one afternoon to hike up to Emerald Pools, but failed to return by dinner time. A two-day search came up with his name in the summit register, and then his body below where he had strayed from the route on the descent, in the dark. The Lady Mountain Trail was closed and dismantled in the early 1960's because of numerous incidents on its exposed climbs.

July 25, 1931–Falling Fatality on Cathedral Mountain

Having climbed The Great White Throne, Ronald C. Orcutt turned his attention to Cathedral Mountain. Solo, he failed to return for dinner, and the nearby trail crew went out a-lookin'. They found his body around midnight, and carried it down through the night.

August 13, 1946–Rescue on The Great White Throne

Roger Clubb joined the small club of GWT summiteers, but failed to find the correct descent route and got stuck on a small ledge above a drop, tying himself to a bush using his belt. The next day, a rescue party spied him around noon, then spent five and one-half hours drilling holes in the sandstone and inserting steel rods to use as foot holds. They finally reached him and rappelled from the bush.

Superintendent Charles J. Smith subsequently requested from the National Office permission to ban all mountain climbing in Zion, except by special permit. His request was denied.

September 17, 1961–Flood in the Zion Narrows

Thunderstorm-induced flooding produced the largest flood recorded in twenty-five years. Unfortunately, it found twenty-six members of the Scotowa Expedition hiking the North Fork Narrows. Twenty-one eventually walked out, but five were swept to their deaths.

September 5, 1965–Flash Flood in the Zion Narrows

Labor Day weekend, 1965, found parties from Los Angeles, Provo and Salt Lake City enjoying overnight trips in The Narrows. Massive rains early Sunday morning flooded the canyon. Over the next two days, all forty-two hikers eventually made it to safety, but only after many anxious moments, making their way down the flooded river.

June 3, 1973–Search and Rescue in The Narrows

After thirty-two hours, a three-man scuba rescue team located stranded hikers Bob and Harry Pattison in the depths of a very flooded Zion Narrows. Stranded for five days, the Pattison's had found high ground and stayed put, though by the time rescue arrived they were cold and hungry. Evacuation down the river was effected with the assistance of a rubber raft and ropes.

MORE RECENT INCIDENTS

This second section covers more recent accidents, mostly selected from the NPS Morning Report and edited to make them shorter. These are sorted by location.

Pine Creek

1992-440 Zion (Utah) Rescue

On the afternoon of August 12th, four young Utah men attempted to descend into the Pine Creek Narrows utilizing a rope purchased from a hardware store. Because of the sheerness of the rock face and the numerous pour-offs, full-length climbing ropes, some climbing equipment and some expertise on their use are required for this descent. Despite their lack of all three, the group descended to the first pour-off, leaving a portion of their rope behind. At the second pour-off, three of the youths descended to the end of the now shortened rope, then dropped into a plunge pool. The fourth member decided not to take the plunge and was therefore able to retreat and report that his companions were unable to get out of the pool. Four rangers and a local climber responded, rappelled to the trio, demonstrated ascending techniques, and belayed the youths out of the canyon—their first ascent, conducted on vertical rock in the dark. The rescue operation was completed at 11:00 PM.

2001-157— Zion National Park (UT)—Rescue

Four visitors entered the slot canyon on Pine Creek around 1 PM. on April 22nd. None of them had a wet suit, and the only descending gear they had with them consisted of two lengths of webbing. After passing the second rappel, they realized that they were not equipped to continue down the canyon. One person was able to climb back up the canyon and alert a ranger. The park's SAR team responded, and team member Bo Beck rappelled about 100 feet from the canyon rim to the stranded party. Each of the three people was then raised to the rim. There were no injuries. The leader of the group was cited for failing to obtain a canyoneering permit.

2002-202— Zion National Park (UT)—Rescue–Pine Creek

The park's SAR team responded to a rappelling accident in the Pine Creek slot canyon at 2 PM. on June 1st. A 51-year-old man had been descending a 100-foot rappel at the end of the slot canyon when he lost control and fell the final 20 feet to the ground. Rescuers reached the injured man at 3:30 PM. and a park medic provided advanced life support (ALS). The patient was placed in a litter and an 800-foot guiding line system was used to raise him and an attendant 600 feet to the canyon's rim. He was then carried a mile to the main park road, then transported to a hospital in St. George. Doctors determined that he'd suffered a fractured left tibia, compressed lumbar vertebrae, and second-degree rope burns on both hands. Seventeen people were involved in the rescue, which concluded at 10 PM.

2002-388— Zion National Park (UT)—Rescue–Pine Creek

Park staff responded to a report of a rappelling accident in Pine Creek Canyon at 3:30 PM. on August 11th. A 50-year-old man had been descending into the slot canyon from the north rim when he found that his rope end did not reach to the canyon floor. When he attempted to stop his downward movement, he turned upside down and rappelled off the end of his rope, falling 15 feet to the canyon floor. EMS personnel reached him at 5 PM. and provided ALS. The man and an attendant were raised 100 feet to the rim. Rescuers got him to the trailhead at 9 PM. He was taken by park ambulance to a hospital in St. George, where he was found to have fractures to four ribs and to his left femur in two locations. The leader of the five-person group was issued a citation for not having a canyoneering permit.

Left Fork (The Subway) and Right Fork

1992-555 Zion (Utah) SAR; Fatality

At 3:15 PM. on October 10th, David Bryant, 32, of Salt Lake City, fell about 30 feet and suffered major injuries while attempting to rappel into the canyon of the Left Fork of North Creek. Bryant and two companions had tied their rope off on a small piñon pine near the canyon rim. His companions rappelled down safely; the 220-pound Bryant slipped when he attempted to descend, however, and the shock to the line pulled the tree out. Bryant fell backwards and landed on rock.

Among the dozen people at the location was a doctor. He determined Bryant had a pulse, but was not breathing. The doctor fashioned an airway out of the handle of a plastic milk jug, intubated him, and began ventilations. A member of the party hiked out for help. The park received the call at 4:45 PM. and immediately requested a helicopter from Nellis AFB. Bryant was hoisted out and arrived at a hospital in St. George at 8:30 PM. Although he still had a pulse at the time, doctors soon pronounced him dead.

2000-430— Zion National Park (UT)—Multiple Rescues–Left Fork

On the afternoon of July 19th, rangers responded to a report of a visitor with a broken leg on the Upper Left Fork of North Creek. Rangers Cindy Purcell and Scott Cooper found 51-year-old Robert Sproul 0.5 mile below Russell Gulch. Sproul had jumped 6 feet from a boulder and suffered what appeared to be an angulated fracture to his lower right leg. Due to the narrow slot canyon, a short-haul extrication was not possible. The park's technical rescue team and gear were flown by a BLM contract helicopter to the rim, and Sproul, Purcell and Cooper were raised 475 feet to the rim through heavy brush and over cliff bands. Upon reaching the rim, Sproul was transported by a medivac helicopter to a local hospital. Rescue operations were conducted entirely in the dark and took until daybreak to complete. The rescue team came upon another incident while being flown out of the area—a 33-year-old male with a severely sprained ankle at the head of Russell Gulch. He was flown out in the contract helicopter.

2000-571— Zion National Park (UT)—Rescue–Right Fork

Anne G, 26, and Quentin C, 25, were rescued from a slot canyon on North Creek on Wednesday, September 6th. G and C headed out for a three-day canyoneering trip down the right fork of the creek on September 2nd. By mid-morning on the 3rd, they realized that they were off-route in a difficult slot canyon with numerous pools. Once they realized that they were unable to climb back up or continue down the canyon, they stopped and waited for rescuers. They were reported overdue when they failed to appear for work; the park was notified late on Tuesday afternoon. A helicopter search was begun and they were found after a space blanket was spotted in the bottom of the narrow canyon. The helicopter landed nearby and rangers rappelled to the pair. Rangers taught them how to ascend a rope and assisted them out of the 400-foot-deep canyon. Canyoneering is a sport requiring special equipment and a variety of skills, including map reading, rappelling, ascending ropes, and prior experience. Said ranger Kurt Spears: "Rappelling is not the only skill needed to safely negotiate these canyons. We're seeing a lot of people without skill or experience. You can't rely on just reading a route description."

2001-151— Zion National Park (UT)–Rescue–The Subway

On Saturday, April 14th, 9:30 AM, two park teams were called out to rescue a group of visitors stranded on the "Subway" canyoneering route. A party of ten had begun a day trip on the route the previous day. After traveling halfway into the canyon, they realized they were unprepared for the technical and water obstacles that they were encountering. Eight of them decided to wait for rescue, while two others continued on. The two exited the drainage the next morning and contacted dispatch. Rescue teams entered the upper and lower sections of the canyon, and the upper team contacted the group around 2 PM. Members of the two teams assisted them through the remainder of the canyon, exiting around 8 PM. There were no injuries.

2002-332— Zion National Park (UT)—Rescue–Russell Gulch

On Tuesday, July 23rd, rangers conducted a demanding technical rescue of an injured hiker from Russell Gulch near the upper starting point for the popular Left Fork of North Creek, also known as The Subway. Garrett B, 19, of Perry, Utah, fell 30 feet while hiking with his parents and three friends and sustained a fracture to his lower right leg. The accident occurred around 3 PM.—park dispatch was contacted at 7:15 PM. Rangers organized a search and rescue team and hiked into the area, reaching B. about 9:30 PM. Because of darkness, the technical nature of the planned extraction route, and the fact that it was not an immediate, life-threatening injury, rangers decided to wait until morning to make the rescue safer for all involved. They stayed with B through the night, then began rescue operations at 6 AM. the following morning. B was secured to a litter and raised to the canyon rim via a 400-foot guiding line, then carried 0.25 mile to where a helicopter could transport him to the Kolob Terrace Road. An ambulance transported B to a hospital in St. George.

2002-451— Zion National Park (UT)—Rescue–Left Fork

The park's SAR team located and rescued a stranded Canadian couple from a ledge in Russell Gulch on Thursday, September 5th. Michael and Cynthia S of British Columbia had obtained a permit to hike the popular Subway route two days previously. While hiking to The Subway, they strayed from their route and descended into Russell Gulch. They lowered themselves down the first rappel by webbing, which proved to be too short. Michael was unable to hold on; he slid down the webbing, then fell about 15 feet into a pool of water, sustaining burns on his hand and a laceration to the back of his head. Cynthia followed and received similar burns to her hands, a laceration around one eye, and an abrasion to one arm. The couple was then stuck on the ledge, unable to go up or down.

A helicopter was employed to find the S's, but strong winds prevented it from being used to shuttle rescuers and gear to the site. Two SAR team members hiked to the site and determined the S's were in good shape medically despite their falls. The rest of the SAR team arrived with rescue gear and extracted them from the gulch. They were brought back to their car, where the S's opted to drive themselves to the Dixie Regional Medical Center to have their burns examined. This incident provided a good illustration of the importance of informing others about planned outings. The permit system provided the information needed to locate and rescue the lost and stranded hikers. (Editor's Note: It rained torrentially the night after their rescue.)

Hidden Canyon

1992-436 Zion (Utah) Rescue–Hidden Canyon

Effie S, 28, of New Haven, Connecticut, fell approximately 25 vertical feet and suffered head, face and leg injuries while in Hidden Canyon on the morning of August 11th. A 20-person rescue team responded. Due to the narrowness of the canyon, two members of the party had to be utilized to relay radio messages. It took the remaining 18 rescuers almost eight hours to move the patient to the trailhead, arriving at that point a half hour after midnight. Maneuvers through high angle boulder fields and a number of vertical litter lowerings were required during the descent through the canyon. After exiting the canyon, rescuers had to belay the litter for almost a half mile along the trail, which has vertical drops of 200 feet. S was taken to a local hospital, treated, and released.

2000-563— Zion National Park (UT)—Rescue–Hidden Canyon

Robert W, a 55-year-old visitor from England, was descending a slope in Hidden Canyon around 3:30 PM. on the afternoon of September 4th when he lost control while sliding down a rock face and sustained a compound fracture of his lower right leg. The accident was reported to the park and initial responders were on scene by 5 PM. They found W in a small alcove at the base of a 30-foot rock obstacle. Park medics treated him and prepared him for a three-quarter-mile technical carryout down the canyon to the Observation Point trail. The carryout team arrived at the Weeping Rock parking lot at 8:30 PM. and transferred W. to an ambulance. He was taken to a hospital in St. George. This was the third visitor injury in a week requiring an evacuation from a slot canyon.

2002-041— Zion National Park (UT)—Rescue–Hidden Canyon

On the afternoon of February 17th, a 25-year-old woman who was hiking alone fell 6 feet and struck her head while climbing down a rock obstacle in Hidden Canyon. Visitors heard her calling for help and found her a short time later. They controlled the bleeding from a head laceration and sent a person to the trailhead to summon help. Park SAR personnel reached the woman around 5 PM. Park medics provided Advanced Life Support and littered the woman to the trailhead, put in a park ambulance and taken to St. George. Doctors determined she had an intracranial hemorrhage, so she was flown to Las Vegas for further treatment.

The Narrows and Orderville Canyon

1992-437 Zion (Utah) Rescue–The Narrows

Just after 1:00 PM. on August 11th, Michael N of El Toro, California, reported that his wife, 47, and his son and two daughters, all in their mid 20s, were in trouble in Zion Narrows and needed assistance. The family planned a one night campout in The Narrows over August 9th and 10th; they'd hiked about ten hours the first day, but had not quite reached the park boundary, four miles from the trailhead. They camped, then continued downstream on Monday, the 10th, but covered less than four miles. During the hike, N and his wife had become separated from the rest of the family because of flash floods. N's wife, who weighed 230 pounds and was taking medication for her heart, began having cardiac problems and injured her leg. N hiked out through the rest of The Narrows on Tuesday without seeing his children, and reported the situation to rangers.

While arrangements were being made to secure a helicopter, the son hiked out of The Narrows to report that his two sisters had returned to help their mother. In doing so, one of his sisters had fallen and apparently broken her tailbone, so was now unable to hike out on her own. FIREPRO personnel Eric Lutz and Koby Barnhurst were dispatched to the trailhead to hike downstream to the three women, and reached them despite considerable difficulty with flash floods. They spent the night with the N's, providing food and water and assessing their medical situation. At the time of the report, plans were to get the party to the top of Narrows Canyon so that they could be airlifted from the area if necessary.

2000-479— Zion National Park (UT)—Rescue—Orderville

Six members of the park's SAR team hiked into Orderville Canyon on the evening of July 25th in response to a report of a 43-year-old visitor with an ankle injury. Jack R of Clovis, California, had been canyoneering with two friends when he rolled his ankle and suffered a severe fracture. His companions left him behind and hiked 3.5 miles to report the accident. While waiting for help to arrive, R crawled about 0.25 mile down the canyon. Four members of the SAR team spent the night with him and were joined in the morning by six more team members. R was carried out on a litter through several deep pools in The Narrows on the North Fork of the Virgin River, then floated by raft about two miles to Riverside Walk. He was evacuated by ambulance to a hospital and treated for his injury.

2000-618— Zion National Park—Search and Rescue—Orderville

On the evening of September 24th, rangers were notified that 48-year-old Brian S was overdue from a hike in the park. S's wife took them to the point where she'd dropped him off just after noon, a spot four miles south of the Orderville Canyon trailhead between Englestead and Birch Hollows. S had been on foot for 10 hours at the time of the report and was not prepared for an extended trip. A search was begun the following morning; a dog team and later a helicopter were utilized. S was found by helicopter at 11 AM. He was uninjured but stuck several hundred feet below the rim of Englestead Hollow. S had rappelled down several cliff bands, but did not have the requisite equipment to continue. The park's technical rescue team was flown in by helicopter. S was raised to the rim and evacuated. The guidebook that S was using did not provide him with adequate information to find the correct route.

2000-647— Zion National Park (UT)—Rescue–The Narrows

On October 11th, an air and ground search was begun for a four-person party that was overdue from an overnight trip through The Narrows. Rain caused the Virgin River to increase in flow from 50 to 250 cubic feet per second. A search helicopter located the party that afternoon in The Narrows section of the river's canyon near the exit of Mystery Canyon. Ground searchers contacted the party and escorted them out of the canyon. The foursome stayed on an isolated area of high ground within the canyon until the river flow dropped to a level that they could manage.

2002-164— Zion National Park (UT)—Rescue–Orderville

Rangers evacuated an injured hiker from The Narrows on May 7th. At approximately 3:55 PM., the park dispatch office received notification of an injured hiker in Orderville Canyon. The park SAR team found Chris E, from Spokane, Washington, with an injured ankle and unable to walk. They splinted his ankle, placed him on a litter, then put him in an inflatable rescue raft for evacuation from The Narrows. The rescue effort was completed at 9:45 PM.

E had been day-hiking in The Narrows and was exploring the lower reaches of Orderville Canyon when he jumped down and injured his ankle. He was not wearing sturdy footwear with good ankle support, as is recommended for hikers in The Narrows. The inflatable rescue raft was designed and built especially for Zion National Park for rescues such as this one. This incident marked the first use for the new raft; members of the SAR team were very pleased with its performance.

Miscellaneous

1993-510—Zion—Kolob Creek–Drownings, Rescue

On July 14th, a group of five Explorer scouts and three leaders from Salt Lake City headed out from Lava Point for a four-day hike into the park through Kolob Creek to the Zion Narrows. The group had hiked in two miles and rappelled into Kolob Creek when Dave Fleisher, 24, got caught in a hydraulic at the base of a rappel. Kim Ellis, another of the group's leaders, pulled him out, but was in turn sucked into the pool, where he hit his head and disappeared. Ellis' body was recovered by Mark Brewer, 35, the third leader, who tried but failed to resuscitate him. The hikers left Ellis' body on the bank and hiked another 150 yards, where Fleisher was swept over a waterfall and sucked into another whirlpool. He did not resurface.

Brewer decided the group shouldn't risk further rappels and should instead await rescue. Their ropes and dehydrated food were lost in the creek, so the hikers huddled in an alcove and shared food from the one remaining backpack. The group was reported missing on Sunday, July 18th, and was spotted the following evening, largely because the party alerted searchers by lighting a fire with glue and burning plastic, thereby sending black smoke into the air. Rescuers rappelled into the canyon wall and used a hand winch to hoist the six survivors to the rim.

1999-19— Zion National Park—Falling Fatality–Lodge Canyon

On Thursday, January 21st, Sasha S, 20, of Springdale, Utah, was killed when she fell 150 feet while climbing the Mountain of the Sun canyoneering route. S was climbing with a group of friends and was near the end of the route. She was trying to release a jammed rope from their previous rappel when a rock dislodged, causing her to lose her balance and fall. The remaining members of the group did not have a rope long enough to complete the final rappel. At 6 PM., an employee of Zion Lodge heard shouting from the cliffs above the lodge and contacted park dispatch. John Hannon, the first ranger to arrive on scene, found S's body. The others in the group tied ropes, a sling, belts and packs together and lowered them to rescuers, who attached a 300-foot rope which they pulled up to them. They then rappelled down. S's body was removed that evening. The five-hour operation was conducted in darkness by 15 park employees from all divisions and three climbers from the local community who train with park staff. (Note: This is the last rappel in Lodge Canyon).

2002-143— Zion National Park (UT)–Rescue–Heaps Canyon

On Sunday, April 28th, Dave H and his companions were descending Heaps Canyon. They were completing their descent when H lost control on the final, 300-foot rappel. Park dispatch was notified of an injured person near Upper Emerald Pools. The SAR team was immediately dispatched. The first ranger reached H just before 8 PM. and found that he was suffering from head, back and leg injuries. Two park medics stabilized him, and an EMS helicopter from Page was dispatched to the park to assist with the evacuation. The SAR team began the evacuation around 10 PM., carrying H across a boulder field and down the Emerald Pools trail to the trailhead. He was flown to Dixie Regional Medical Center in St. George.

2004-11—Thanksgiving Rescue in Behunin

(This last incident is sourced by direct communication with Zion SAR staff.)

The Zion SAR team was called out one evening just before Thanksgiving. Zion

Lodge employees had heard shouts of help from stranded canyoneers in Behunin. The rescue team headed up to the last rappel in the dark. What they found there astounded them. A little water was flowing out of Behunin and forming ice, including icicles hanging off the backpack of a young canyoneer hanging on a rope, halfway down the last rappel.

J and S had started the descent that morning, expecting a dry canyon and few difficulties. Close to dark, when setting up the rope for the last rappel, J had secured one end of the rope to the anchor, then tossed the rest of the rope into the air. The other end of the rope, which should have reached the ground, had stuck itself in a crack a few feet below the top. J rappelled halfway down the last drop before noticing that the rope end was stuck, and was unable to pull it free. Without the tools or training to ascend the rope, the canyoneer was left hanging in space, 80 feet above the ground and 80 feet from the top.

At the top of the rappel, S had been unable to assist her friend other than by shouting for help. With the waterfall flowing a few feet away, ice had formed on J's back and backpack. Only by luck had their calls for help been heard by some of the few people in Zion Canyon that evening.

Luck was on their side in another way. Hiking around to the top and descending the canyon to reach the stranded canyoneers would have taken four hours at least—time J did not have. By a stroke of luck, hanging from the anchor was a second rope left by another party earlier in the month. The rope had an inch-thick coating of ice on it, so J and S had not thought of using it, but it now provided a way to send gear up to S.

The SAR team quickly sent a radio up to S. and determined she was competent enough to help with the rescue. They then sent up a large rescue pulley, loaded with a 300-foot rope, that S. secured to the top anchor with locking carabiners. J was still coherent enough to clip himself into the end of the 300-foot rope, and the rangers lifted him a few feet so he could unclip from his tangled rappel rope. They lowered him to the ground and wrapped him in blankets. The team then pulled the rope up and lowered S. to the ground. Pulling the rescue rope was easy, but the tangled rope, the ice-covered rope that saved J's life, and the pulley were left to winter-over at the end of Behunin, and provoke curiosity in the first canyoneers to descend the canyon in the spring.

Bibliography

Brereton, Thomas and Dunaway, James *Exploring the Backcountry of Zion National Park: Off-Trail Routes.* Springdale, Utah: Zion Natural History Association. (Revised and Updated by Bob Lineback): 1988 edition. ISBN 0-915630-25-7

Eves, Robert L. *Water, Rock, and Time–The Geologic Story of Zion National Park.* Springdale, Utah: Zion Natural History Association, 2005. ISBN 0-915630-42-7

Farabee, Charles R "Butch" *Death Daring and Disaster–Search and Rescue in the National Parks* Niwot, Colorado: Roberts Rinehart Publishers, June 1999. ISBN 1-57098-202-3

Garate, Donald T. *The Zion Tunnel–From Slickrock to Switchback.* Springdale, Utah: Zion Natural History Association, 1989. ISBN 0-945630-26-5

Gregory, Herbert E. *Geology and Geography of the Zion Park Region–Utah and Arizona.* Geological Survey Professional Paper 220. Washington DC: US Government Printing Office: 1950.

Gregory, Herbert E. *Geologic and Geographic Sketches of Zion and Bryce Canyon National Parks.* (4th edition) Springdale, Utah: Zion-Bryce Natural History Association: August 1956.

Hamilton, Wayne L. *Geological Map of Zion National Park, Utah.* Springdale, Utah: Zion Natural History Association. 1987 ISBN 0-915630-10-9

Hamilton, Wayne L. *The Sculpturing of Zion–with a Road Guide to the Geology of Zion National Park.* Springdale, Utah: Zion Natural History Association, 1984 (revised edition, 1995). ISBN 0-915630-13-3

Ranney, Wayne *Carving Grand Canyon–Evidence, Theories and Mystery* Grand Canyon, Arizona: Grand Canyon Association: 2005. ISBN 0-938216-82-1

Woodbury, Angus M. *A History of Southern Utah and Its National Parks.* Salt Lake City, Utah: Utah State Historical Society, Vol XII, Nos 3-4, July-October 1944–Revised and reprinted 1950.

National Park Service, Denver Service Center *Zion National Park–General Management Plan.* Washington DC: Department of the Interior, 2001.

Western Heritage Conservation, Inc. *The Outstanding Wonder–Zion Canyon's Cable Mountain Draw Works.* Springdale, Utah: Zion Natural History Association, 1981.

Acknowledgements

No book comes together without significant help from friends, and this effort is no exception.

For specific help on the book, thank you to: Steve Ramras, Steve Lewis, and Brian Cabe, plus Ray O'Neil and Cindy Purcell of the National Park Service.

For help in so many other ways (and in no particular order): Alicia Scotter, Steve Brezovec, Kurt and Melody Bellock, Jeff Nish, Hank Moon, Scott Holley, Jonathan Zambella, Dean Woods, Jill Woods, Bo Beck, Steve Allen, Rich Carlson, Dave Black, Kris Nosack, Rick Thompson, Roger and Jane Arhart, Kylin LaPlante, Shane Burrows, Dr. Pepper, Kip Marshall, Stephen King, David Muench, Michael Kelsey, Dennis Maw, Kelly Oldroyd, Chris Avery, John Muir, Gustav Mahler, David Brower, Jerry Garcia, Patty Rambert and Royce D. Trapier.

Index

CAPITALS: CANYON or TRAIL
Plain: Text
Bold: Map
Italics: Photo
C: Color page

Z

Opposite: *Tom Jones, Lin Alder and Chris Avery below the last rappel in Heaps. Photo by Lin Alder/Alderphoto.com*

ATLAS

The Author

Photo by Lin Alder / *AlderPhoto.com*

TOM JONES has been exploring the canyons of Zion for 20 years. His engineering degree from MIT, his need to tinker and experiment, and his love of the outdoors have led him to invent interesting canyoneering and climbing equipment. He founded Imlay Canyon Gear, where he designs, produces, markets and sells innovative canyon-specific gear.

Tom shares his canyoneering knowledge, skills and ethics through his website, *CanyoneeringUSA.com*, and by organizing canyon fests and service projects. He is the chairman of the Zion Canyoneering Coalition.

He makes his home just east of Zion in Mount Carmel, Utah.